TRANSMISSION

COMMUNICATION AND HUMAN VALUES

TRANSMISSION

Toward a Post-Television Culture

2nd Edition

edited by Peter d'Agostino
David Tafler

SAGE Publications
International Educational and Professional Publisher
Thousand Oaks   London   New Delhi

For information address:

SAGE Publications, Inc.
2455 Teller Road
Thousand Oaks, California 91320

SAGE Publications Ltd.
6 Bonhill Street
London EC2A 4PU
United Kingdom

SAGE Publications India Pvt. Ltd.
M-32 Market
Greater Kailash I
New Delhi 110 048 India

Printed in the United States of America

Library of Congress Cataloging-in-Publication Data

Main entry under title:

Transmission: Toward a post-television culture / edited by Peter
    d'Agostino, David Tafler.—2nd ed.
        p. cm.—(Communication and human values)
    Rev. ed. of: Transmission: theory and practice for a new
television aesthetics. 1st ed.
    Includes bibliographical references and index.
    ISBN 0-8039-4268-0 (cl.)—ISBN 0-8039-4269-9 (pb)
    1. Television broadcasting—Social aspects. 2. Television
broadcasting—Political aspects. I. d'Agostino, Peter, 1945-
II. Tafler, David.   III. Series: Communication and human values
(Thousand Oaks, Calif.)
PN1992.6.T73   1995
302.23'45—dc20   94-27937

95   96   97   98   99   10   9   8   7   6   5   4   3   2

Sage Production Editor: Tricia K. Bennett

DEDICATED TO

PASQUALE D'AGOSTINO
1900-1985

ABRAHAM TAFLER
CLAIRE S. TAFLER

Contents

Preface

It is almost a decade since the initial publication of *Transmission*. Originally subtitled "Theory and Practice for a New Television Aesthetics," *Transmission* now reflects a shift in emphasis toward a post-television culture. The focus is on television and on the related systems that have evolved and have been absorbed into the fabric of daily life, from automated banking and video games to computerized war. The glow from these cathode ray tubes, light-emitting diodes, and liquid crystal displays projects an ever increasing realm of mediated consciousness throughout a continually enveloping electronic landscape.

In this vein, the title, as well as the approach, to this book were inspired primarily by the work of Raymond Williams and Walter Benjamin that set a broad base for cultural studies. Williams contributed to the study of television by looking at its origins, content, and flow. He critiqued a culture that was becoming more and more technologically determined.

> Unlike all previous communications technologies, radio and TV were systems devised for transmission and reception as abstract processes, with little or no definition of preceding content. . . . It is not only that the supply of broadcasting facilities preceded the demand; it is that the means of communication preceded its content. (Williams, 1975, p. 25)

Benjamin's early analysis of photography and film explored the social, economic, and political implications of works of art in an "age of mechanical reproduction." This investigation has been extended here to TV, hypermedia, and virtual reality in an age of electronic transmission.

With the content and contextualization of new technologies shaping ever evolving perspectives, philosophical questions continue to emerge as to what is real and what is not, from Plato's Cave to this oxymoron called *virtual reality*. When foraging along the electronic spectrum, it becomes necessary to reframe those philosophical questions and reconsider the inherent meanings and current uses of terms like *virtuality, reality,* and *actuality*. Issues concerning race, gender, and ethnicity as well as the erosion and possible reclamation of oral traditions firmly rooted in the past and still manifested in the present are also addressed in this volume.

The actual events-wars, individual crises, and the myriad of topics that thematically drive the chapters in this book are not, however, the primary subject of our text. The emphasis here is on the mediation of the events being analyzed. We envision *Transmission* to be an interference pattern within the prepackaged flow of technologically determined ideology. Charting the territory of a post-television culture and suggesting alternative structures may yield something beyond the sterility and predictability of a pervasive high-tech culture.

Transmission is intended as a multidimensional source book, and not a homogeneous blend. The reader is therefore encouraged to cross reference, compare the sometimes dialectical positions of the authors and work toward one's own synthesis of ideas presented.

Peter d'Agostino

Reference

Williams, R. (1975). *Television: Technology and cultural form.* New York: Schocken.

Acknowledgments

Transmission compiles the work and concerted efforts of its many contributors. It has been informed by the authors in the previous edition and those in this current volume. Four of the chapters, by Erik Barnouw, Deirdre Boyle, John Carey and Pat O'Hara, and Todd Gitlin were also part of the initial publication. Deepest gratitude is extended to all of the authors and publishers who have provided material for this book. Our series editor Bob White provided the faith to proceed while his critical feedback motivated us to stop and reconsider our ideas before committing them to print. Thanks are also extended to the past and present editorial staff at Sage (Ann West, Sophy Craze, Astrid Virding, and Tricia Bennett) for their guidance and patience during the editing process.

To my wife, Deirdre Dowdakin, and my daughters, Brita and Lia, for their love, support, and understanding. —P. d'A.

To my family and friends for their love and support. —D. T.

CHAPTER 1 SOURCE: "Lost Generations" originally appeared in *Timeshift on Video Culture*, ©1991 Sean Cubitt. Reprinted by permission of the author and Routledge Press.

CHAPTER 2 SOURCE: "Surrealism Without the Unconscious" originally appeared as Chapter 3, "Surrealism Without the Unconscious," in *Postmodernism, or, The Cultural Logic of Late Capitalism,* by Fredric Jameson, ©1991 Duke University Press. Reprinted by permission of the author and Duke University Press.

CHAPTER 3 SOURCE: "Women Watching Television: Issues of Class, Gender, and Mass Media Reception" originally appeared as parts of Chapter 1, "Theoretical Framework," and "Conclusion: Television Reception as a Window on Culture" in *Women Watching Television,* by Andrea Press, ©1991 University of Pennsylvania Press. Reprinted by permission of the author and the University of Pennsylvania Press.

CHAPTER 4 SOURCE: "The Whole World Is Watching" appeared in the 1st edition of *Transmission: Theory and Practice for a New Television Aesthetics* (New York: Tanam Press, 1985) as a revised version of the Introduction in *The Whole World Is*

Introduction

PETER D'AGOSTINO
DAVID TAFLER

Transmission presents an overview, a shifting territory previously known as television. Inside its borders, a multiplicity of events for the exchange of information transpire across an expanding spectrum, come from divergent sources, rush toward a number of applications. While the word *transmission* may still refer to the technological apparatus of television, to the sociopolitical structures of the medium, and ultimately to the exchange of information, in a post-television culture, television no longer means television. An omnipresence now pervades every facet of daily life; CRTs (cathode ray tubes) dot the landscape and occupy the hubs of all human activity, from the office to the ballpark, from transportation platforms to transporting vehicles, from libraries to supermarkets, from ATMs to research laboratories. Television has now become a bank machine, security monitor, information terminal, computer interface. No longer a formidable household icon, television comes unhinged; it no longer stands alone as it did at a time when the family gathered in front of the living room screen, twisted the dials, and chose their favorite programs. The individual now holds a remote, separates from the body, and plunges into cyberspace.

The rubric of an electronic information superhighway heralds the arrival of a post-television culture. With the option of going on-line, people turn to the " 'net" to form their community.[1] Defined by common interests, perhaps by their economic status or other factors determining privileged access, individuals form alliances that transcend geographic location, history, routine. They communicate on-screen using language or other abstract symbols. Initially, nothing matters but the message.

Only later might visual or other kinesic factors enter into a relationship. The old boundaries disappear.

Today, television's interface, everywhere intertwined with everyday activity, separate channels in separate spaces, public and private jurisdictions at work and at home, marks an individual's activity beyond the physical constraints of absence and presence at the edges of the network. Ambivalences correspond with the onslaught of yet newer technologies, generating the constant buzz out there.

With the proliferation of channels, with the growing number of on-line network services, with the increasing number of voices addressing the same issues, screening the same images, the viewer-participant now receives and sends abbreviated reports, continuously and often instantaneously, about an exploding number of remote affairs transpiring on a shrinking planet. Ranging from weather forecasts to war reports, this information from other regions and other places offers little of immediate personal consequence and detracts from issues of more concentrated significance. Little in-depth analysis takes place.

When it comes to war and other national traumatic events, a hyper-dramatization characterizes the media scenario. Television networks work to expunge and exploit the horror. When satellite hook-ups eliminate the temporal span between the battlefield and the living room, the networks remain constrained by censorship. The active players then become the tools, the military hardware, the aerial representations of (sexual) projectiles hurtling against some unknown other. The respective agents of power compete for time on the television screen. Alternating visits with conflicting generals measure the distance in the conflict. Disremembered before it begins, the theater misses the historical issues that go beyond the boundaries of the televised conflict. If memory plays no role in television, then television has limitless license to bend the collective consciousness in ways only possible when no tether holds the audience logic.

The historical framework defining television experience adjusts and shifts. These shifts have come about rapidly. Technology changes terminology and new paradigms shape the evolution of new tools. Tomorrow, television again becomes something else. Along the proposed electronic highways, interactive multimedia raises questions of information rich and information poor. Visionary propositions and technological advances must be tempered by the realities of control and ownership that serve the political and economic interests of the communication industry rather than those of the public. Auxiliary devices create the impression of alternatives.[2] How can telecommunication technologies be put to the service of people; how can they flourish and survive with their resources intact?

Not long ago, television's window on the world, its limited network spectrum, became a fixed icon on the landscape, its seasons simulated the artificial passage of time, its programming served as a harbinger of trends. Years of programming went by with scores of researchers documenting how television technology molded social habits, political strategies, marketing campaigns; fueled professional sports; corrupted society's values; and consumed elective time. From this historical vantage point, the status of television appeared stable.

The media continue to structure overall consciousness. As part of the distribution process, they filter and frame activity, produce meaning, shape discourse, introduce, play out, emphasize, and exclude certain vital information until the very reality on the screen becomes a metadrama, recognizable but detached from everyday life.

Mainstream television, still driven by the loud voices of multinational corporate power brokers, however, represents only one reality, familiar but inappropriate. Mainstream television culture continues to pretend to represent the whole community. On the screen, that reality obscures cultural difference, more difficult to discern but ever present. Weighing in, a post-television environment can no longer simply satisfy its constituents with endless replays of the same old traumas. While mass-distributed television programming shrinks to accommodate a smaller audience, television, a world watering hole, must reflect and shape the tensions, questions, and shifting values of a world in rapid transition.

On the reception side, individuals resist television, understand its difference as part of their daily lives, in their private spaces, accepted unconsciously. Through critical interpretation, viewers bring their own background to the reception experience, thus breaking the hegemonic foothold of the medium. Active screening, not to mention production activity, helps to temper television's predominant influences.

Accommodating to this resistance, television plays on gender relations, on class differences, through positing conformity and encouraging resistance. Television undercuts its own critique by creating a homogenized mainstream reality. Within each socioeconomic cycle, television plays off the audience in front of the screen. As a domestic medium, television moves into the family and unravels the myriad relationships: daughter-mother, father-son, husband-wife, among siblings, and between children and parents of the opposite sex. Outside the family, television stereotypes and reassures constituents of each class grouping. Radical messages simply replay themselves as exotic entertainment, advertising gone MTV, encouraging consumption of yet more bourgeois ideology. In the end, television annihilates difference by appropriating factions outside the social center.

That oscillation between involvement and detachment, between the de facto world and the de jure, signals the pleasure of the encounter with the television medium. People sometimes resist this anesthetized pleasure and grab hold of technologies that provide the means for resistance. Along with new hopes, the transformation of electronic media into multiuse utensils raises new challenges and demands new ways of thinking.

David Antin (1975) once described television as "video's frightful parent" (p. 58). In a post-television environment, television first turns to video. Video offers the possibilities for breaking television's hold. Video inhabits the neighborhoods of "broken experience" and not the domestic world of sitcoms and soap operas. Off stage, its presence shapes the ethical standard, the environment outside the window. Video and television, each one encircles the other, watches the other, defines and contextualizes the other's relations to the world outside itself. Video indicts television's fiction. Television derides home videos. Where each steps out, the other calls attention to that masquerade until the Rodney King tape shows up. Here, video shockingly makes itself present by indicting the silence of passive consumption.

In earlier ruptures, radical groups like TVTV (Top Value Television) used video to break the boundaries of television. In the process, they triggered the networks' move to ENG (electronic news gathering). On the residual edges of this new frontier, video made possible the dream of reclaiming some lost territory, staking claim to new turf where the rules and regulations have not yet been invented. Technological limitations became the foundation for breaking with stylistic norms, those conventional approaches to interacting with people in the surrounding community.

With new technologies fueling the transformation of the Portapak, the camcorder ushers in the first explosion of new stylistic codes and constructions. Video revolutionizes television. In a post-television culture, video is propagated through the spread of cameras and their accompanying monitors. To maintain a meaningful identity, smaller communities in the inner city and in the outlying rural areas use video to build a new anchor for maintaining their values, for establishing their own codes and signs, defining their own reality as it may appear on and beyond the electronic screen.

Video activism means undermining the credibility of the message by exposing the vehicle that delivers that message. In the process, other languages evolve. On this level, information flow yields to format. Opportunities for information access compete with applications generating immediate pleasure. Surrounded, the community finds itself consumed from within.

A critical historic moment rests within the space of time in which the alternate group can produce a novel approach and the appropriation of that approach by mainstream agencies. In that constant process of exploration, a process that means staying one step ahead of the flood, an interactive environment emerges where people maintain a commitment to resisting the effects of television's constantly evolving content and form.

Apparently, for some groups, the distances remain great. Their efforts to build their own language emerge from a long-standing cultural posture when encountering all new experiences, particularly electronic experiences. With indigenous people, such as the Aboriginal peoples of Australia, other factors enter into the equation, for example, landscape, vegetation, movement that corresponds to the flow of a given story. Differences lie in the size of the community; the spread between notions of urban, suburban, and rural; needs, messages, relations within the family—who stays home and who watches when.

New interactive television networks emerge in the bush for bridging these differences. Questions remain, however, about the very nature of interactive television. Not only do concerns focus on substitution—not only does interactive television replace the telephone or face-to-face encounters—they focus on whether a unique communication medium such as interactive television can change the mind-set of a community, its people's relationship to space, to time, to their own reality, to their relations with others, to their notion of community.

At the bottom, there remains the question of control. Who controls the tools often determines the nature of the system put in place. Increasingly complex technologies facilitate user-friendly exchanges, but they operate at the mercy of an army of service technicians, system regulators, corporate entities designing the respective interfaces, changing the parameters of the exchange. In the end, communication becomes something else. Who knows where that destination lies.

Video, a temporal medium, captures transition, embodies degeneration. Video lies along the ideological interface, the divide separating government and commerce, regulation and restlessness, control and freedom. Mediating difference and not based on preserving values, video negotiates change. A post-television culture requires new thinking and new theories of experience.

As other high-tech applications proliferate, they threaten to accelerate the eradication of cultural difference. Each new system's material reality makes claims on its users. Each new wave proportionately affects the language, ritual, influence, and power among communities. Borders change; territories diminish. As distances diminish, the collision among social forces disrupts, fragments, and eventually destroys contingent customs and practices, particularly those predicated on earlier, now outmoded networks of time and space.

While technology may destabilize frontiers, does high technology inevitably destroy tradition? Can an indigenously developed telepresence accommodate newer technologies and thus maintain the traditional bridges sustaining older cultures? "The electronic age is also an age of 'secondary orality,' the orality of telephones, radio, and television, which depends on writing and print for its existence" (Ong, 1982, p. 3). This notion of "secondary orality" harbors the potential for the continuity of oral cultures without the disruptive and arbitrary shifts to literacy.

Significant upheavals often mask the less perceptible, more gradual changes transpiring within an everyday environment. On a micro level, the conjunction of electronic windows wedding the television with the telephone, coaxial with fiber optic, with the computer-driven CD, laser disc, CD ROM, alter overall viewer reception habits by further fragmenting attention and communication. Traveling the internal conduits within an expanding body, 24-hour electronic traffic patterns serve as the social matrix. Presence and absence become meaningless. Even in the receiver's absence, answering machines, modems, and FAX terminals continue to downlink messages for future referencing.

Electronic corridors secured by access privileges, the doors and hallways, the screen portals of the future yield to those carrying the appropriate assigned digits on the global highways: those individuals in constant contact, personalized, monitored, and approved; those individuals privileged and equipped to enter the proper pathways for moving through the circuit. Input devices proliferate and hierarchical differences mark the playing field. Security buffers telecommunication stations.

Artificial intelligence operations match producer-user systems. Power gateways designate the information recipients, and allocate resources accordingly.

The university lies within the ghetto. Cars with phones roll by homes where people have difficulty paying for their basic telephone service. Computers in police cars help sustain the steeper thresholds between the haves and have-nots. Everybody carries a gun. Computers on the beach pacify the old outcasts, while the channel surfers, oblivious of their presence, continue to ride back and forth across the airwaves. The tools do not guarantee access. Once access becomes available, the users do not necessarily avail themselves of the myriad opportunities placed before them. People continue to pursue prescribed objectives; they adhere to well-charted pathways. Only a venturesome few go beyond.

Safe within the conceptual lodge, the young navigate future relationships, free from disease and unwelcome confrontation. Growing up on the electronic grid, taking the phenomena for granted, the youngest generation acquires its own language screaming "CD" or "TV" before knowing how to say "mommy" or "dada." These synaptic shifts have profound consequences. When the computer appears in the baby's room, the television set follows the phonograph, follows the telephone, follows the desktop computer, to the scrap heap of historical nostalgia. In cyberspace, no one can hear you beyond the screen.

Separating space from time, becoming involved in the machine, technology shapes aesthetics, aesthetics become the currency for navigating through the technosphere, a virtual reality of artifice and new structured convention. The chapters in this volume range across this terrain, from topics exploring television's relationship with domestic and international conflagrations, to topics surrounding the implementation of new technologies such as interactive networks and virtual landscapes. Aesthetic values, gender and race issues, class determinants motivate the selection of material and inform its discussion.

The organization of the book matches chapters that now have some historical bearing with chapters focused on more contemporary issues that arise from similar concerns. Without dwelling on individual programs or tapes, the book moves across the television terrain examining the impact of video on commercial television, the relationship of media to the social causes it (mis)represents, the effects of new communication tools on participating constituents.

In the opening chapter, **"Lost Generations,"** Sean Cubitt pinpoints the interplay between television and video. Television embodies a society situated in front of the screen. Captivated by narcissistic impulses, television's play updates and perpetually revises the psychoanalytic play on the body within its social relations, focusing on death, on the environment. In contrast to "being" there for a society in transition, video straddles change by constantly becoming something else.

Cubitt argues that alternative media must escape the demands of popular sentiment to arrive at a true democracy of the individual image. Measuring television's specific historical and material conditions means evaluating the symbolic language and manipulated communication, dialectical struggle, and psychoanalytic angst, all against the lifestyle and postmodern setting of the suburban environment. At the end of science, the *danse macabre* of ecological disaster, the mediasphere extends the grip of wanton consumption and eventual annihilation toward a future woven between dystopian technocratic nightmares and its own profound self-interrogation.

Here, outside the commercial boundaries, outside of its own marketplace, art production builds meaning while straddling a world organized by territories, constrained by boundaries. Art represents a time and place beyond the constancy of the media facade. Cubitt propounds a negation of television's eternal presence, to release/recognize the historical imagination/historical change. Cubitt argues that video's "indefiniteness . . . becomes its field of possibility." About difference, dialogue, place, and time, video works toward discovering/elaborating the terms on which the future might emerge. In a postmodernist chronology, the question becomes this: What comes after video?

Once again, historical circumstances might tend to repeat themselves. Looking back at the turn of the last century, motion pictures, collective dream machines, stretched the conceptual thresholds of the industrial revolution. Cultural change took off in an inflamed environment of the imagination. In the context of a world often disrupted by war, financial upheaval, and concomitant cycles of technological, political, and social revolution, technological innovation fueled militarism, imperialism, colonialism, and other forms of adventurous exploitation. The players, meanwhile, fueled technological development.

On the cusp of the twenty-first century, when processing speed sucks up memory at the speed of light, digital instruments supplant analog systems. A cognitive apparatus predicated on a sequence of single points conjoined across a three-dimensional grid, a computer's simplified set of instructions impedes the imagination. With everything becoming bits and bytes, margins separating transmission and reception shrink. The desktop computer station becomes the post-television future. The simple act of watching means settling for software options. One can no longer simply discover oneself in the act of watching. The viewer reaches out for the joystick. The targeted audience grabs the remote and hopscotches across the sterile spectrum, a capitalist wasteland of shopping channels and shopping malls. In between, the commodities range from born-again religion to reborn politicians. Outside, the physical parameters of the universe change forever; new principles take hold.

In his chapter, **"Surrealism Without the Unconscious,"** Fredric Jameson plots mainstream consciousness along aesthetic and technological axes. Technology defines the materiality of the contemporary media, its artistic mode, and social institution. Of all media, according to Jameson, video fully embodies the postmodern, the art form of late capitalism. With culture and media entwined, video lies at the locus of a new social and economic conjuncture. Unlike commercial television's simulacrum of fictive time, video's rigorously nonfictive machine language, machine time (television flow), depersonalizes the subject into a quasi-paralyzed member of the cultural apparatus.

At that juncture, fringe and center dematerialize within a reactivated signifying system. Video disturbs historical reception through its reexamination of the "consciousness industry." Video's space time specificity arrests commercial television's exemplary unity. Video splits into video and television. Jameson argues television lacks memory. While memory plays no role in postmodernism, after postmodernism, after video, there's no presence. In that structural degeneration defines video's inherent status, the video text itself represents transition. No video masterpieces can emerge as a new canon.

Jameson goes on to acknowledge video's relationship to computer and information technology, to videotext. In the ceaseless interaction among signs and logos, reproductive technology can break with its automatic referentiality. In establishing some autonomy from the referent, reference and reality disappear. Meaning becomes problematized.

What remains of television, television programming stitches together the many contradictory threads to sustain the complex social-economic-political environment. Television, positioned unconsciously as reality, remains a domestic medium. It presumes family, presumes that women are preoccupied with family. Television focuses around familylike groupings more than around individuals. Therefore television does not attribute to the viewer the same powerful voyeuristic gaze when compared with the film viewer. Television submits to a collective discourse. Insofar as women develop different relations than men, more in tune with family and friends, television may appear to draw women into a more involved relationship, "becoming subject to its discourse." In fact, women negotiate their experience with television in different ways depending on their respective socioeconomic class and/or generation. On both a conscious and an unconscious plateau, women organize, often resist, and occasionally absorb the subject(s) of their fascination.

As an affective system, quasi-private/public television momentarily placates deep-seated human needs: the imagination, desire, and guilt-free consumption. Andrea Press's chapter, **"Women Watching Television: Issues of Class, Gender, and Mass Media Reception,"** scrutinizes the integration of gender and class in the metamorphosis of television. It raises the question: To what extent do respective constituents have the ability to generate their own meaning(s) within prevailing and marginal media systems? Press examines how viewer resistance, or lack of resistance, to culture's often hegemonic messages operates within television, the most salient instrument of that struggle.

The media's negotiation, management, and comprehension of reality make their own processed image into the reported movement. From that representation, the audience formulates its positions and chooses its eventual actions.

Todd Gitlin, in **"The Whole World Is Watching,"** analyzes the effects of these framing mechanisms on the world at large with regard to a hegemonic ideology that attempts to naturalize the artificiality of media conventions. Gitlin critiques the role of mass media as core systems for the distribution of ideology. Focusing on the complex relationship of television news and the New Left of the 1960s, Gitlin looks at the way the media frames actual events and deforms their social meaning. Through media instruments, the public world penetrates the private sphere, the sanctuary of the home. Within that body, the synchronic array of ceaseless imagery shapes residual values, emotions, and the very language of the individual/group discourse. The flow remains one sided. Individuals have no leverage over what constitutes information. Mediated meanings fall into concrete patterns that hover back and forth over the same familiar territory, a distant territory. Meanwhile, the mediators bypass relevant news to the community when the hook lacks the magic to fall into those categories that titillate the viewer for a moment of his or her attention. As a consequence, nothing on the screen mobilizes public attention for any meaningful duration.

In a post-television environment, other voices reach the screen. Accompanying the spread of satellite dishes, cable systems, and other forms of electronic distribution, the conjoining of specialized communication tools with everyday media appliances has begun to notably alter the cultural practices of the most remote communities in the bush as well as lend a voice to their disenfranchised brothers and sisters in the larger cities. Collapsing the differences between larger and smaller communities, media centers disassemble the output of the large media machines and permit individuals to form their own constituencies.

A new level of cynicism accompanies this access. Television plays out the omniscient myth of an ever-presence waiting for the viewer to tap. On both sides of the screen, the text implicates its participants in the production of force. "Wasted time, being wasted," the spectator remains trashed. Television, about being-not-at-home, tries to locate the certainty, the "in" of being-in-the-world. Surveilling, being under surveillance, television's interrupted discourse seeks to recapture its own rupture.

Avital Ronell's **"Video/Television/Rodney King: Twelve Steps Beyond *The Pleasure Principal*"** compares television to a shock absorber, to a drug in its relation to law, in its relations to itself as force, alternately stimulating and tranquilizing. She uses the Rodney King case to examine "television watching the law watch video." She discusses the strategy of reducing the videotape of the beating into a photograph, where it lacks the force of the moving narrative. In the hemorrhaging of meaning, television's call to consciousness reverts to video's call of conscience—the "interpellation that takes place between television and video, the way the one calls the other to order, which is one way of calling the other to itself."

A large global population sown together by satellite can no longer sustain regional hatred, rampant exploitation of human and natural resources, and imperialist forays into neighboring territories. When the respective territories of individual and group, large and small community conflict, the electronic highway will channel the respective constituents' frustration and anxiety. To this end, it weaves and strokes and makes benign most of the explosive forces operating within the combined social body by channeling specific messages onto carefully formatted and regulated tracks. Yet, while reaching for the stars, the global community continues to fight medieval battles. With no place to hide, the problems turn in on themselves. With time running out, the challenges defy solutions.

Out of the 1950s come fear, imagination, and suppression. Out of the fear of the hydrogen bomb and the fascination with Sputnik, imagination overtakes reality. Media goes with the imagination by ignoring, masking, or revising earlier history. Erik Barnouw's **"The Case of the A-Bomb Footage"** chronicles the history of film footage of the devastation of Hiroshima and Nagasaki. Filmed by independent Japanese filmmakers, the footage was confiscated by occupation authorities and remained "classified material" in Washington until 1968. After obtaining permission from the National Archives to review the films, Barnouw edited the material into the documentary *Hiroshima-Nagasaki, August 1945*. The chapter concludes with a description of the television premiere of the program on the 25th anniversary of the Hiroshima bombing.

The Hiroshima-Nagasaki documentary chronicles the reality of a modern world gone awry in waging war and suffering devastation. The electric effect on audiences foretold the fascination with televised images of the Vietnam War on the nightly news and its antiseptic aftermath, "smart" bombs and their adjoining cameras during the Gulf War. Yet, network television at the time ignored the independent documentary until forced to take notice.

Marita Sturken's chapter, **"The Television Image and Collective Amnesia: Dis(re)membering the Persian Gulf War,"** examines late twentieth-century high-tech conflicts in light of earlier twentieth-century military-industrial relationships fueling the incipient shape of television. On the outskirts of the Persian Gulf War, the media's military technospeak displays the fleeting images of television coverage from the margins of the battlefield. When compared with the edited photographic/filmic footage of previous wars, most television viewing experience was forgettable as empty spectacle. Nevertheless, the vicarious experience of the bomber, of the smart bomb, of the fiery night spectacles of SCUDS versus Patriot missiles, obscures the pain of individual suffering experienced by soldiers and civilians. As a consequence, a collective amnesia sets in of a war not remembered but occasionally reexperienced through television reruns.

Globally, television mobilizes attitudes and opinions. Locally, it markets commodities and mainstream positions. While many voices come from multiple directions, each program's structural format plays a major role in shaping and accommodating new social alignments particularly when it comes to race, gender, and Third World constituents' struggles.

With television now a source of entertainment sometimes called news, a computer screen, arcade, and money dispenser, security watchdog, and departure/arrival board, has it become impossible to upset cultural practices, shift aesthetic parameters, and aspire toward noncommercial objectives that affect social organization and its reception?[3] Perhaps video art's relationship to television still allows it a unique position from which to play, replay, recontextualize television experience. Caught between camps, video practice occupies no distinct communicative or aesthetic function. Not adhering to format and genre models, video's frontiers remain unstable. Each new camera design invokes different applications by different populations. In a medium that blends imagination and reality, a medium that perpetually recontextualizes information, there are no absolutes.

In her chapter, **"Guerrilla Television,"** Deirdre Boyle looks at some of the earlier "video documentarians" who created a new style of alternative television. Her primary focus is on the 1970s group TVTV (Top Value Television) and their innovative programs *Four More Years* and *Lord of the Universe*. After chronicling the rise of the group, Boyle discusses the reasons for its eventual demise and the subsequent impact on the alternative TV movement.

Video made television portable. Video became the new frontier. The Portapak led to the first generation of video pioneers/artists. Video gangs or media groups were like an extended family. Eventually, the artists and documentarians split. In the early years, guerrilla television embraced art as documentary and stressed innovation and critical relationships to television. Video theater preexisted public access. The lack of editing tools made video vérité the only style, an aesthetic dictated by equipment. TVTV's adaptive and creative attitude in *Four More Years* broke ground by pointing the camera away from the podium during the Republican national political convention to reelect President Nixon. The tape experimented with graphics and wide-angle lenses. It was the beginning of electronic news gathering (ENG).

As a catalyst, video generates transition. Portable, more affordable electronic instruments offer a small window of opportunity for recouping television experience. The use of accessible tools permits the development of a new rhetorical standard enabling small communities to revise and sustain their sense of identity. Communities with limited resources can now begin to build texts that fortify their own practices, some passed down from generation to generation, others generated by contemporary circumstances, some perhaps recovered. These recitations help to mediate relationships, fortify identity, contribute to the sense of belonging and purpose most individuals require to operate successfully within their respective societies. A home videomaker captures the Rodney King incident and exposes it to the world.

Laurie Ouellette's chapter, **"Will the Revolution Be Televised? Camcorders, Activism, and Alternative Television in the 1990s,"** focuses on the incendiary efforts of independent groups to use new media technology to promote an ideologically self-aware, critical analysis positioned outside of the standard discourse that reifies conventional practice(s). Today, activists use video to document their own demonstrations. They develop programming for local and national cable access with the intent of publicizing their causes and/or subverting the messages of mainstream media. Groups such as Paper Tiger Television have spawned a number of media collectives to resist mainstream media's normal viewing habits. The community becomes a producer as well as a consumer of images. Community producers build alternative structures while simultaneously recontextualizing the commercial media industries.

With the creation of the national cable access satellite network Deep Dish TV, diversified programming has spread to numbers of satellite dish owners and cable system operators across the United States. Wraparound shows, panel discussions, and phone-in programs work to build an interactive dimension to the media discussion. While gradually restructuring the minute patterns of individual behavior, electronic media transforms the broad dynamic interactivity of larger social factions and groups.

Eric Michaels's **"The Aboriginal Invention of Television in Central Australia 1982-1986"** focuses on the use of video by the Warlpiri people, who, engulfed by Eurocentric forces and yet resident on the margins, ask the pivotal question facing all Third World communities besieged by new technologies: "Can video make our culture strong? Or, will it make us lose our Law?" Can varying modes of cultural production continue across media? What happens when varying modes of media production cross cultures?

Not all bodes well. The broad-scale distribution of carefully crafted, self-regulated tools has a downside. In a contracting world, real-time visual telecommunication accelerates the homogeneous nightmare. As high-tech applications proliferate, they threaten to accelerate the eradication of cultural difference. Telecommunication tools' built-in governors structure their attendant use and discourse.

Once constructed, the signal requires distribution. Each transmission center makes claims on its users. When a fringe community transmits its own signal via the center, modifications to the original message may adjust it to the extent that it ceases to exist. Each new wave proportionately affects the language, ritual, influence, and power among communities. As a means for an alternative voice, each new technical inroad marks a small part of the fall from those fundamental thresholds that hold the line against the future erosion of indigenous cultures.

A post-television discourse must reconstitute frontiers; it must inhibit high technology's destruction of fragile tradition. A post-television manifesto must challenge indigenous groups to establish their telepresence, to assimilate newer technologies while maintaining the traditional bridges sustaining their older cultures. While history preexists television, it does not operate as some a priori force. Revising applications and their concomitant tools can modify, perhaps alter, each wave of change. Because specific tendencies only become discernible in time, the timely recognition and comprehension of new communication paradigms require an evolutionary approach when examining this subtle metamorphosis.

At the core lies the question of the shifting interface. Across the global, within the local community, the electronic media distort culturally determined reference points. Questions of proximity, of the relationships among individuals within the community, remain dormant in the effort to present the subject as relevant to its reception, to integrate the audience within the text. Questions of time remain constrained despite the broken barriers, the oceans, the ranges, the routine of day and night. A post-television environment bridges these disproportions. Its technological shifts have a profound effect. The aftermath triggers a self-reflexive wake, a moment for reexamining the social, cultural climate, its erosion and reclamation.

A child interacting with the screen rewires centuries of cognition, of consciousness, with limitless consequences. The console at the viewer's fingertips directs an array of auditory-visual events, on the electronic screen, radio, tape deck, CD player, and CB. Projections of the past, and of what yet remains ahead, peel away from the ephemeral bubble that encloses the wide-eyed time traveler. Wars and other regional conflagrations appear and disappear leaving their human scars and ecodevastation.

The cybernetic platform of the immediate future may be found on the ground. Switching on or off the designated pathways, the driver will integrate certain immediate features of the grid while bypassing what lies beyond his or her use and/or fascination. Mapping positions, recursions, loop procedures, deflect attention. Endless, limitless corridors exhaust the explorer. Avoiding entrapment, the viewer moves off the track.

Other spectators occupy auxiliary stations on either side of the screen. A seamless experience of desire and expectation separates the active grazer from the outside scavenger who assembles the inchoate discards compiled from the other's actions. No longer equal, each potential interactor will either compete for control of the remote or separate into her own modular unit. Each new module becomes an arena for renewed privilege and competition. Television's metamorphosis from windows to microchip passageways transforms the environment into a multidimensional earth station.

While the body resists fragmentation for the sake of love and procreation, the family tether continues to unravel in myriad ways. In its place, the simultaneity of networked experience shared by users around the globe becomes a new tabernacle for the virtual community.

It does not seem likely that a utopian juncture will emerge where society can successfully accommodate the individual within a regulated system of transmission and reception. Nevertheless, a new paradigm for processing experience and practice remains a fundamental necessity for survival. John Carey and Pat O'Hara's **"Interactive Television"** surveys the brief history of the actual and simulated forms of two-way TV. Interactive television, still largely an unrealized concept, dates to the technological origins of television in the 1920s, to the home-studio interviews with Edward R. Murrow, to the plastic drawing screens attached by children to their TVs in the 1950s, picturephone in the 1964-1965 New York World's Fair, 1960s and 1970s pilot projects. Carey and O'Hara provide a detailed account of the Berks Community Interactive Cable TV system in operation since 1975 and designed primarily for use by senior citizens in Reading, Pennsylvania.

The Reading system began with a clear understanding of local conditions, needs, and resources. From its originating sites—neighborhood communication centers, city hall, various administrative offices, schools, and with telephone hookups for home participation—the system established a center-to-center to home talk format. With one camera at each location, each shot transition meant a shift in location. With no reaction shots manipulated by a director, the system remained crude but direct. Over time, shared codes of behavior evolved. Communication patterns became more consistent and efficient.

No single instrument or application fully embodies the shifting televisual climate though the word *interactive* has been increasingly thrown about. Interactive media have a multifaceted history. They cover a wide span of diverse systems. Some operations offer new territory while others recycle in new formats the limited choices of older systems. Hierarchical differences separate these systems, which range from multiple choice modules in the home to talk-feedback formats that encourage an open exchange of ideas.

The early interactive laser disc art installations of the 1980s took advantage of their systemic novelty to engage viewer-participants in an open-ended encounter. The encounter challenged viewer-participants to build a unique experience specific to their situation. David Tafler's chapter, **"Boundaries and Frontiers: Interactivity and Participant Experience—Building New Models and Formats,"** begins with the pioneers at the MIT Media Lab and later focuses on those interactive video laser disc experiments where a reception-based approach prevailed over other technologically determined efforts.

Some exploratory efforts and pockets of resistance operate along the electronic margins, in the digital arts and sciences. Here, a final platform exists for engaging and contesting new influences, for making self-connections guided by originating spiritual, ideological, aesthetic, and social standards.

Electronic art, the site of collision, of struggle, a breeding ground of renewed resistance against the rituals of passive consumption, ploughs the narrow, electronic/mathematic corridors spawned by engineers and technicians in their quest designing industrial applications, sustains the psychological, ecological, and sociological concerns on the cultural edge.

In a digital future, absolute values yield fleeting images that haunt the mind. Virtual realities form a vicarious environment for collective experience. Television projects the present, frames the past, and alludes to an empty future ready to be filled with forgettable spectacle. Maintaining a perspective on the state of the art means articulating a strategy for continually reassessing that experience in front of the screen. As the experience evolves, that strategy must change to accommodate this transition. Not only does this reflexive process never end, it accelerates over time.

The electronic interface, a sophisticated feedback loop, works to reduce time by increasing input-output frequency. The present immediately becomes past performance. Once removed, never in absolute contact, the individual deduces his or her conditions through a series of readings predicated on direct or indirect experience.

In essence, never on the screen or within the controls, the interface resembles a cognitive membrane, a prelude to remembering, an ephemeral territory that circumscribes the individuals' relationship to the machine, to ancestral forms of communication, to marks left on the stones, to voices passed down through generations upon generations of storytelling.

On those tracks, the body remains subject to deprivation and desire: when phenomenological contradictions accentuate the mind-body split, when cyberadventures compete with CAT scans, when virtual realities clash with dramatic representations of countless tragedies from all over the neighborhood, from all over the globe, those latent pressures threaten to overwhelm the spirit and consume the planet.

Peter d'Agostino's chapter, **"Virtual Realities: Recreational Vehicles for a Post-Television Culture?"** looks to the future by examining the poetics, technics, and politics of high-tech models, projections, and fantasies. The technofuture platform harbors all sorts of utopian possibilities and dystopian problems. At the end of the century, questions of what constitutes the cybernetic body—its theology, memory, and overall intelligence; its environment, day-to-day routine, and leisure—arise from the visions conjured by contemporary dreamers. In fact, many of the ideas surrounding media, virtual reality, recreation, and escape have been around for some time. To what degree will these visions anticipate the freedoms afforded versus the controls implanted?

Never alone, television accompanies other outreach devices. RVs, called recreational vehicles or caravans, bring the safety and reassurance of the home, with all of its running water and electronic apparatuses, to the outback. Borders change; territories diminish. As distances diminish, the collision among social forces disrupts, fragments, and eventually destroys contingent customs and practices, particularly those predicated on earlier, now outmoded networks of time and space.

The chapters in this volume renegotiate the electronic screen, from its mass implementation as a narrowly defined home output station to its more global presence and universal concept as a multiuse conduit and instrument. *Transmission* explores an understanding of reflexivity, its impact on the complex interrelationship of structure and content within the context of new television/video practice, a practice that continues to expand in proportion to the growing tele-electronic dimension of everyday experience.

No single anthology can, in and of itself, embody the full range of ideas percolating around a complex communication subject. This book makes an effort to address the interstices binding the tools with the users, to examine how relationships change within the family, within our society, how individuals bring their own experience to bear, thus breaking with the hegemonic foothold of the media.

A different future challenges the accepted frames. By both constructing and deconstructing messages, this anthology works against building a foundation for defining where television has been. Instead, *Transmission* looks at the array of forces moving the contemporary video landscape forward. It monitors the progress of this ongoing transformation by staking out the issues that mark this future. *Transmission* looks forward.

Notes

1. The " 'net" refers to Internet, Compuserve, Prodigy, America On-Line, and any number of other on-line subscriber services.

2. Periodically, efforts to generate new alternatives meet with limited success. As of this writing, a non-PBS public support television station, WYBE in Philadelphia, struggles to survive. Meanwhile, Philadelphia community groups battle for the realization of public access, previously promised and contracted when the local cable franchises reached their respective agreements with the city.

3. Academies sustain old practices. As a result, values endure. Unlike this century's technology's more recent art forms, painting remains a high art form precisely because it is preindustrial. Its handmade status gives it value. Ironically, despite mass production, replication, and transmission, or as a consequence of it, a commodity remains valuable when it remains collectable on the marketplace. In the not too distant future, day-to-day exhibition and media saturation will perhaps no longer prioritize collection over transmission.

References

Antin, D. (1975). Video: The distinctive features of the medium. In *Video art*. Philadelphia: University of Pennsylvania, ICA.

Ong, W. J. (1982). *Orality and literacy: The technologizing of the word*. New York: Methuen.

It is easy to envisage a culture in which the aesthetic relation is no longer based on finished texts, but on the ways in which a programme can be manipulated by its users, so that the true computer art would not be like existing show-reels, but actual pieces of software for the user to create with.

1

Lost Generations

SEAN CUBITT

No one said it was going to be easy. Certain themes are persistent in the self-analysis of video activists: access, work-practices, end-users. The spirit of critique (and self-criticism) which at times can seem so intro-spective and even petty marks the sector off as different, not only from others but from itself. But this endless self-questioning is also func-tional—it makes us constantly conscious that *we* must make the culture in which we wish to live, according to *all* the strategies that we can employ. This is not a quest in the classical sense: there is no definite end in sight. It is not teleological, guided by an historical goal, but eschalogical, governed by the principle of hope. It is science as defined by Lacan, the practice of disbelief. To disbelieve is to test every proposition against multiple, conflicting, even contradictory cases, and ultimately to challenge ideals of knowledge which we hold. Such a practice subjects the nature and notion of knowledge to change through social practice, in this instance the social practice of video, and writing about video. The task of such a materialist practice is not to prove but to disprove. Video practice, with its transparent manipulations of image and sound and its particular temporal relations, is forced to take change into account, as other media may but are not forced to.

Enmeshed in the Symbolic, video is also imbricated in the production of history and cannot claim eternity like other media, not least because of the phenomena of lost generations, as the material moves from master to submaster, to broadcast, to timeshift, where it begins to degenerate with every play. Moreover, video must test the probity, the fragility, the reality of its sources and itself at every turn, for example in Gary Hill's *Why Do Things Get in a Muddle,* whose radically disturbing account of entropy relies less on Gregory Bateson's texts than on the technique of getting the performers to recite their lines backwards prior to reversing them into 'normal' speech. This is not simply a matter of techniques which other media may but also may not employ: it is a question of the ways in which video, whether as art, as campaign material or as timeshift, partakes of the processes of becoming not as a matter of choice, but as a function of its specific historical and material conditions. This becomes an ethical position, defining itself against any refusal to question, any wilful ignorance which exceeds the powers of imposed stupidity. Acceptance of the comfortable banalities is acquiescence in the evils worked everyday in the name of our comfort. Video, as a practice which excludes the metaphysics of Being underlying broadcasting's eternal presence, denies that cosy, finally sadistic apathy.

This has to do with seizing the practice of radical critique as our own. . . . [T]hat has been at the risk of an equally radical confusion. The intensity of self-questioning (as distinct from self-reflection) in the independent sector raises methodical doubt to the level of cultural *raison-d'être*. Moreover, confusion may not be all bad: the 'logic' of cultural capitalism is all too clear, too neat, too rational. To think for ourselves is the first duty. The mediation of 'public opinion' carried out by dominant media produces the homogeneity on which the status quo depends. Alternative media must escape the statistical norms of polls and pundits to arrive at a democracy of the image.

The core function of television is the resolution of conflict between the giver of laws and the ill-fitting, rebellious subjects that cannot be totally suborned to its narcissistic Imaginary. Narcissistic because power, like the narcissism of the infant child, recognises no limits, no rules: those arrive only with the Oedipus complex, with its first act of legislation, the prohibition against incest, on which sexual difference, according to psychoanalysis, is premised. Imaginary because it is embroiled entirely in self-image, excluding the Symbolic world of language and communication which, however ruled and regulated, is always a matter of other people. In its classical phase, when most closely related to Christianity, science attempted to reveal and to conquer nature: Mother Nature. In the period in which we live this Oedipal rape is resituated in another set of projects designed to rebuild a pre-Oedipal phase of wholeness. Total immersion in the mother's body through the absorbative properties of the video monitor (cf. Skirrow 1986); reformulation of the maternal body through the imagination of the ecosphere as totality; recovery of infantile conditions through legislation like the Education Reform Act, which seeks to restore the classroom conditions of our rulers' childhood (and, in a more round about way, via broadcasting deregulation, imaged on the model of the impact of commercial and US army stations on the BBC of our governors' youth). The mode of survival after the great western systems have failed—religion, science, the humanism possible before Auschwitz—must be an artifice. For the rulers, that artifice must be one which offers to absolve, to wipe out difference, to collapse the Symbolic into the Imaginary. Broadcasting homogenises, and through its Imaginary community proposes an absolution by producing a series of perpetual Others in order to produce a register of the Same. Guerrilla media plunge into a universe of boundaries and their transgression, of difference and heterogeneity. The refusal to be the Same, and the insistence on (decentred) individuality form the second necessary condition of democratic media.

The term 'art' is one which is treated gingerly on the Left. My preferred definition has been that art is that field of practices which is retailed through galleries—an instrumental and in many ways dismissive description, one which follows the lines of film theory as it cast off the literary notions of author, creativity and genius. Yet it is to art, to the aesthetic domain, that a secular age turns for the production of profound meanings which might help us understand our status in the universe and our relations to ourselves and others. The secret of religion is that it recognises that these yearnings for 'a time beyond us, yet ourselves' (Stevens 1955: 165) are properly popular, and form an important element of the field of popular pleasures. The intellectual Left has still to lose its puritanism. It has remained variously colonialist, knowing, coy and patronising about popular pleasures. It is essential to recognise in ourselves and others the actually existing terms of pleasure, and to seek out that passionate involvement which is now almost entirely left to the dominant media.

Lacan as analyst of masculinity contends that what artists share as a problematic is the *'manque à être'*, the paucity of being in the world which bedevils the Lacanian—male—subject. We—men—are constantly hailed by ego ideals of ability, of assurance, of fullness to ourselves. But the obdurate reality of our beings is always and in various ways less than those ideas. The experience of lack which is the core of Lacan's psychoanalysis is the heartland, again in Lacan's analysis, of spirituality: the yearning for fulfillment, the proximity of annihilation. The roots of a passionate culture thrive, not in a comfortable mulch of pious wishes, but at the foot of that other tree on which Christ's despair speaks for the human condition: 'My God, My God, why hast Thou forsaken Me?'

We have survived: survived the Death of God, the end of science, the decline of the west, even ecological disaster. Carnival today, perhaps to this extent different from the medieval carnivals described by Bakhtin, is a kind of *danse macabre* which, once a year, tries to reclaim a sense of place from the anonymity of the streets. It is a celebration of where we are now, a celebration of survival, a bid for making these spaces we inhabit Home. This is where video is posed its awesome task—to reverse that trend, to make Home the site of carnival. The fear and loathing that once surrounded the nomad witnessed by the prayers of the Gaelic monks for protection from the Vikings is with us still in the rhetoric of Thatcher, who in a 1978 speech on immigration announced that 'The British character has done so much for democracy, for law, and done so much throughout the world that if there is any fear that it might be swamped, people are going to react.' (This speech gave the Metropolitan Police the name for 'Operation Swamp', the massive presence in Brixton which sparked the uprisings of 1981.) In the modern period, this becomes allied with the cult of the anonymous, wandering, amorphous 'man of the crowd' from Poe to Launder and Gilliat's *Millions Like Us,* and undergoes a further transformation in the age of suburbia, the private car and the domestic leisure centre. In the dialectic of displacement, the displaced serve the function of validating Others, proving our rootedness by calling for us to act as hosts. In this exchange, the powerful get more power. Surrounding the airports with immigration controls and customs regulations, binding our movements and the potential of the electronic image to surveillance by closed-circuit television: they still do not trust us to fly. The holiday-maker sneaking in an extra bottle or a gram of hash has a tactic of refusal, but as de Certeau argues, tactics are for the weak: the strong have strategies, and strategies depend upon the occupation of a place—be it geographical, institutional or discursive—a place which 'permits one to capitalise on acquired advantages, to prepare for future expansions, and to give . . . an independence in relation to the variability of circumstances. It is a mastery of time by the founding of an autonomous place' (de Certeau 1980).

Although the postmodern suburb is not locatable within geographical space (since one suburb is much the same as every other), it is tied to other communities of interest through the car, the telephone, the (carefully selected) dinner guests and institutional sites such as schools and supermarkets. For a segment of society, these communities of interest constitute the local. For others living in the inner-city, the Third World of the suburban psyche, geographical territory is the major marker of cultural identity. The postmodern thesis of the mediasphere fails to recognise the *localisation* of power within the hurtling images. It extends the totalitarian grip of capital by the same token—insistent on the ontological nature of the phenomena it describes, giving hyperreality a metaphysical status as the end beyond which we may not move spatially or even historically. Such fatalism is an alibi for style in the place of journalism, allegory in the place of analysis and observation in the place of action. It is a strategy of pessimism from a position of power: promising, in the work of Baudrillard, Deleuze and Guattari and, even more so, among their North American avatars, the fullness of 'consumer society' to itself, the availability of satisfactions, the fulfillment of desire and so, as desire is the motor of history, the end of history and the beginning of time as a pure, uninflected extension of the western present. Alternative media, by contrast, must be specific to their time and place, must recognise the parameters of their specificity, and build their strategies on that.

Negation appears to me the most useful tool we have in hand for understanding historical processes in an epoch in which history is largely ignored or abandoned as unusable in a sinister and simplistic discourse of 'That was then, this is now.' The celebrants as well as the Cassandras of the postmodern operate in a shifting terrain of verb tenses which work through simple, ugly and constraining binaries—'In the past . . . but now', 'nowadays . . . in the future'—without either specifying the thresholds at which these momentous changes are to take (or have taken) place, or how the two thresholds relate to each other. At the same time, the modern is held to cover a period as extended as Foucault's Classical Age, starting in the sixteenth century, or as curtailed and amorphous as 'the twentieth century' or 'pre-war'. The return of chronology, and an unquestioning transfer of the epistemological break from the discursive to the material universe, goes hand in hand with the abandonment of the world beyond western Europe and North America, possibly adding Australia and Japan.

Television . . . proposes itself as the eternal present, while video makes that proposal leaky and finally untenable. But in that case, we have to argue a position dangerously close to the weird chronologies of postmodernism: after video, no more presence. Yet that does not mean that we have no alternative but to accommodate ourselves to ahistoricism and the abolition of the local. The alternative to presence is not the simulacral, but process and becoming, the micro and the macro of historical struggle. The role of negation is to refuse the givenness of the world that presents itself to us, mediately and immediately: to recognise the specificity of what is now becoming, here, in its relations to more global historical change. What I would propose is a kind of ecological model. The most successful political alternative of the 1980s and 1990s, one which offers a *grand récit* despite Lyotard's strictures, ecology provides more than an ethics of shopping, though that is in itself a remarkable achievement.

'The Butterfly Effect' is the term given by meteorologists to the idea that even the minuscule drafts created by the fluttering of a butterfly's wings have eventual effects in the closed system of the weather: just as nothing is forgotten in the Freudian unconscious, so the atmosphere retains every breath, every draft, every local condition as a part of its macrosystemic permutations. It is an effect illuminated with great elegance in Steve Hawley's tape *The Extent of Three Bells,* in which the comet-tails produced on video equipment by the movement of candle flames across a darkened room is choreographed with the music of traditional bell-ringing. The dialogics systematised by Todorov out of Bakhtin and Volosinov suggest a parallel cultural model: not a word, not a sign that is lost in the global movements of the cultural formation. Utterances may be mislaid, repressed or denied, but their effects cannot be lost, destroyed or, ultimately, forgiven.

I remember a science fiction story, misplaced in the library of memories, in which, despite fears of changing history, a machine is sent back from contemporary New York to observe the origins of life on this planet. As the machine returns, the triumphant demonstrator waves a long purple tentacle over his head: 'There, you see', it says, 'Nothing has changed!' Our memories are ourselves, and we have charge of creating memories. But the process of remembering is also a field of contradiction, of renegotiation and dispute, biography and ideology. And memory—say in the form of DNA—can be unkind and (since it is a code) misleading, open to polysemy: transsexuals among others have every reason to distrust the pairings of amino acids in the double helix, the material of genetic coding that determines biological sex. None the less, the raw material on which we work and the ways we know to work upon it are our common lot. Our work is then a common one, though riven through by contradiction at every level.

Within that field of contradiction there are nodes of power, institutionally-based discourses capable of regimenting the entire panjandrum—almost. As Enzensberger writes in 'A Critique of Political Ecology' (in Enzensberger 1988), the difference between materialist and ecologist is the determination on the part of the former that the distinction human/natural is inadequate to comprehend (accurately enough for successful action) the flux through and around the complex relations of people with their environments. In particular, human discourse is structured in dominance: we make our own histories but not in conditions of our own choosing. As the ecosystem must take account of every movement throughout its totality, however mediated by intervening actions, so we must work with the whole sphere of the social, but also with the weight of history. Video work is about difference, about dialogue, about place and about time.

Time has a particular set of relevances to video. The new medium belongs to the world described by Benedict Anderson (1983) as the era of print capitalism: a period in which the older circular time of agrarian societies gives way to the linear time of industrial society. Electronic media bolt this new temporal axis together with space. As Robert C. Allen argues (1985), electronic media tend towards paradigmatic rather than syntagmatic time, where the syntagm refers to the ordering of images and sound in linear time, but the paradigm operates a system of cross-referencing with other sights and sounds far more spatial in its orientation. The most familiar combined form is in machine memory, where a frame-store, for example, might hold not only the history of work on a particular project, but also all the other images which have been grabbed and manipulated in the process. But there are other forms of historical imagination: horror, the imagination of finality; the time of boredom and self-disgust most poignantly caught in the suicide note of the poet Mayakovsky: 'the love boat/ has crashed against the everyday' (quoted in Shklovsky 1972: 201); the intoxication of the endless paradigmatic present. To these we might also add Braudel's *longue durée,* the huge historical epochs over which climates, trade routes and modes of production change, and the awesome scale of astronomical time. What is productive is the interplay of these timescales. It is essential to realise that the ancient scales persist, just as sailors still navigate with the Ptolemaic system, alongside the most recent. Machine memory, the Foucauldian archive of images as much as the computer frame-store, is largely information as opposed to knowledge, and to that extent the word memory is a misnomer. K. S. Gill (1986) argues that this conforms to a distinction between economic and social wealth creation, or between capitalist accumulation and the distribution of wealth. The point is to create the structures through which such information becomes knowledge, and to seize control of local knowledge.

This, of course, sits at the borders of legality. Hacking is a seed bed of the new electronic culture: the lure of William Gibson's hacker dystopias (1986; 1987; 1989) is the sense of entry into and disturbance of the hardware. On the one hand, we could argue with Whitby (1986) and Weizenbaum (1984) that 'One of the reasons someone might become a compulsive programmer is that a programmer has total and complete control over his/her program . . . software engineers regard disobedient programs as very dangerous things (except perhaps from the extreme fringe of AI work)' (Whitby 1986: 120). This should remind us of Skirrow's (1986) thesis concerning video games and the maternal body: the narcissistic relation to video is one of power, and nothing is so frustrating to that emotional attachment to the VDU than a fault that interferes with the pleasures of mastery. At the same time, there is the lure of disobedience, and of the potential for unleashing unforeseen processes, the call of chaos. Paik entered these arenas in his early work. Yet the more advanced and user-friendly the machinery becomes, the less possible it is to gain entry to the programming software. Expensive paint systems, for example, will not let you determine the possibilities or shift their parameters. The future may belong to the treated image— the camera has never been the sole device for making moving-image media, and its role is diminishing daily—but there is no 'access' to the means of its treatment, other than forcible entry. A great deal of the future of electronic media will lie in the hands of engineers, software architects, programmers: it is easy to envisage a culture in which the aesthetic relation is no longer based on finished texts, but on the ways in which a programme can be manipulated by its users, so that the true computer art would not be like existing show-reels, but actual pieces of software for the user to create with. The designer of the Quantel Paintbox would be the real artist, not the producers of flying logos and credit sequences that use it.

This new relation to the machine, however, opens another whole element in the theory of democratic media: the technological relation and the ways it relates to the extremities of human experience. Between the strangeness of our relations to ourselves, to each other and to the biosphere of local space, there subsists an instant of uncomprehending awe, the experience of the sublime that reframes and undercuts our comprehension of the Beautiful and the Good. The best, as Lacan observes (1986: 256), is the enemy of the good—and of goods. Sublimity puts us in awe—since the question persists after the death of God, in awe of what?—in awe of the mismatch between the poverty of the world we have created, and the wealth of the means at our disposal to change it.

Todorov's account of Bakhtin's 'philosophical anthropology' devolves upon the relation of self and other, the impossibility of solipsism. My perception of myself is necessarily partial: to be perceived as a totality, I depend on others, for example to witness my birth or my death:

> The very being of man (exterior as interior) is a *profound communication.*
> *Being* signifies *communication.* . . . Being signifies being for an other and,
> through them, for oneself. Man does not possess a sovereign internal
> territory, he is entirely and always on a frontier; looking inside himself, he
> looks *into the eyes of an other* or *through the eyes of another.*
>
> (Mikhail Bakhtin, 'Concerning the Revision of the Book on Dostoyevsky', 1961; in
> Todorov 1981: 148)

The functions of this other, witness to life and to birth, had long been the province of divinity. In a secular world, the same function must be transferred to the totality of the human world, visibly manifest in the ecology of language, in which, as in the global ecosystem, each utterance only takes place as a result of, in concert with and in relation to, every other utterance. For us, however, the issue is one of the relation of this complex to the audio-visual media, the new complex of self, Other and machine that finds such popular expression in the horror genre.

If horror as a cultural affect continues to act consistently, it is because we still internalise and visit upon ourselves, our bodies and our planet— all now refigured in the guise of objects, of Others—in fantasy and reality, the fantastic wrath of the abandoned *infans*. The guards at Treblinka played at fort-da with human identity (and indeed with the identities of the dogs they trained to attack men's genitals): in the cultural forms of horror we play the game with our own bodies—dismembered, returned to wholeness. Re-enacting compulsively the moment of loss on the figure of our bodies—and Whitehouse is quite wrong: identification is *always* with the victim, *never* with the perpetrator—we perform a psychic act of denial, a *Verneinung,* on our relations with ourselves.

Because film and tape have recorded what, in any decent world, should never have occurred; because this English language has been fouled with utterances—commands, remembrances, cries—that should never have been spoken; because uniforms clothe the torturers and smiles cover the tracks of gun-runners and arms dealers; because, all the same, we must speak, and work through images, and wear clothes and use the language of our bodies, because we are always already in the Symbolic, I must speak. And in speaking there is a virtually existential imperative to try to produce, even if it is only for myself, a way of speaking and acting that allows of respect, for my others and so for myself. The beautiful precision of these media—language, video—is marred, even invalidated by the uses to which they have been put. Perhaps this is the appeal of synthetic images generated by computer, the secret of their cleanness: that they emerge, or so it appears, from the mathematic universe of machine codes and Boolean algebra. They do not belong to us but to the dark interiors of the devices we have made, whose capabilities already exceed what uses we can make of them. In the new dialectic between the human and the machine that characterises the late twentieth century, replacing Lévi-Strauss's dialectic of nature and culture, it is the machine that is clean, and we ourselves the unclean.

Kristeva's work on abjection carries us further towards an understanding of what this might mean for us. The abject—which seems very close to *Das Ding* in Lacanian usage—is that which you try to expel in involuntary vomiting, but it is also your 'self' that you expel and abject. Abjection is therefore a kind of narcissistic crisis, as revulsion hurls us away from that which marks the limits of our being: birth, death, dirt. Two causes bring about this crisis:

> *A too great severity on the part of the Other,* confounded with the One and the Law. And *the failure of the Other* which becomes apparent in the breakdown of objects of desire. In each case, the abject appears in order to uphold the 'I' in the Other. The abject is the violence of mourning for an object that is always already lost. The abject smashes the wall of repression and its judgements. It resituates the ego at those abominable limits from which, in order to be, it had detached itself—it resituates it in the non-ego, in the drive, in death. Abjection is a resurrection which passes through death (of the ego).
>
> (Kristeva 1980: 22)

In the wake of the cult of hygiene which blossomed in the mid-twentieth century, we have assumed all the dirt, leaving the machines clean: it is they, in some senses, who become our Other, confounded with the rule-giving, paternal figure of the One (whose unity underpins the ideologies of being, presence and identity) and the Law. In a moral order in which objects, having initially been produced as objects, are then categorized and hierarchised, the abject revolts at separation.

Yet via our technologies, we can be resituated at the brink of that loss. And it is in this nexus that the relation between the body, and its 'loathsome' interiors, with the machine enters into the play. At the limit between life and death arrives a third term, that which has never lived. The ambiguity recycles in android movies, the inside-out Freddy of the *Elm Street* series, in graphic novels and techno-pop. It emerges in fantasies of the future: cloning, for example, and the figure of the cyborg. And it is present in such areas as reproductive technologies (cf. Corea 1986) and medical practice generally. Corea argues that the control over birth acts also as a control over death, a bid for immortality through gene-cloning, prosthesis (cf. McLuhan's 'prosthetic media') and transplant surgery. We can thus arrive at a thesis of 'unmournable death' (Hayles 1987: 80), a refusal to accept death, the deaths of others or our own, which takes the form of unsuccessful repression, taken up and obliterated by the dominant media, which cannot provide a substitute for the older rituals through which our forebears laid their ghosts. Freud analyses unsuccessful mourning and melancholia alike as disguises for an unwillingness to come to terms with the hatred felt by a subject for its mourned object:

> On the one hand a strong fixation to the loved object must have been present; on the other hand, in contradiction to this, the object cathexis must have had little power of resistance. As Otto Rank has aptly remarked, this contradiction seems to imply that object-choice has been effected on a narcissistic basis, so that the object cathexis, when obstacles come in its way, can regress to narcissism.
>
> (Freud [1917] 1984: 258)

A major function of new video will be to negotiate that mourning which we have never been able to conclude, to create forms in which the relation to death can be expressed, in which we can face the founding loss on which our culture and society is based. The alternative is a final act of mania, a withdrawal of the emotional bond to the objects of our affections ('object-cathexis') that returns us to a primary narcissism let loose in the nursery of universal destruction.

The centre-out model of broadcasting criticised by Enzensberger ('Constituents of a Theory of the Media', in Enzensberger 1988) is unable to handle process. Stuck in its eternal present, it has become static, able to increase quantitatively but not qualitatively through the addition of non-terrestrial channels. It seeks its novelties from the domain of video practice as narrowly defined: the world of community, campaign and artists' video provides the raw materials (and sometimes the personnel) for youth programming, advertising, pop video and new modes of documentary. It is in the margins that the nub of the culture now appears, a decentralised centre. The vital organs of the culture, the messy, vulnerable organs that keep us alive, are on the outside.

Video is not whole, though in its reference to reality it at times hypostatises a whole real preceding its activities, sometimes the real of television, sometimes that of the political world. Its wholeness and its reality however lie outside of each individual work, even outside the domain of video practice—including viewing—in general. Built in an aesthetics of difference, contemporary video practice encompasses as much as TV, and also includes TV itself, in a field of radical heterogeneity. The point of analysing it is not to restore it to wholeness, nor to celebrate the end of global modes of thinking, but to indicate its relation to the material absence of wholeness, and to the two routes which it takes to achieving some kind of alternate solidity, through intertextuality (and therefore intersubjectivity), and through reference to a common negativity vis-à-vis the accepted presentation of realities. Perhaps another route might be through what was described above . . . as an ethical imperative, the critique of homogeneity as the apathetic acceptance of (the injustices which provide) comfort.

To take control of a means (but not the means) of production in this world is to make a qualitative shift from the ossifying forms of multinational and corporate capital in broadcasting to a more chaotic system, one whose 'organisation' exceeds the forms of previous systems through increasing levels of self-organisation. It is to assert with Whitehead the primacy of relations in the processes of innovation, that each new existent receives its identity from its relations with others, and adds to them all their new relations with itself (Whitehead 1969: 26ff.): that individual or small group activity is not without its significance, or the need to take responsibility for what is undertaken. This in turn implies again that relations are also relations of struggle, mapped through contradictions in the actual situations in which we act, not in abstract models of homogeneity.

Prigogine and Stengers note that

> The specific form in which time was introduced into physics, as a tendency towards homogeneity and death, reminds us more of ancient mythological and religious archetypes than of the progressive complexification and diversification described by biology and the social sciences. . . . The rapid transformation of the technological mode of interaction with nature, the constantly accelerating pace of change experienced by the nineteenth century, produced a deep anxiety. This anxiety is still with us and takes various forms, from the repeated proposals for a 'zero-growth' society or for a moratorium on scientific research to the announcement of 'scientific truths' concerning our disintegrating universe.
>
> (Prigogine and Stengers 1988: 116)

The often observed prevalence of pessimism as a cultural form in the 1980s has a longer heritage, which the previous quotation locates in the evolution of the theory of entropy. Such a pessimism undoubtedly underpins Baudrillard, and to some extent the claims of right-wing 'ecology' (the coca-colonialism of population control, the 'one-worldism' of Gorbachev): the crisis is now, 'we' must all pull in 'our' belts, we are all on this ship together (but some of the bastards are travelling first class). The mythologising of eco-disaster allows for a politics of crisis management in which social contradiction is pushed aside in favour of short-term solutions of often the most Draconian kind (cf. Ryle 1988).

Ecological disaster here stands in as the acceptable vision of the death of God: here, someone must pay, but the someone is clearly anyone other than the global ruling class. In the Thatcherite version, it works as the otherwise unavailable mourning, undertaken in the spirit of a patrician stewardship of the Earth (the same rhetoric as employed by the aristocratic landowners of Norfolk in the East Anglian Filmmakers' documentary *The Poacher*). What we need to distinguish between are the rhetoric of 'green' policies (often driven through at the expense, for example, of Amazonian peasants or 'dirty'-industry workers), especially as they recruit from the pessimism of the nineteenth century or from the residual needs of populations for a sense of the sublime, and the possibility of building an ecological perspective on aesthetics, especially here in video. The first is a reaction to the 'failure of the Other' cited by Kristeva (1980: 22): the second is a response to the unavailability of the lost object, a readiness to face the physical and material reality of death, dirt and decay as the ambit within which the human subject operates, and a grasp on the intersubjectivity which makes us human.

Lyotard has spent some time examining the shape of the sublime in relation to death. In a 1984 catalogue essay he describes a suite of works by the American Barnett Newman:

> In 1966, Newman shows the fourteen *Stations of the Cross* at the Guggenheim. He gives them the subtitle *Lamma Sabachtani,* the cry of distress which the crucified Christ hurls towards God: why have You abandoned me? 'This question without a reply', he writes in the accompanying *Notice,* 'has been with us for so long—since Jesus—since Abraham—since Adam—it is the original question'. Jewish version of the Passion: the reconciliation of existence (and therefore of death) with signification has not taken place. The Messiah, bringer of meaning, always makes us wait. The only answer ever heard to the questioning of the abandoned is not *Know why,* but: *Be.*
>
> (reprinted in Lyotard 1988: 98)

The increasingly Kantian note which, as Meaghan Morris observes in her essay on 'Postmodernity and Lyotard's Sublime' (in Morris 1988), pervades his recent writings on politics and culture, is far removed from the realm of popular pleasures. The harsh return to a Greenbergian aesthetics of the purity of painting in and for itself denotes a severe elitism in his approach, one that moreover reaches its apotheosis in the instant, not of becoming, but of Being, that supremely metaphysical and monolithic state.

Maybe, in place of the sublime (a quality, it could be argued, of the art work itself), we should argue awe as the entity to be analysed, a quality of the subject/object relation in which the object loses its limits as object, invading the processes that constitute the subject, in a movement in which the subject also bleeds over into the object. Such a thesis would site horror as an effect in the imagination of one's own dissolution. One of the great truisms of popular wisdom is that if you dream of falling, you must wake before you hit the bottom: impact only occurs in the dream at the moment of the real dreamer's death. This tale is symptomatic of the relation of awe: the moving (*movance*—a movement defined not by the points from and to which it travels but by the activity of moving) between identification and loss of subjectivity beyond the exchange of ego for ego-ideal in visual pleasure: a horror which, in its finality, reduces to common humanity (beyond regimes, for example, of sexual and racial difference) while simultaneously insisting on the dreamer's own specificity, absolute difference.

I wonder whether Eisenstein's 'montage of effects' has reemerged as the montage of affects in the pyrotechnic cinema of Spielberg and Lucas, and in the contemporary horror film. Their popularity would then be legible in terms of a loss of self which they offer in the spectacle of the destruction of objects, the imagination of finality, the engagement, not of knowledge, but of ignorance: destruction of the self in the eyes of others, an end in as well as of language. As mentioned above, every cinema usher knows that audiences identify with victims: fear is the attraction. That is the confrontation which Viola urges in *I Do Not Know What It Is That I Am Like* and its images of decay. This is me, in some sense which precludes (precedes?) meaning: awe in the face of the faceless. Beyond the postmodern play of identity is the unaddressed, unaddressable realm of non-identity: no dissolution into infinite semiosis, but the finality of one's own death, one's own birth, one's own fragile and passionate materiality: the zero-state of animal consciousness—no identity, no oneness, no incompletion, no entropy: the further side of experience that can only be spoken of in the negative.

Nor is this phenomenal obverse of the totalitarian nature of language and culture purely individual, though it starts in each different person and has its roots there in the most intimate hinterland between body and mind. Citing Fanon's dictum that 'It is to the zone of occult instability where the people dwell that we must come' (Fanon 1967: 182-3), James Donald argues that the politics of 'such a shadowy borderland' might learn from the 'sublime'

> an attention to the materiality and limits of representation, and to their inevitable inadequacy to the idea of totality, and so also a certain pragmatic modesty. And, not least, from the transgressive and creative aspects of popular culture it might learn not only the impossibility of political closure but also the critical possibilities of social and cultural heterogeneity for an aspiration towards community that always remains to be brought into being.
>
> (Donald 1989: 248-9)

The popular sublime demands just such a deference, not to the theological command to 'Be', but, precisely, to the processes of emergence and disappearance, of arrival and fading that mark video as their own. Video cannot, and should not try, to imagine the future—the traditional role of the final chapter of books on new technologies—but to set up the terms on which the future might emerge: to seize that initiative back from the 'global postmodern' (in Stuart Hall's phrase in a talk at the 'Changing Identities' conference, London, May 1989) which exists, in the main, precisely to halt the emergence of the new through its prose-lytising theories of sameness. Transgression, it should be recalled, is not some tidy mess on the gallery floor, assimilable into the deft and inane paradoxes of postmodernism, but potentially violent, ugly, foul, disgusting: beyond the regimen of taste that regulates the tasteful and the kitsch alike, it will above all not be nice. I think that I will probably loathe it in its emergence.

There is, however, every risk of becoming prescriptive as to what kind of video practice might be entailed by the strictures outlined in this chapter. While recognising the issues in the impact of magnetic media on the environment—energy-efficient? ozone-friendly? biodegradable? safe work-stations?—what I have in mind is a democracy of the media, in which management in all its forms—corporate, governmental, psy-chic—gives way to a serious and responsible play from which evolu-tion, even through the kind of radical instability described in Prigogine's chaos theory, can produce the grounds on which cultural and techno-logical means of communication are opened up for play and for change. To do so, we must give up the melancholia prevalent in the culture, finish mourning the body of the all-knowing God who for so long legitimated religion and science, recognise the powers that oppress us for what they are and begin to dismantle them. The radical questioning at the heart of contemporary video practice is part and parcel of these processes.

The replicability of video, as it loses generations, means that, in art terms, it loses value: ubiquity at the price of unicity. But as it approaches the finite limit of lost generations, the valueless approaches the price-less. The moments, their transitoriness marked in the edits, the new metaphysical space of the image-generator, these do not promise a utopia. What can be said of an audio-visual culture in which the adverts cost more, use better equipment and compete seriously for talent with the programmes? Is this the rationale for the ascendancy of style over content and the deteriorating status of the referential?

And yet: work is being done. It is important to operate between impossibility and utopia: pessimism of the intellect, optimism of the will, in Gramsci's slogan. Video succeeds when it is heteroclite, when it moves by contradiction, from document to generation, from medium to material, from simple grapheme to complex lexicon and back. Video has already added to Metz's five codes of cinema (writing, speech, sound, music and image) with image-grabbing, treated images, multi-ple-perspective images, the interfacing of cel and stop-frame animation with computer technology, tapes based in photocopying technologies or ultrasound scanning. . . . Video's strength is its ability to cut across the interstices, to play upon the contradictions, of the regimes of looking and hearing that structure the dominant audio-visual world. Its very weakness, its indefiniteness, becomes its field of possibility: the necessity of pluriform tactics, since no structure of power presents it with a strategy. Video is strong because it evades, is larger than, exceeds, avoids, slips by and away from, cannot be accounted for in the discourses (including this one) about it.

To resume: video is out of control, at least in the software zone. The hardware is still open to remaking, and a generation of artist-technicians is in the making, for whom software architectures and chip design will be potential areas for creative work. The problem is that such creativity is most immediately rewarded inside transnational corporations, rewarded in any case fiscally. You can't blame someone for accepting £40,000 a year as a paint-box editor in exchange for that creativity. But someone, somewhere has to break the circuit: to be prepared for a culture of the one-off machine, owned and built outside the structures of corporate capital. Artists generally are getting access only to machinery a generation out of date. The few technician-artists working with the emerging generations are so constrained by the commercial imperatives of hugely expensive research and development programmes that the artistic potentials of the machines take second place, let alone their role as social rather than economic capital. We need a generation of image-generation for its own sake to break the cycle. It seems poignant to have to argue this tired ideology, and to have to suggest that through it alone, the full commercial potential of the new computers will be realised. Taking the longer view: capital demands, in the UK at least, returns in two or three years. Software applications call for a far further horizon. Finally, capital cannot deliver on its promises.

Cable, satellite, opto-electronics, 4D animation . . . the capability for so much and the delivery (not only in the peculiar circumstances of the United Kingdom) so trivial. Artists have ceased to be sources, have made themselves conduits: no longer the unacknowledged legislators, they are the unofficial magistrates of a cultural regime they are no longer invited to understand or to help make. The dominant is a stagnant and dying culture whose highest aim—and even this it lacks the courage to realise—is to become decadent, as if it imagined a moment beyond itself and its own barrenness, the grounds for a new and fundamentally alien growth.

To confound this depressing prognosis, video will in all probability become transfixingly lovely. The emergent Europe of the 1990s will enter a new and quite probably capitalist or metacapitalist phase that will throw up new Jimi Hendrixes, new Frieda Kahlos, new Pablo Picassos of the electronic image. For the best part of this century, the majority, if not indeed the totality, of artists worth the time of day have been profoundly at odds with the dominant presuppositions of capital and its workings, though most have had to make a virtue of coming to terms with the non-negotiable. At the time of writing, capital has rarely seemed more triumphant in attracting the best talent. If this situation continues, we are doomed to a bland, inhuman, sadistic and narcissistic spiral. It is so easy to deflect aspiration for the best into acceptance of the good(s); to redirect yearning for the sublime into nostalgia for the womb. Yet in its triumph, capital cannot help making enemies, and it is they who will provide the greatest contribution to the species, or to whatever it might be that they will find to sing. The electronic media, for viewers as much as producers, like the social formation as a whole, is so productive of contradictions that there remains, in the absence of faith and of charity, that hope which baffles rational comprehension—hope that we could be surprised again, face the possibility of change so profound that nothing will ever be the Same again.

References

[Editors' Note: The following references have been extracted from the larger reference list of the source book in which this chapter originally appeared, and have been adapted slightly in style.]

Allen, R. C. (1985). *Speaking of soap operas.* Chapel Hill: University of North Carolina Press.

Anderson, B. (1983). *Imagined communities: Reflections on the origin and spread of nationalism.* London: Verso.

Corea, G. (1986). *The mother machine: Reproductive technologies from artificial insemination to artificial wombs.* New York: Harper & Row.

de Certeau, M. (1980). On the oppositional practices of everyday life. *Social Text, 3.*

Donald, J. (1989). The fantastic, the sublime and the popular: Or, what's at stake in vampire films. In J. Donald (Ed.), *Fantasy and the cinema.* London: British Film Institute.

Enzensberger, H. M. (1988). *Dreamers of the absolute: Essays on ecology, media and power.* London: Radius.

Fanon, F. (1967). *The wretched of the earth.* Harmondsworth: Penguin.

Gibson, W. (1986). *Neuromancer.* London: Gratton.

Gibson, W. (1987). *Count zero.* London: Gratton.

Gill, K. S. (Ed.). (1986). *Artificial intelligence and society.* London: John Wiley.

Hayles, K. (1987). Cyborgs: Postmodern phantasms of mind and body. *Discourse, 9.*

Kristeva, J. (1980). *Pouvoirs de l'horreur: Essai sur l'objection.* Paris: Seuil.

Lacan, J. (1986). *Le Séminaire: Vol. 7. L'éthique de la psychoanalyse.* Paris: Seuil.

Lyotard, J.-F. (1988). *L'inhumaine: Causeries sur le temps.* Paris: Galilée.

Metz, C. (1977). *Psychoanalysis and cinema: The imaginary signifier.* London: Macmillan.

Michaels, E. (1986). *Aboriginal invention of television: Central Australia 1982-86* (report). Canberra: Australian Institute of Aboriginal Studies.

Morris, M. (1988). *The pirate's fiancée: Feminism, reading, postmodernism.* London: Verso.

Prigogine, I., & Stengers, I. (1988). *Order out of chaos: Man's new dialogue with nature.* London: Flamingo.

Ryle, M. (1988). *Ecology and socialism.* London: Radius.

Shklovsky, V. (1972). *Mayakovsky and his circle.* London: Pluto.

Skirrow, G. (1986). Hellivision: An analysis of video games. In C. MacCabe (Ed.), *High theory/low culture.* Manchester: Manchester University Press.

Stevens, W. (1955). *Collected poems.* London: Faber and Faber.

Todorov, T. (1981). *Mikhaïl Bakhtine: le principe dialogique, suivi de Écrits du Cercle de Bakhtine.* Paris: Seuil.

Weizenbaum, J. (1984). *Computer power and human reason.* Harmondsworth: Pelican.

Whitby, B. (1986). The computer as cultural artefact. In K. S. Gill (Ed.), *Artificial intelligence and society.* London: John Wiley.

Whitehead, A. N. (1969). *Process and reality: An essay in cosmology.* New York: Free Press.

Commercial television is not an autonomous object of study; it can only be grasped for what it is by positioning it dialectically over against that other signifying system which we have called experimental video, or video art.

2

Surrealism Without the Unconscious

FREDRIC R. JAMESON

It has often been said that every age is dominated by a privileged form, or genre, which seems by its structure the fittest to express its secret truths; or perhaps, if you prefer a more contemporary way of thinking about it, which seems to offer the richest symptom of what Sartre would have called the "objective neurosis" of that particular time and place. Today, however, I think we would no longer look for such characteristic or symptomatic objects in the world and the language of forms or genres. Capitalism, and the modern age, is a period in which, with the extinction of the sacred and the "spiritual," the deep underlying materiality of all things has finally risen dripping and convulsive into the light of day; and it is clear that culture itself is one of those things whose fundamental materiality is now for us not merely evident but quite inescapable. This has, however, also been a historical lesson: it is because culture has *become* material that we are now in a position to understand that it always *was* material, or materialistic, in its structures and functions. We postcontemporary people have a word for that discovery—a word that has tended to displace the older language of genres and forms—and this is, of course, the word *medium,* and in particular its plural, *media,* a word which now conjoins three relatively distinct signals: that of an artistic mode or specific form of aesthetic production, that of a specific technology, generally organized around a central apparatus or machine; and that, finally, of a social institution. These three areas of meaning do not define a medium, or the media, but designate the distinct dimensions that must be addressed in order for such a definition to be completed or constructed. It should be evident that most traditional and modern aesthetic concepts—largely, but not exclusively, designed for literary texts—do not require this simultaneous attention to the multiple dimensions of the material, the social, and the aesthetic.

It is because we have had to learn that culture today is a matter of media that we have finally begun to get it through our heads that culture was always that, and that the older forms or genres, or indeed the older spiritual exercises and meditations, thoughts and expressions, were also in their very different ways media products. The intervention of the machine, the mechanization of culture, and the mediation of culture by the Consciousness Industry are now everywhere the case, and perhaps it might be interesting to explore the possibility that they were always the case throughout human history, and within even the radical difference of older, precapitalist modes of production.

Nonetheless, what is paradoxical about this displacement of literary terminology by an emergent mediatic conceptuality is that it takes place at the very moment in which the philosophical priority of language itself and of the various linguistic philosophies has become dominant and well-nigh universal. Thus, the written text loses its privileged and exemplary status at the very moment when the available conceptualities for analyzing the enormous variety of objects of study with which "reality" presents us (now all in their various ways designated as so many "texts") have become almost exclusively linguistic in orientation. Media analysis in linguistic or semiotic terms therefore may well appear to involve an imperializing enlargement of the domain of language to include nonverbal—visual or musical, bodily, spatial—phenomena; but it may equally well spell a critical and disruptive challenge to the very conceptual instruments which have been mobilized to complete this operation of assimilation.

As for the emergent priority of the media today, this is scarcely a new discovery. For some seventy years the cleverest prophets have warned us regularly that the dominant art form of the twentieth century was not literature at all—nor even painting or theater or the symphony—but rather the one new and historically unique art invented in the contemporary period, namely film; that is to say, the first distinctively mediatic art form. What is strange about this prognosis—whose unassailable validity has with time become a commonplace—is that it should have had so little practical effect. Indeed, literature, sometimes intelligently and opportunistically absorbing the techniques of film back into its own substance, remained throughout the modern period the ideologically dominant paradigm of the aesthetic and continued to hold open a space in which the richest varieties of innovation were pursued. Film, however, whatever its deeper consonance with twentieth-century realities, entertained a merely fitful relationship to the modern in that sense, owing, no doubt, to the two distinct lives or identities through which, successively (like Virginia Woolf's *Orlando*), it was destined to pass: the first, the silent period, in which some lateral fusion of the mass audience and the formal or modernist proved viable (in ways and resolutions we can no longer grasp, owing to our peculiar historical amnesia); the second, the sound period, then coming as the dominance of mass-cultural (and commercial) forms through which the medium must toil until again reinventing the forms of the modern in a new way in the great auteurs of the 1950s (Hitchcock, Bergman, Kurosawa, Fellini).

What this account suggests is that however helpful the declaration of the priority of film over literature in jolting us out of print culture and/or logocentrism, it remained an essentially modernist formulation, locked in a set of cultural values and categories which are in full post-modernism demonstrably antiquated and "historical." That film has today become postmodernist, or at least that certain films have, is obvious enough; but so have some forms of literary production. The argument turned, however, on the priority of these forms, that is, their capacity to serve as some supreme and privileged, symptomatic, index of the zeitgeist; to stand, using a more contemporary language, as the cultural *dominant* of a new social and economic conjuncture; to stand—now finally putting the most philosophically adequate face on the matter—as the richest allegorical and hermeneutic vehicles for some new description of the system itself. Film and literature no longer do that, although I will not belabor the largely circumstantial evidence of the increasing dependency of each on materials, forms, technology, and even thematics borrowed from the other art or medium I have in mind as the most likely candidate for cultural hegemony today.

The identity of that candidate is certainly no secret: it is clearly video, in its twin manifestations as commercial television and experimental video, or "video art." This is not a proposition one proves; rather, one seeks, as I will in the remainder of this chapter, to demonstrate the interest of presupposing it, and in particular the variety of new consequences that flow from assigning some new and more central priority to video processes.

One very significant feature of this presupposition must, however, be underscored at the outset, for it logically involves the radical and virtually a priori differentiation of film theory from whatever is to be proposed in the nature of a theory or even a description of video itself. The very richness of film theory today makes this decision and this warning unavoidable. If the experience of the movie screen and its mesmerizing images is distinct, and fundamentally different, from the experience of the television monitor—something that might be scientifically inferred by technical differences in their respective modes of encoding visual information but which could also be phenomenologically argued—then the very maturity and sophistication of film conceptualities will necessarily obscure the originality of its cousin, whose specific features demand to be reconstructed afresh and empty-handed, without imported and extrapolated categories. A parable can indeed be adduced here to support this methodological decision: discussing the hesitation Central European Jewish writers faced between writing in German and writing in Yiddish, Kafka once observed that these languages were too close to each other for any satisfactory translation from one into the other to be possible. Something like this, then, is what one would want to affirm about the relationship of the language of film theory to that of video theory, if indeed anything like this last exists in the first place.

Doubts on that score have frequently been raised, nowhere more dramatically than at an ambitious conference on the subject sponsored by *The Kitchen* in October 1980, at which a long line of dignitaries trooped to the podium only to complain that they couldn't understand why they had been invited, since they had no particular thoughts about television (which some of them admitted they watched), many then adding, as in afterthought, that only one halfway viable concept "produced" about television occurred to them, and that was Raymond William's idea of "whole flow."[1]

Perhaps these two remarks go together more intimately than we imagine: the blockage of fresh thinking before this solid little window against which we strike our heads being not unrelated to precisely that whole or total flow we observe through it.

For it seems plausible that in a situation of total flow, the contents of the screen streaming before us all day long without interruption (or where the interruptions—called *commercials*—are less intermissions than they are fleeting opportunities to visit the bathroom or throw a sandwich together), what used to be called "critical distance" seems to have become obsolete. Turning the television set off has little in common either with the intermission of a play or an opera or with the grand finale of a feature film, when the lights slowly come back on and memory begins its mysterious work. Indeed, if anything like critical distance is still possible in film, it is surely bound up with memory itself. But memory seems to play no role in television, commercial or otherwise (or, I am tempted to say, in postmodernism generally); nothing here haunts the mind or leaves its afterimages in the manner of the great moments of film (which do not necessarily happen, of course, in the "great" films). A description of the structural exclusion of memory, then, and of critical distance, might well lead on into the impossible, namely, a theory of video itself—how the thing blocks its own theorization becoming a theory in its own right.

My experience, however, is that you can't manage to think about things simply by deciding to, and that the mind's deeper currents often need to be surprised by indirection, sometimes, indeed, by treachery and ruse, as when you steer away from a goal in order to reach it more directly or look away from an object to register it more exactly. In that sense, thinking anything adequate about commercial television may well involve ignoring it and thinking about something else; in this instance, experimental video (or alternatively, that new form or genre called MTV, which I cannot deal with here). This is less a matter of mass versus elite culture than it is of controlled laboratory situations: what is so highly specialized as to seem aberrant and uncharacteristic in the world of daily life—hermetic poetry, for example—can often yield crucial information about the properties of an object of study (language, in that case), whose familiar everyday forms obscure it. Released from all conventional constraints, experimental video allows us to witness the full range of possibilities and potentialities of the medium in a way which illuminates its various more restricted uses, the latter being subsets and special cases of the former.

Even this approach to television via experimental video, however, needs to be estranged and displaced if the language of formal innovation and enlarged possibility leads us to expect a flowering and a multiplicity of new forms and visual languages: they exist, of course, and to a degree so bewildering in the short history of video art (sometimes dated from Nam June Paik's first experiments in 1963) that one is tempted to wonder whether any description or theory could ever encompass their variety. I have found it enlightening to come at this issue from a different direction, however, by raising the question of *boredom* as an aesthetic response and a phenomenological problem. In both the Freudian and the Marxist traditions (for the second, Lukács, but also Sartre's discussion of "stupidity" in Sartre's *Journal of the Phony War*), "boredom" is taken not so much as an objective property of things and works but rather as a response to the blockage of energies (whether those be grasped in terms of desire or of praxis). Boredom then becomes interesting as a reaction to situations of paralysis and also, no doubt, as defense mechanism or avoidance behavior. Even taken in the narrower realm of cultural reception, boredom with a particular kind of work or style or content can always be used productively as a precious symptom of our own existential, ideological, and cultural limits, an index of what has to be refused in the way of other people's cultural practices and their threat to our own rationalizations about the nature and value of art. Meanwhile, it is no great secret that in some of the most significant works of high modernism, what is boring can often be very interesting indeed, and vice versa: a combination which the reading of any hundred sentences by Raymond Roussel, say, will at once dramatize. We must therefore initially try to strip the concept of the boring (and its experience) of any axiological overtones and bracket the whole question of aesthetic value. It is a paradox one can get used to: if a boring text can also be good (or interesting, as we now put it), exciting texts, which incorporate diversion, distraction, temporal commodification, can also perhaps sometimes be "bad" (or "degraded," to use Frankfurt School language).

Imagine at any event a face on your television screen accompanied by an incomprehensible and never-ending stream of keenings and mutterings: the face remaining utterly without expression, unchanging throughout the course of the "work," and coming at length to seem some icon or floating immobile timeless mask. It is an experience to which you might be willing to submit out of curiosity for a few minutes. When, however, you begin to leaf through your program in distraction, only to discover that this particular videotext is twenty-one minutes long, then panic overcomes the mind and almost anything else seems preferable. But twenty-one minutes is not terribly long in other contexts (the immobility of the adept or religious mystic might offer some point of reference), and the nature of this particular form of aesthetic boredom becomes an interesting problem, particularly when we recall the differ-

ence between the viewing situation of video art and analogous experience in experimental film (we can always shut the first one off, without
sitting politely through a social and institutional ritual). As I have
already suggested, however, we must avoid the easy conclusion that this
tape or text is simply bad; one wants immediately to add, to forestall
misconceptions, that there are many, many diverting and captivating
videotexts of all kinds—but then one would also want to avoid the
conclusion that those are simply better (or "good" in the axiological
sense).

There then emerges a second possibility, a second explanatory temp-
tation, which involves authorial intention. We may then conclude that
the videomaker's choice was a deliberate and conscious one, and that
therefore the twenty-one minutes of this tape are to be interpreted as
provocation, as a calculated assault on the viewer, if not an act of
outright aggressivity. In that case, our response was the right one:
boredom and panic are appropriate reactions and a recognition of the
meaning of that particular aesthetic act. Apart from the well-known
aporias involved in concepts of literary intent and intention, the thematics of such aggressivity (aesthetic, class, gender, or whatever) are
virtually impossible to reestablish on the basis of the isolated tape itself.

Perhaps, however, the problems of the motives of the individual
subject can be elided by attention to the other type of mediation
involved, namely, technology and the machine itself. We are told, for
instance, that in the early days of photography, or rather, of the da-
guerreotype, subjects were obliged to sit in absolute immobility for
periods of time which, although not long as the crow flies, could
nonetheless be characterized as being relatively intolerable. One imag-
ines the uncontrollable twitching of the facial muscles, for example, or
the overwhelming urge to scratch or laugh. The first photographers
therefore devised something on the order of the electric chair, in which
the heads of their portrait subjects, from the lowliest and most banal
generals all the way to Lincoln himself, were clamped in place and
immobilized from the back for the obligatory five or ten minutes of the
exposure. Roussel, whom I've already mentioned, is something like a
literary equivalent of this process: his unimaginably detailed and minute description of objects—an absolutely infinite process without principle
or thematic interest of any kind—forces the reader to work laboriously
through one sentence after another, world without end. But it may now
be appropriate to identify Roussel's peculiar experiments as a kind of

anticipation of postmodernism within the older modernist period; at any rate, it seems at least arguable that aberrations and excesses which were marginal or subordinate in the modernist period become dominant in the systemic restructuration that can be observed in what we now call postmodernism. It is nevertheless clear that experimental video, whether we date it from the work of the ancestor Paik in the early 1960s or from the very floodtide of this new art which sets in in the mid 1970s, is rigorously coterminous with postmodernism itself as a historical period.

The machine on both sides, then; the machine as subject and object, alike and indifferently: the machine of the photographic apparatus peering across like a gun barrel at the subject, whose body is clamped into its mechanical correlative in some apparatus of registration/reception. The helpless spectators of video time are then as immobilized and mechanically integrated and neutralized as the older photographic subjects, who became, for a time, part of the technology of the medium. The living room, to be sure (or even the relaxed informality of the video museum), seems an unlikely place for this assimilation of human subjects to the technological: yet a voluntary attention is demanded by the total flow of the videotext in time which is scarcely relaxed at all, and rather different from the comfortable scanning of the movie screen, let alone of the cigar-smoking detachment of the Brechtian theatergoer. Interesting analyses (mostly from a Lacanian perspective) have been offered in recent film theory of the relationship between the mediation of the filmic machine and the construction of the viewer's subjectivity—at once depersonalized, and yet still powerfully motivated to reestablish the false homogeneities of the ego and of representation. I have the feeling that mechanical depersonalization (or decentering of the subject) goes even further in the new medium, where the auteurs themselves are dissolved along with the spectator (a point to which I will return shortly in another context).

Yet since video is a temporal art, the most paradoxical effects of this technological appropriation of subjectivity are observable in the experience of time itself. We all know, but always forget, that the fictive scenes and conversations on the movie screen radically foreshorten reality as the clock ticks and are never—owing to the now codified mysteries of the various techniques of film narrative—coterminous with the putative length of such moments in real life, or in "real time": something a filmmaker can always uncomfortably remind us of by returning occasionally to real time in this or that episode, which then threatens to project much the same intolerable discomfort we have ascribed to certain videotapes. Is it possible, then, that "fiction" is what is in question here and that it can be defined essentially as the construction of just such fictive and foreshortened temporalities (whether of film or reading), which are then substituted for a real time we are thereby enabled momentarily to forget? The question of fiction and the fictive would thereby find itself radically dissociated from questions of narrative and storytelling as such (although it would retain a key role and function in the practice of certain forms of narration): many of the confusions of the so-called representation debate (often assimilated to a debate about realism) are dispelled by just such an analytic distinction between fiction effects and their fictional temporalities, and narrative structures in general.

At any rate, in that case what one would want to affirm is that experimental video is not fictive in this sense, does not project fictive time, and does not work with fiction or fictions (although it may well work with narrative structures). This initial distinction then makes other ones possible, as well as interesting new problems. Film, for example, would clearly seem to approach this status of the nonfictive in its documentary form; but I suspect for various reasons that most documentary film (and documentary video) still projects a kind of residual fictionality—a kind of documentary constructed time—at the very heart of its aesthetic ideology and its sequential rhythms and effects. Meanwhile, alongside the nonfictional processes of experimental video, at least one form of video clearly does aspire to fictionality of a filmic type, and that is commercial television, whose specificities, whether one deplores or celebrates them, are also perhaps best approached by way of a description of experimental video. To characterize television series, dramas and the like, in other words, in terms of the imitation of this medium of other arts and media (most notably filmic narrative) probably dooms one to miss the most interesting feature of their production situation: namely, how, out of the rigorously nonfictive languages of video, commercial television manages to produce the simulacrum of fictive time.

As for temporality itself, it was for the modern movement conceived at best as an experience and at worst as a theme, even though the reality glimpsed by the first moderns of the nineteenth century (and designated by the word ennui) is surely already this temporality of boredom we have identified in the video process, the ticking away of real time minute by minute, the dread underlying irrevocable reality of the meter running. Yet the involvement of the machine in all this allows us now perhaps to escape phenomenology and the rhetoric of consciousness and experience, and to confront this seemingly subjective temporality in a new and materialist way, a way which constitutes a new kind of materialism as well, one not of matter but of machinery. It is as though, rephrasing our initial discussion of the retroactive effect of new genres, the emergence of the machine itself (so central to Marx's organization of *Capital*) deconcealed in some unexpected way the produced materiality of human life and time. Indeed, alongside the various phenomenological accounts of temporality, and the philosophies and ideologies of time, we have also come to possess a whole range of historical studies of the social construction of time itself, of which the most influential no doubt remains E. P. Thompson's classic essay[2] on the effects of the introduction of the chronometer into the workplace. Real time in that sense is objective time; that is to say, the time of objects, a time subject to the measurements to which objects are subject. Measurable time becomes a reality on account of the emergence of measurement itself, that is, rationalization and reification in the closely related sense of Weber and Lukács; clock time presupposes a peculiar spatial machine—it is the time of a machine, or better still, the time of the machine itself.

I have tried to suggest that video is unique—and in that sense historically privileged or symptomatic—because it is the only art or medium in which this ultimate seam between space and time is the very locus of the form, and also because its machinery uniquely dominates and depersonalizes subject and object alike, transforming the former into a quasi-material registering apparatus for the machine time of the latter and of the video image or "total flow." If we are willing to entertain the hypothesis that capitalism can be periodized by the quantum leaps or technological mutations by which it responds to its deepest systemic crises, then it may become a little clearer why and how video—so closely related to the dominant computer and information technology of the late, or third, stage of capitalism—has a powerful claim for being the art form par excellence of late capitalism.

These propositions allow us to return to the concept of total flow itself and to grasp its relationship to the analysis of commercial (or fictive) television in a new way. Material or machine time punctuates the flow of commercial television by way of the cycles of hour and half-hour programming, shadowed as by a ghostly afterimage by the shorter rhythms of the commercials themselves. I have suggested that these regular and periodic breaks are very unlike the types of closure to be found in the other arts, even in film, yet they allow the simulation of such closures and thereby the production of a kind of imaginary fictive time. The simulacrum of the fictive seizes on such material punctuation much as a dream seizes on external bodily stimuli, to draw them back into itself and to convert them into the appearance of beginnings and endings; or, in other words, the illusion of an illusion, the second-degree simulation of what is already itself, in other art forms, some first-degree illusory fictiveness or temporality. But only a dialectical perspective, which posits presences and absences, appearances and realities, or essences, can reveal these constitutive processes: for a one-dimensional or positivistic semiotics, for example, which can only deal in the sheer presences and existent data of segments of commercial and experimental video alike, these two related yet dialectically distinct forms are reduced to cuts and lengths of an identical material to which identical instruments of analysis are then applied. Commercial television is not an autonomous object of study; it can only be grasped for what it is by positioning it dialectically over against that other signifying system which we have called experimental video, or video art.[3]

The hypothesis of some greater materiality of video as a medium suggests that its analogies are perhaps better sought for in other places than the obvious cross-referencing of commercial television or fiction or even documentary film. We need to explore the possibility that the most suggestive precursor of the new form may be found in animation or the animated cartoon, whose materialistic (and paradoxically nonfictive) specificity is at least twofold: involving, on the one hand, a constitutive match or fit between a musical language and a visual one (two fully elaborated systems which are no longer subordinate to one another as in fiction film), and, on the other, the palpably produced character of animation's images, which in their ceaseless metamorphosis now obey the "textual" laws of writing and drawing rather than the "realistic" ones of verisimilitude, the force of gravity, etc. Animation constituted the first great school to teach the reading of material signifiers (rather than the narrative apprenticeship of objects of representation—characters, actions, and the like). Yet in animation, as later in experimental video, the Lacanian overtones of this language of material signifiers is inescapably completed by the omnipresent force of human praxis itself; suggesting thereby an active materialism of production rather than a static or mechanical materialism of matter itself as some inert support.

As for total flow, meanwhile, it has significant methodological consequences for the analysis of experimental video, and in particular for the constitution of the object or unity of study such a medium presents. It is, of course, no accident that today, in full postmodernism, the older language of the "work"—the work of art, the masterwork—has everywhere largely been displaced by the rather different language of the "text," of texts and textuality—a language from which the achievement of organic or monumental form is strategically excluded. Everything can now be a text in that sense (daily life, the body, political representations), while objects that were formerly "works" can now be reread as immense ensembles or systems of texts of various kinds, superimposed on each other by way of the various intertextualities, successions of fragments, or, yet again, sheer process (henceforth called textual production or textualization). The autonomous work of art thereby— along with the old autonomous subject or ego—seems to have vanished, to have been volatilized.

Nowhere is this more materially demonstrable than with the "texts" of experimental video—a situation which, however, now confronts the analyst with some new and unusual problems characteristic in one way or another of all the postmodernisms, but even more acute here. If the old modernizing and monumental forms—the Book of the World, the "magic mountains" of the architectural modernisms, the central mythic opera cycle of a Bayreuth, the Museum itself as the center of all the possibilities of painting—if such totalizing ensembles are no longer the fundamental organizing frames for analysis and interpretation; if, in other words, there are no more masterpieces, let alone their canon, no more "great" books (and if even the concept of good books has become problematic)—if we find ourselves confronted henceforth with "texts," that is, with the ephemeral, with disposable works that wish to fold back immediately into the accumulating detritus of historical time—then it becomes difficult and even contradictory to organize an analysis and an interpretation around any single one of these fragments in flight. To select—even as an "example"—a single videotext, and to discuss it in isolation, is fatally to regenerate the illusion of the masterpiece or the canonical text and to reify the experience of total flow from which it was momentarily extracted. Video viewing indeed involves immersion in the total flow of the thing itself, preferably a kind of random succession of three or four hours of tapes at regular intervals. Indeed, video is in this sense (and owing to the commercialization of public television and cable) an urban phenomenon demanding video banks or museums in your neighborhood which can thus be visited with something of the institutional habits and relaxed informality with which we used to visit the theater or the opera house (or even the movie palace). What is quite out of the question is to look at a single "video work" all by itself; in that sense, one would want to say, there are no video masterpieces, there can never be a video canon, and even an auteur theory of video (where signatures are still evidently present) becomes very problematical indeed. The "interesting" text now has to stand out of an undifferentiated and random flow of other texts. Something like a Heisenberg principle of video analysis thereby emerges: analysts and readers are shackled to the examination of specific and individual texts, one after the other; or, if you prefer, they are condemned to a kind of linear *Darstellung* in which they have to talk abut individual texts one at a time. But this very form of perception and criticism at once interferes with the reality of the thing perceived and intercepts it in mid-lightstream, distorting all the findings beyond recognition. The discussion, the indispensable preliminary selection and isolation, of a single "text" then automatically transforms it back into a "work," turns the anonymous videomaker[4] back into a named artist or auteur, and opens the way for the return of all those features of an older modernist aesthetic which it was in the revolutionary nature of the newer medium to have precisely effaced and dispelled.

In spite of these qualifications and reservations, it does not seem possible to go further in this exploration of the possibilities of video without interrogating a concrete text. We will consider a twenty-nine-minute "work" called *AlienNATION,* produced at the School of the Art Institute of Chicago by Edward Rankus, John Manning, and Barbara Latham in 1979. For the reader this will evidently remain an imaginary text; but the reader need not "imagine" that the spectator is in an altogether different situation. To describe, afterward, this stream of images of all kinds is necessarily to violate the perpetual present of the image and to reorganize the few fragments that remain in the memory according to schemes which probably reveal more about the reading mind than the text itself: do we try to turn it back into a story of some kind? (A very interesting book by Jacques Leenhardt and Pierre Józsa [*Lire la lecture* (Paris: Le Sycamore, 1982)] shows this process at work even in the reading of "plotless novels"—the reader's memory creates "protagonists" out of whole cloth, violates the reading experience in order to reassemble it into recognizable scenes and narrative sequences, and so forth.) Or, at some more critically sophisticated level, do we at least try to sort the material out into thematic blocks and rhythms and repunctuate it with beginnings and endings, with graphs of rising and falling emotivity, climaxes, dead passages, transitions, recapitulations, and the like? No doubt; only the reconstruction of these overall formal movements turns out differently every time we watch the tape. For one thing, twenty-nine minutes in video is much longer than the equivalent temporal segment of any feature film; nor is it excessive to speak of a genuine and a very acute *contradiction* between the virtually drug like experience of the present of the image in the videotape and any kind of textual memory into which the successive presents might be inserted (even the return and recognition of older images is, as it were, seized on the run, laterally and virtually too late for it to do us any good). If the contrast here with the memory structures of Hollywood-type fiction films is stark and obvious, one has the feeling—more difficult to document or to argue—that the gap between this temporal experience and that of *experimental* film is no less great. These op art tricks and elaborate visual montages in particular recall the classics of yesteryear such as *Ballet mechanique;* but I have the impression that, above and beyond the difference in our institutional situation (art movie theater here, television monitor either at home or in a museum for the videotext), these experiences are very different ones, and in particular that the blocks of material in film are larger and more grossly and tangibly perceptible (even when they pass by rapidly), determining a more leisurely sense of combinations than can be the case with these attenuated visual data on the television screen.

One is therefore reduced to enumerating a few of these video materials, which are not themes (since for the most part they are material quotations form a quasi-commercial storehouse somewhere), but which certainly have none of the density of Bazinian mise-en-scène either, since even the segments which are not lifted from already existing sequences, but which have obviously been filmed explicitly for use in this tape, have a kind of shabbiness of low-grade color stock which marks them somehow as "fictional" and staged, as opposed to the manifest reality of the other images-in-the-world, the image objects. There is therefore a sense in which the word *collage* could still obtain for this juxtaposition of what one is tempted to call "natural" materials (the newly or directly filmed sequences) and artificial ones (the pre-cooked image materials which have been "mixed" by the machine itself). What would be misleading is the ontological hierarchy of the older painterly collage: in this videotape the "natural" is worse and more degraded than the artificial, which itself no longer connotes the secure daily life of a new humanly constructed society (as in the objects of cubism) but rather the noise and jumbled signals, the unimaginable informational garbage, of the new media society.

First, a little existential joke about a "spot" of time, which is excised from a temporal "culture" that looks a little like a crepe; then experimental mice, voice-overed by various pseudoscientific reports and therapeutic programs (how to deal with stress, beauty care, hypnosis for weight loss, etc.); then science fiction footage (including monster music and camp dialogue), mostly drawn from a Japanese film, *Monster Zero* (1965). At this point the rush of image materials becomes too dense to enumerate: optical effects, children's blocks and erector sets, reproduction of classical paintings, as well as mannequins, advertising images, computer printouts, textbook illustrations of all kinds, cartoon figures rising and falling (including a wonderful Magritte hat slowly sinking into Lake Michigan); sheet lightning; a woman lying down and possibly under hypnosis (unless, as in a Robbe-Grillet novel, this is merely the photograph of a woman lying down and possibly under hypnosis); ultramodern hotel or office building lobbies with escalators rising in all directions and at various angles; shots of a street corner with sparse traffic, a child on a big wheel and a few pedestrians carrying groceries; a haunting closeup of detritus and children's blocks on the lakeshore (in one of which the Magritte hat reappears, in real life: poised on stick in the sand); Beethoven sonatas, Holst's *Planets,* disco music, funeral parlor organs, outer space sound effects, the *Lawrence of Arabia* theme accompanying the arrival of flying saucers over the Chicago skyline; a grotesque sequence as well in which friable orange oblongs (that resemble Hostess Twinkies) are dissected with scalpels, squeezed by vises, and shattered by fists; a leaky container of milk; the disco dancers in their habitat; shots of alien planets; closeups of various kinds of brush strokes; ads for 1950s kitchens; and many more. Sometimes these seem to be combined in longer sequences, as when the sheet lightning is overcharged with a whole series of opticals, advertisements, cartoon figures, movie music, and unrelated radio dialogue. Sometimes, as in the transition from a relatively pensive "classical music" accompaniment to the stridence of mass-cultural beat, the principle of variation seems obvious and heavy-handed. Sometimes the accelerated flow of mixed images strikes one as modeling a certain unified temporal urgency, the tempo of delirium, let's say, or of direct experimental assault on the viewer-subject; while the whole is randomly punctuated with formal signals—the "prepare to disconnect" which is presumably designed to warn the viewer of impending closure, and the final shot of the beach, which borrows a more recognizably filmic connotative language—dispersal of an object world into fragments, but also the touching of a kind of limit or ultimate edge (as in the closing sequence of Fellini's *La Dolce Vita*). It is all, no doubt, an elaborate visual joke or hoax (if you were expecting something more "serious"): a student's training exercise, if you like; while such is the tempo of the history of experimental video that insiders or connoisseurs are capable of watching this 1979 production with a certain nostalgia and remembering that people did that kind of thing in those days but are now busy doing something else.

The most interesting questions posed by a videotext of this kind—and I hope it will be clear that the text *works,* whatever its value or its meaning: it can be seen again and again (at least partly on account of its informational overload, which the viewer will never be able to master)—remain questions of value and of interpretation, provided it is understood that it may be the absence of any possible response to those questions which is the historically interesting matter. But my attempt to tell or summarize this text makes it clear that even before we reach the interpretative question—"what does it mean?" or, to use its petit bourgeois version, "what is it supposed to represent?"—we have to confront the preliminary matters of form and reading. It is not evident that a spectator will ever reach a moment of knowledge and saturated memory from which a formal reading of this text in time slowly disengages itself: beginnings and thematic emergences, combinations and developments, resistances and struggles for dominance, partial resolutions, forms of closure leading on to one or another full stop. Could one establish such an overall chart of the work's formal time, even in a very crude and general way, our description would necessarily remain as empty and as abstract as the terminology of musical form, whose problems today, in aleatory and post-twelve-tone music, are analogous, even though the mathematical dimensions of sound and musical notation provide what look like more tangible solutions. My sense is, however, that even the few formal markers we have been able to isolate—the lakeshore, the building blocks, the "sense of an ending"—are deceptive; they are now no longer features or elements of a form but signs and traces of older forms. We must remember that those older forms are still included within the bits and pieces, the bricolated material, of this text: Beethoven's sonata is but one component of the bricolage, like a broken pipe retrieved and inserted in a sculpture or a torn piece of newspaper pasted onto a canvas. Yet within the musical segment of the older Beethoven work, "form" in the traditional sense persists and can be named—the "falling cadence," say, or the "reappearance of the first theme." The same can be said of the film clips of the Japanese monster movie: they include quotations of the SF form itself: "discovery," "menace," "attempted flight," and so forth (here the available formal terminology—in analogy to the musical nomenclature—would probably be restricted to Aristotle or to Propp and his successors, or to Eisenstein, virtually the only sources of a neutral language of the movement of narrative form). The question that suggests itself, then, is whether the formal properties within these quoted segments and pieces are anywhere transferred to the videotext itself, to the bricolage of which they are parts and components. But this is a question that must first be raised on the microlevel of individual episodes and moments. As for the larger formal properties of the text considered as a "work" and as temporal organization, the lakeshore image suggests that the strong form of an older temporal or musical closure is here present merely as a formal residue: whatever in Fellini's ending still bore the traces of a mythic residue—the sea as some primordial element, as the place at which the human and the social confront the otherness of nature—is here already long since effaced and forgotten. That content has disappeared, leaving but a faint aftertrace of its original formal connotation, that is, of its syntactical function as closure. At this most attenuated point in the sign system the signifier has become little more than a dim memory of a former sign, and indeed, of the formal function of that now extinct sign.

The language of connotation which began to impose itself in the preceding paragraph would seem to impose a reexamination of the central elaboration of this concept, which we owe to Roland Barthes, who elaborated it, following Hjemslev, in his *Mythologies,* only in his later "textual" work to repudiate its implicit differentiation of first- and second-degree languages (denotation and connotation), which must have come to strike him as a replication of the old divisions between aesthetic and social, artistic free play and historical referentiality— divisions which essays like *Le Plaisir du texte* were concerned to evade or escape. No matter that the earlier theory (still enormously influential in media studies) ingeniously reversed the priorities of this opposition, assigning authenticity (and thereby aesthetic value) to the denotative value of the photographic image, and a guilty social or ideological functionality to its more "artificial" prolongation in advertising texts that take the original denotative text as their own new content, pressing already existent images into the service of some heightened play of degraded thoughts and commercial messages. Whatever the stakes and implications of this debate, it seems clear that Barthes's earlier, classical conception of how connotation functions can be suggestive for us here only if it is appropriately complicated, perhaps beyond all recognition. For the situation here is rather the inverse of the advertising one, where "purer" and somehow more material signs were appropriated and readapted to serve as vehicles for a whole range of ideological signals. Here, on the contrary, the ideological signals are already deeply embedded in the primary texts, which are already profoundly cultural and ideological: the Beethoven music already includes the connotator of "classical music" in general, the science fiction film already includes multiple political messages and anxieties (an American Cold War form readapted to Japanese antinuclear politics, and both then folding into the new cultural connotator of "camp"). But connotation is here—in a cultural sphere whose "products" have functions that largely transcend the narrowly commercial ones of advertising images (while no doubt still including some of those and surely replicating their structures in other ways)—a polysomic process in which a number of "messages" coexist. Thus the alternation of Beethoven and disco no doubt emits a class message—high versus popular or mass culture, privilege and education versus more popular and bodily forms of diversion—but i[t] also continues to vehiculate the older content of some tragic gravity, the formal time sense of the sonata form itself, the "high seriousness" of the most rigorous bourgeois aesthetic in its grappling with time, contradiction, and death; which now finds itself opposed to the relentless temporal distraction of the big city commercial music of the postmodern age that fills time and space implacably to the point where the older "tragic" questions seem irrelevant. All these connotations are in play simultaneously. To the degree to which they appear easily reducible to some of the binary oppositions just mentioned (high and low culture), and to that degree alone, we are in the presence of a kind of "theme," which might at the outside limit be the occasion for an interpretative act and allow us to suggest that the videotext is "about" this particular opposition. We will return to such interpretive possibilities or options later on.

What must be excluded, however, is anything like a process of demystification at work in this particular videotext: all its materials are degraded in that sense, Beethoven no less than disco. And although, as we will shortly make clear, there is a very complex interaction at work here between various levels and components of the text, or various languages (image versus sound, music versus dialogue), the political use of one of these levels against another (as in Godard), the attempt somehow to purify the image by setting it off against the written or spoken, is here no longer on the agenda, if it is even still conceivable. This is something that can be clarified, I believe, if we think of the various quoted elements and components—the broken pieces of a whole range of primary texts in the contemporary cultural sphere—as so many logos, that is to say, as a new form of advertising language which is structurally and historically a good deal more advanced and complicated than any of the advertising images with which Barthes's earlier theories had to deal. A logo is something like the synthesis of an advertising image and a brand name; better still, it is a brand name which has been transformed into an image, a sign or emblem which carries the memory of a whole tradition of earlier advertisements within itself in a well-nigh intertextual way. Such logos can be visual or auditory and musical (as in the Pepsi theme): an enlargement which allows us to include the materials of the sound track under this category, along with the more immediately identifiable logo segments of the office escalators, the fashion mannequins, the psychological counseling clips, the street corner, the lakefront, *Monster Zero,* and so forth. "Logo" then signifies the transformation of each of these fragments into a kind of sign in its own right; yet it is not yet clear what such new signs might be signs of, since no product seems identifiable, nor even the range of generic products strictly designated by the logo in its original sense, as the badge of a diversified multinational corporation. Still, the term *generic* is itself suggestive if we conceive of its literary implications a little more broadly than the older, more static, tables of "genres," or fixed kinds. The generic cultural consumption projected by these fragments is more dynamic and demands some association with narrative (itself now grasped in the wider sense of a type of textual consumption). In that sense, the scientific experiments are narratives fully as much as *Lawrence of Arabia;* the vision of white-collar workers and bureaucrats mounting flights of escalators is no less a narrative vision than the science fiction film clips (or horror music); even the still photograph of sheet lightning suggests a multiple set of narrative frames (Ansel Adams, or the terror of the great storm, or the "logo" of the Remington-type western landscape, or the eighteenth-century sublime, or the answer of God to the rainmaking ceremony, or the beginning of the end of the world).

The matter grows more complicated, however, when we realize that none of these elements or new cultural signs or logos exists in isolation; the videotext itself is at virtually all moments a process of ceaseless, apparently random, interaction between them. This is clearly the structure which demands description and analysis, but it is a relationship between signs for which we have only the most approximate theoretical models. It is indeed a matter of apprehending a constant stream, or "total flow," of multiple materials, each of which can be seen as something like a shorthand signal for a distinct type of narrative or a specific narrative process. But our immediate questions will be synchronic rather than diachronic: how do these various narrative signals or logos intersect? Is one to imagine a mental compartmentalization in which each is received in isolation, or does the mind somehow establish connections of some kind; and in that case, how can we describe those connections? How are these materials wired into one another, if at all? Or do we merely confront a simultaneity of distinct streams of elements which the senses grasp all together like a kaleidoscope? The measure of our conceptual weakness here is that we are tempted to begin with the most unsatisfactory methodological decision—the Cartesian point of departure—in which we begin by reducing the phenomenon to its simplest form, namely, the interaction of two such elements or signals (whereas dialectical thinking asks us to begin with the most complex form, of which the simpler ones are considered derivatives).

Even in the case of two elements, however, suggestive theoretical models are few enough. The oldest one is, of course, the logical model of *subject* and *predicate,* which, divested of its propositional logic—

with its statement sentences and truth claims—has in recent times been rewritten as a relationship between a *topic* and a *comment*. Literary theory has for the most part been obliged to confront this structure only in the analysis of metaphor, for which I. A. Richards's distinction between a *tenor* and a *vehicle* seems suggestive. The semiotics of Peirce, however, which seeks insistently to grasp the process of interpretation—or semiosis—in time, usefully rewrites all these distinctions in terms of an initial sign in relationship to which a second sign stands as an *interpretant*. Contemporary narrative theory, finally, with its operative distinction between the fable (the anecdote, the raw materials of the basic story) and the mise-en-scène itself, the way in which those materials are told or staged; in other words, their *focalization*.

What must be retained from these formulations is the way in which they pose two signs of equal nature and value, only to observe that in their moment of intersection a new hierarchy is at once established in which one sign becomes something like the material on which the other one works, or in which the first sign establishes a content and a center to which the second is annexed for auxiliary and subordinate functions (the priorities of the hierarchical relationship here seeming reversible). But the terminology and nomenclature of the traditional models do not register what surely becomes a fundamental property of the stream of signs in our video context: namely, that they change places; that no single sign ever retains priority as a topic of the operation; that the situation in which one sign functions as the interpretant of another is more than provisional, it is subject to change without notice; and in the ceaselessly rotating momentum with which we have to do here, our two signs occupy each other's positions in a bewildering and well-nigh permanent exchange. This is something like Benjaminian "distraction" raised to a new and historically original power: indeed, I am tempted to suggest that the formulation gives us at least one apt characterization of some properly postmodernist temporality, whose consequences now remain to be drawn.

For we have not yet sufficiently described the nature of the process whereby, even allowing for the perpetual displacements we have insisted on, one such element—or sign or logo—somehow "comments" on the other or serves as its "interpretant." The content of that process, however, was already implicit in the account of the logo itself, which was described as the signal or shorthand for a certain kind of narrative. The microscopic atomic or isotopic exchange under study here can therefore be nothing less than the capture of one narrative signal by another: the rewriting of one form of narrativization in terms of a different, momentarily more powerful one, the ceaseless renarrativization of already existent narrative elements by each other. Thus, to begin with the most obvious examples, there does not seem much doubt that images like the fashion model or mannequin sequences are strongly and crudely rewritten when they intersect with the force field of the science fiction movie and its various logos (visual, musical, verbal): at such moments the familiar human world of advertising and fashion becomes "estranged" (a concept to which we will return), and the contemporary department store becomes as peculiar and as chilling as any of the institutions of an alien society on a distant planet. In much the same way, something happens to the photograph of the recumbent woman subject when it is surcharged with the profile of sheet lightning: sub specie aeternitatis, perhaps? culture versus nature? at any event, the two signs cannot fail to enter into a relationship with each other in which the generic signals of one begin to predominate (it is, for example, somewhat more difficult to imagine how the image of the woman under hypnosis could begin to draw the lightning stroke into its thematic orbit). Finally, it seems evident that as the image of the mice and the associated texts of behavioral experiments and psychological and vocational counseling intersect, the combination yields predictable messages about the hidden programming and conditioning mechanisms of bureaucratic society. Yet these three forms of influence or renarrativization—generic estrangement, the opposition of nature and culture, and the pop psychological or "existential" culture critique—are only a few of the provisional effects in a much more complex repertoire of interactions which it would be tedious, if not impossible, to tabulate (others might, however, include the high and low cultural opposition described earlier, and also the most diachronic alternation between the shabby and "natural" directly filmed street scenes and the flow of stereotypical media materials into which they are inserted).

Questions of priority or unequal influence can now be raised in a new way, one which need not be limited to the evidently central matter of the relative priority of sound and image. The psychologists distinguish between auditory and visual forms of recognition, and the former being apparently more instantaneous and working by means of fully formed auditory or musical gestalts, while the latter is subject to an incremental exploration which may never crystallize into something appropriately "recognizable." We recognize a tune all at once, in other words, while the flying saucers which ought to allow us to identify the generic class of a film clip may remain the object of some vague geometric gaze which never bothers to slot them into their obvious cultural and connotational position. In that case, it is clear how auditory logos would tend to dominate and rewrite visual ones, rather than the other way round (although one would have liked to imagine some reciprocal "estrangement" of the science fiction music by the photographs of mannequins, for example, in which the former is turned back into late twentieth-century cultural junk of the same substance as these last).

Above and beyond this simplest case of the relative influence of signs from distinct senses and distinct media, there persists the more general problem of the relative weight of the various generic systems themselves in our culture: is science fiction a priori more powerful than the genre we call advertising, or than the discourse that offers images of bureaucratic society (the rat race, the office, the routine), or the computer printout, or that unnamed "genre" of visuals we have called op art effects (which probably connote a good deal more than the new technology of graphics)? Godard's work seems to me to turn on this question, or at least to pose it explicitly in various local ways; some political video art—such as that of Martha Rosler—also plays with these unequal influences of cultural languages to problematize familiar cultural priorities. The videotext under consideration here, however, does not allow us to formulate such issues as problems, since its very formal logic—what we have called the ceaselessly rotating momentum of its provisional constellations of signs—depends on effacing them: a proposition and a hypothesis that will lead us on into those matters of interpretation and aesthetic value that we have postponed until this point.

The interpretive question—"what is the text or work about?"—generally encourages a thematic answer, as indeed in the obliging title of the present tape, *AlienNATION*. There it is and now we know: it is the alienation of a whole nation, or perhaps a new kind of nation organized around alienation itself. The concept of alienation had rigor when specifically used to articulate the various concrete privations of working-class life (as in Marx's Paris manuscripts); and it also had a specific function at a specific historical moment (the Khrushchev opening), which radicals in the East (Poland, Yugoslavia) and the West (Sartre) believed could inaugurate a new tradition in Marxist thinking and practice. It surely does not amount to much, however, as a general designation for (bourgeois) spiritual malaise. But this is not the only reason for the discontent one feels when, in the midst of splendid postmodernist performances like Laurie Anderson's *USA,* the repetition of the word *alienation* (as it were, whispered in passing to the public) made it difficult to avoid the conclusion that this was indeed what that also was supposed to be "about." Two virtually identical responses then follow: so that's what it was supposed to mean; so that's all it was supposed to mean. The problem is twofold: alienation is, first of all, not merely a *modernist* concept but also a modernist *experience* (something I cannot argue further here, except to say that "psychic fragmentation" is a better term for what ails us today, if we need a term for it). But the problem's second ramification is the decisive one: whatever such a meaning and its adequacy (qua meaning), one has the deeper feeling that "texts" like *USA* or *AlienNATION* ought not to have any "meaning" at all in that thematic sense. This is something everyone is free to verify, by self-observation and a little closer attention to precisely those moments in which we briefly feel that disillusionment I have described experiencing at the thematically explicit moments in *USA.* In effect, the points at which one can feel something similar during the Rankus-Manning-Latham videotape have already been enumerated in another context. They are very precisely those points at which the intersection of sign and interpretant seems to produce a fleeting message: high versus low culture, in the modern world we're all programmed like laboratory mice, nature versus culture, and so forth. The wisdom of the vernacular tells us that these "themes" are corny, as corny as alienation itself (but not old-fashioned enough to be camp). Yet it would be a mistake to simplify this interesting situation and reduce it to a question of the nature and quality, the intellectual substance, of the themes themselves; indeed, our preceding analysis has the makings of a much better explanation of such lapses.

We tried to show, indeed, that what characterizes this particular video process (or "experimental" total flow) is a ceaseless rotation of elements such that they change place at every moment, with the result that no single element can occupy the position of "interpretant" (or that of primary sign) for any length of time but must be dislodged in turn in the following instant (the filmic terminology of "frames" and "shots" does not seem appropriate for this kind of succession), falling to the subordinate position in its turn, where it will then be "interpreted" or narrativized by a radically different kind of logo or image content altogether. If this is an accurate account of the process, however, then it follows logically that anything which arrests or interrupts it will be sensed as an aesthetic flaw. The thematic moments we have complained about above are just such moments of interruption, of a kind of blockage in this process: at such points a provisional "narrativization"—the provisional dominance of one sign or logo over another, which it interprets and rewrites according to its own narrative logic—quickly spreads out over the sequence like a burn spot on the film, at that point "held" long enough to generate and emit a thematic message quite inconsistent with the textual logic of the thing itself. Such moments involve a peculiar form of reification, which we might characterize equally well as a *thematization*—a word the late Paul de Man was fond of, using it to characterize the misreading of Derrida as a "philosopher" whose "philosophical system" was somehow "about" writing. Thematization is then the moment in which an element, a component, of a text is promoted to the status of official theme, at which point it becomes a candidate for that even higher honor, the work's "meaning." But such thematic reification is not necessarily a function of the philosophical or intellectual quality of the "theme" itself: whatever the philosophical interest and viability of the notion of the alienation of contemporary bureaucratic life, its emergence here as a "theme" is registered as a flaw for what are essentially formal reasons. The proposition might be argued the other way around by identifying another possible lapse in our text as the excessive dependence on the "estrangement effects" of the Japanese SF film clips (repeated viewings, however, make it clear that they were not so frequent as one remembered). If so, we have here to do with a thematization of a narrative or generic type rather than a degradation via pop philosophy and stereotypical doxa.

We can now draw some unexpected consequences from this analysis, consequences that bear not only on the vexed question of interpretation in postmodernism but also on another matter, that of aesthetic value, which had been provisionally tabled at the outset of this discussion. If interpretation is understood, in the thematic way, as the disengagement of a fundamental theme or meaning, then it seems clear that the postmodernist text—of which we have taken the videotape in question to be a privileged exemplar—is from that perspective defined as a structure or sign flow which resists meaning, whose fundamental inner logic is the exclusion of the emergence of themes as such in that sense, and

which therefore systematically sets out to short-circuit traditional interpretative temptations (something Susan Sontag prophetically intuited
in the appropriately titled *Against Interpretation,* at the very dawn of
what was not yet called the postmodern age). New criteria of aesthetic
value then unexpectedly emerge from this proposition: whatever a
good, let alone a great, videotext might be, it will be bad or flawed
whenever such interpretation proves possible, whenever the text slackly
opens up just such places and areas of thematization itself.

Thematic interpretation, however—the search for the "meaning" of
the work—is not the only conceivable hermeneutic operation to which
texts, including this one, can be subjected, and I want to describe two
other interpretive options before concluding. The first returns us to the
question of the referent in an unexpected fashion, by way of that other
set of component materials to which we have so far paid less attention
than to the quoted inscribed and recorded spools of canned cultural junk
which are here interwoven: those (characterized as "natural" materials)
were the segments of directly shot footage, which, above and beyond
the lakeshore sequence, essentially fell into three groups. The urban
street crossing, to begin with, is a kind of degraded space, which—distant, poor cousin in that to the astonishing concluding sequence of
Antonioni's *Eclipse*—beings faintly to project the abstraction of an
empty stage, a place of the Event, a bounded space in which something
may happen and before which one waits in formal expectation. In
Eclipse, of course, when the event fails to materialize and neither of the
lovers appears at the rendezvous, place—now forgotten—slowly finds
itself degraded back into space again, the reified space of the modern
city, quantified and measurable, in which land and earth are parceled
out into so many commodities and lots for sale. Here also nothing
happens; only the very sense of the possibility of something happening
and of the faint emergence of the very category of the Event itself is
unusual in this particular tape (the menaced events and anxieties of the
science fiction clips are merely "images" of events or, if you prefer,
spectacle events without any temporality of their own).

The second sequence is that of the perforated milk carton, a sequence
which perpetuates and confirms the peculiar logic of the first one, since
here we have in some sense the pure event itself, about which there's
no point crying, the irrevocable. The finger must give up stopping the
breach, the milk must pour out across the table and over the edge, with
all the visual fascination of this starkly white substance. If this quite

wonderful image seems to me to revert even distantly to a more properly filmic status, my own aberrant and strictly personal association of it with a famous scene in *The Manchurian Candidate* is no doubt also partially responsible.

As for the third segment, the wackiest and more pointless, I have already described the absurdity of a laboratory experiment conducted with hardware store tools on orange objects of indeterminate size which have something of the consistency of a Hostess Twinkie. What is scandalous and vaguely disturbing about this homemade bit of dada is its apparent lack of motivation: one tries, without any great satisfaction, to see it as an Ernie Kovacs parody of the laboratory animal sequence; in any case, nothing else in the tape echoes this particular mode or zaniness of "voice." All three groups of images, but in particular this autopsy of a Twinkie, reminds one vaguely of a strand of organic material which has been woven in among an organic texture, like the wale blubber in Joseph Beuys's sculpture.

Nonetheless, a first approach suggested itself to me on the level of unconscious anxiety, where the hole in the milk carton—following the assassination scene in *The Manchurian Candidate,* where the victim is surprised at a midnight snack in front of the open refrigerator door—is now explicitly read as a bullet hole. I have meanwhile neglected to supply another clue, namely, the computer-generated *X* that moves across the empty street crossing like the sights of a long-range rifle. It remained for an astute listener (at an earlier version of this paper) to make the connection and point out the henceforth obvious and unassailable: the American media public, the combination of the two elements—milk and Twinkie—is too peculiar to be unmotivated. In fact, on November 27, 1978 (the year preceding the composition of his particular videotape), San Francisco Mayor George Moscone and City Supervisor Harvey Milk were shot to death by a former supervisor, who entered the unforgettable plea of not guilty by reason of insanity owing to the excessive consumption of Hostess Twinkies.

Here, then, at last, the referent itself is disclosed: the brute fact, the historical event, the real toad in this particular imaginary garden. To track such a reference down is surely to perform an act of interpretation or hermeneutic disclosure of a very different kind from that previously discussed: for if *AlienNATION* is "about" this, then such an expression can only have a sense quite distinct from its use in the proposition that the text was "about" alienation itself.

The problem of reference has been singularly displaced and stigmatized in the hegemony of the various poststructuralist discourses which characterizes the current moment (and along with it, anything that smacks of "reality," "representation," "realism," and the like—even the word *history* has an *r* in it); only Lacan has shamelessly continued to talk about "the Real" (defined, however, as an absence). The respectable philosophical solutions to the problem of an external real world independent of consciousness are all traditional ones, which means that however logically satisfying they may be (and none of them were ever really very satisfactory from a logical standpoint), they are not suitable candidates for participation in contemporary polemics. The hegemony of theories of textuality and textualization means, among other things, that your entry ticket to the public sphere in which these matters are debated is an agreement, tacit or otherwise, with the basic presuppositions of a general problem field, something traditional positions on these matters refuse in advance. My own feeling has been that historicism offers a peculiarly unexpected escape from this vicious circle or double bind.

To raise the issue, for example, of the fate of the "referent" in contemporary culture and thought is not the same thing as to assert some older theory of reference or to repudiate all the new theoretical problems in advance. On the contrary, such problems are retained and endorsed, with the proviso that they are not only interesting problems in their own right but also, at the same time, symptoms of a historical transformation.

In the immediate instance that concerns us here, I have argued for the presence and existence of what seems to be a palpable referent—namely, death and historical fact, which are ultimately not textualizable and tear through the tissues of textual elaboration, of combination and free play ("the Real," Lacan tells us, "is what resists symbolization absolutely"). I want to add at once that this is no particularly triumphant philosophical victory for some putative realism or other over the various textualizing world views. For the assertion of a buried referent—as in the present example—is a two-way street whose antithetical directions might emblematically be named "repression" and *Aufhebung,* or "sublation": the picture has no way of telling us whether we are looking at a rising or a setting sun. Does our discovery document the persistence and stubborn, all-informing gravitational charge of reference, or, on the contrary, does it show the tendential historical process whereby refer-

ence is systematically processed, dismantled, textualized, and volatilized, leaving little more than some indigestible remnant?

However this ambiguity is handled, there remains the matter of the
structural logic of the tape itself, of which this particular directly filmed
sequence is only a single strand among many, and a particularly minor
one at that (although its properties attract a certain attention). Even if
its referential value could be satisfactorily demonstrated, the logic of
rotating conjunction and disjunction that has been described above
clearly works to dissolve such a value, which cannot be tolerated any
more than the emergence of individual themes. Nor is it clear how an
axiological system could be developed in the name of which we might
then affirm that these strange sequences are somehow better than the
random and aimless "irresponsibility" of the collages of media stereotypes.

Yet another way of interpreting such a tape is conceivable, however—an interpretation that would seek to foreground the process of
production itself rather than its putative messages, meanings, or content. On this reading some distant consonance might be invoked between the fantasies and anxieties aroused by the idea of assassination
and the global system of media and reproductive technology. The
structural analogy between the two seemingly unrelated spheres is
secured in the collective unconscious by notions of conspiracy, while
the historical juncture between the two was burned into historical
memory by the Kennedy assassination itself, which can no longer be
separated from its media coverage. The problem posed by such interpretation in terms of auto-referentiality is not its plausibility: one would
want to defend the proposition that the deepest "subject" of all video
art, and even of all postmodernism, is very precisely reproductive
technology itself. The methodological difficulty lies rather in the way
in which such a global "meaning"—even of some type and status newer
than the interpretive meanings we have touched on above—once again
dissolves the individual text into an even more disastrous indistinction
than the total flow-individual work antimony evoked above: if all
videotexts simply designate the process of production/reproduction,
then presumably they all turn out to be "the same" in a peculiarly
unhelpful way.

I will not try to solve any of these problems; instead I will restage the
approaches and perspectives of the historicism I have called for by way
of a kind of myth I have found useful in characterizing the nature of

contemporary (postmodernist) cultural production and also in positioning its various theoretical projections.

Once upon a time at the dawn of capitalism and middle-class society, there emerged something called the sign, which seemed to entertain unproblematical relations with its referent. This initial heyday of the sign—the moment of literal or referential language or of the unproblematic claims of so-called scientific discourse—came into being because of the corrosive dissolution of older forms of magical language by a force which I will call that of reification, a force whose logic is one of ruthless separation and disjunction, of specialization and rationalization, of a Taylorizing division of labor in all realms. Unfortunately, that force—which brought traditional reference into being—continued unremittingly, being the very logic of capital itself. Thus this first moment of decoding or of realism cannot long endure; by a dialectical reversal it then itself in turn becomes the object of the corrosive force of reification, which enters the realm of language to disjoin the sign from the referent. Such a disjunction does not completely abolish the referent, or the objective world, or reality, which still continue to entertain a feeble existence on the horizon like a shrunken star or red dwarf. But its great distance from the sign now allows the latter to enter a moment of autonomy, of a relatively free-floating Utopian existence, as over against its former objects. This autonomy of culture, this semiautonomy of language, is the moment of modernism, and of a realm of the aesthetic which redoubles the world without being altogether of it, thereby winning a certain negative or critical power, but also a certain otherworldly futility. Yet the force of reification, which was responsible for this new moment, does not stop there either: in another stage, heightened, a kind of reversal of quantity into quality, reification penetrates the sign itself and disjoins the signifier from the signified. Now reference and reality disappear altogether, and even meaning—the signified—is problematized. We are left with that pure and random play of signifiers that we call postmodernism, which no longer produces monumental works of the modernist type but ceaselessly reshuffles the fragments of preexistent texts, the building blocks of older cultural and social production, in some new and heightened bricolage: metabooks which cannibalize other books, metatexts which collate bits of other texts—such is the logic of postmodernism in general, which finds some of its strongest and most original, authentic forms in the new art of experimental video.

Notes

1. Readers of collections like E. Ann Kaplan, *Regarding Television,* American Film Institute No. 2, Maryland, 1983 and John Hanhardt, *Video Culture: A Critical Investigation,* NY, 1986 may find such assertions astonishing. A frequent theme of these articles remains, however, the absence, tardiness, repression, or impossibility of video theory proper.

2. "Time, Work-discipline, and Industrial Capitalism," *Past and Present,* No. 38, 1967.

3. This is a point I have tried to argue more generally about the relationship between the study of "high literature" (or rather, high modernism) and that of mass culture, in "Reification and Utopia in Mass Culture," *Social Text* no. 1, 1977 (reprinted in *The Politics of the Simulacrum,* London).

4. I mean there essentially the good anonymity of handicraft work of the medieval kind, as opposed to the supreme demiurgic subjectivity or "genius" of the modern Master.

In American life, while we pay lip service to the public, for most of us the private is the realm of the real. This reliance on the private realm is particularly salient for women in our society, whose role in the public world is even less legitimated than that of men. . . . Television helps us to bridge the gap between the public and private realms of our lives and to maintain, in our increasingly fragmented lives, a feeling of connection—however precarious—with the social world, even if this connection is emotive rather than substantive.

3

Women Watching Television: Issues of Class, Gender, and Mass Media Reception

ANDREA L. PRESS

The complexity of television viewing can be best accommodated by applying elements of several paradigms which have recently been used in studying responses to the mass media specifically and culture more generally: "hegemony theory" which has characterized an essentially Gramscian-Althusserian Marxist school of mass media study, the British Cultural Studies tradition,1 and the more general tradition of British and American feminist cultural studies to which British Cultural Studies has given rise. In the sections that follow, I offer a brief survey of these theoretical traditions, the combination of which has informed the research I present here.

Unlike many currently working in our field, rather than conceptualizing these two modes of response in an either-or fashion, I stress the need to discuss both viewer resistance to our culture's often hegemonic messages and viewer accommodation to these messages as two integral parts of women's responses to entertainment television, both of which come into play for most women in different situations and at different times. It is my hope that the following discussion, in which I explicate my theoretical position more fully, will give the reader a framework which may help in situating and evaluating the research presented here.

Hegemony Theory and Television

Ideology refers generally to the terrain of ideas so centrally constitutive of our world views that we fail to notice what they are.[2] The hegemonic perspective asserts that television's meanings play some role in solidifying ideologies in capitalist societies such as the United States (Gerbner 1972; Schudson 1978; Tuchman [et al.] 1978; Gitlin 1980, 1983; Schiller 1985). Television, which some may analogously describe to be such an integral part of our lives that we also fail to notice it as we might fail to notice a necessary piece of living room or bedroom furniture, provides, in the context of our private experience, a constant stream of social images that impinge upon our view of the world and upon our very definitions of who we are. Television's unobtrusive nature, amplified by its hidden location in the private sphere, may make it effective in the same way ideologies are effective: unconsciously, both structure our conceptions of self and the social world.

The Italian Marxist Antonio Gramsci developed the concept of hegemony to describe the manner through which the ruling class dominates by securing popular consent to its rule.[3] Gramsci adopted the notion of hegemony to give new importance to struggles within the ideological realm of society, claiming that these were as important as physical coercion by the state apparatuses in maintaining popular support for the ruling class (Boggs 1976:17). One writer defines Gramsci's theory of hegemony as "an order in which a certain way of life and thought is dominant, in which one concept of reality is diffused throughout society in all its institutional and private manifestations, informing with its spirit all taste, morality, customs, religious and political principles, and all social relations, particularly in their intellectual and moral connotations" (Williams 1960:587; quoted in Cammett 1967:204). The theory of hegemony for the first time exposed the institutions of the capitalist superstructure—the family, the church, education, and the mass media—to intensive Marxist scrutiny. In the period since Gramsci's writings came to light, these institutions have been examined, with the theoretical tools he helped develop, in light of their function as bolstering and transmitting ideology. This occurs in complex, mediated ways to be sure, but occurs "functionally" nonetheless (Althusser 1971; Boggs 1976; Adamson 1980).

Gramsci used the example of the United States to illustrate what was, in his view, the best instance of a society in which the ruling classes had achieved, throughout their history, almost complete ideological hegemony (Gramsci 1971; Boggs 1976:50-51). In the United States, capitalist development, in the absence of a feudal past, led to the emergence of a new type of individual and a new type of culture, both of which were permeated with capitalist values, in Gramsci's analysis.

While Gramsci may have overstated the case, it is important that those analyzing values, beliefs, and ideology in the United States take seriously the possibility of capitalist ideological hegemony and seek to explain either resistance to it or the lack of resistance found among specific groups and individuals within them.

Television, Realism, and Everyday Life

From some perspectives, television can be seen to be a particularly salient instrument of hegemony.[4] Surrounded as many of us are by television in our private lives, its images may come to seem more real to us than our own experiences. At the very least, television images compete with our experience and influence our interpretation of it.

Many writers have commented on the realistic nature of television (Gitlin 1980, 1983; Marc 1989).[5] They note that, in our culture, television has become a part of our daily lives. It is accepted into the flow of our routine, or into our everyday division of labor (Kuhn 1982:25). As a result, television may be unique among media in that its images are strongly positioned to be accepted unconsciously by viewers as presenting images of reality, that is, as painting pictures of our world as it truly exists.

Television is a domestic medium. We watch television primarily in the private space of our homes (unlike films, for example, which have until recently been viewed in public movie theaters). Some researchers connect the way television consumption has increased vis-à-vis films to the historical ascendancy of the private over the public sphere (Williams 1974:28-29) in our culture. As society becomes privatized, the images and ideas we consume in the privacy of our homes become increasingly numerous and influential, particularly with the growth of television as a medium that can bring the outside public world into the privacy of our homes.[6]

In American life, while we pay lip service to the public, for most of us the private is the realm of the real.[7] This reliance on the private realm is particularly salient for women in our society, whose role in the public world is even less legitimated than that of men. Such a pattern of attributing primary importance and reality to the private realm, coupled with our almost universal possession and viewing of television sets, points to the possibility that what television portrays impacts heavily on our views of the world and ourselves (Gerbner 1972). It is possible that we rely on television for images of social reality, which may be skewed, however, in demonstrable, ideologically informed ways. Television helps us to bridge the gap between the public and private realms of our lives and to maintain, in our increasingly fragmented lives, a feeling of connection—however precarious—with the social world, even if this connection is emotive rather than substantive.[8]

Due primarily to its domestic location, television presumes a "family audience" (Ellis 1982; Morley 1986; Lembo 1988) and often, since women spend on average more time in the home than do men, a feminine one (Hobson 1982; Modleski 1982). Probably for these reasons, television content has long been preoccupied with portrayals of the nuclear family.[9] But this preoccupation has taken a particular form. The repetitive series convention of television programming makes television, unlike film, particularly suited to presenting the world as stable and unchanging;[10] the result is that both television content as a whole, and its presumed audience, are depicted in a manner biased toward the stability of the nuclear family.

Television's repetitive series format dictates several other important distinctions between television and more public visual media such as film. The narrative, central to traditional Hollywood narrative film, for example, is incidental to television. Whereas narrative film (like other traditional narrative forms) involves movement of an individual spectator through a problem which is resolved at the narrative's conclusion, television narrative works differently. Problems are never really resolved on series television, since the series must live on. Narrative resolution takes place then at a less fundamental level in television than in film, at the level of individual incidents (e.g., clinches, confrontations, or conversations) that are offered to us each week. It is the dilemma that characterizes the television series, not resolution or closure (Ellis 1982).

Consequently, the individual spectator posited by narrative film is either not posited by television in individual format at all or not attributed the same powerful voyeuristic "gaze" that film structurally imparts to its spectator, according to classical film theory.[11] Television, presuming as it does a family or essentially group audience, focuses its situations primarily around family-like groupings rather than around individuals.

We thus might expect it to be more difficult to make strong identifications with individual television characters than with film characters. As a result, the viewer herself has less power than does the spectator of a narrative film; rarely is there one main, powerful, all-knowing character with whom to identify, but rather merely a series of less powerful, more limited egos as objects for identification (Modleski 1982:92). Feminist theorists (Dinnerstein 1976; Chodorow 1978; Flax 1983) have posited a new "female" model for the individual, arguing that women individuate differently from men, maintaining much closer connections to their mothers, children, and others throughout their lives. In some ways, then, television is uniquely suited to the female viewer, uniquely able to draw women into involvement with itself.

Television's characteristic qualities have given rise to hot debates over its potential social power. While some commentators find television's presence in our interior domestic space threatening and invasive (Ellis 1982), others understand television's domestic presence very differently. Some see precisely this feature of the medium as ensuring its submission, above other media, to the terms of our collective discourse, and therefore to individual discourses when these vary from the collective:

> In going out to cinema we tend to submit to its terms, to become subject to its discourse, but television comes to our discourses. The living room as cultural space means differently to different members of the family. . . . These different meanings of the cultural space of viewing result in different social discourses being brought to bear upon television, and thus in different cultural texts being made out of it. (Fiske 1986:212)

In this argument, television is less totalizing than film because it is more directly subjugated to the terms of our discourse, rather than we to its terms. Others agree, arguing that television's particular appropriation of the traditional narrative actually opens this form up to active, give-and-take participation from the viewing audience (Altman 1986:50). This position emphasizes viewers' abilities to resist television's hegemonic meanings with interpretations of their own. In a particular form, this perspective is articulated in some of the works done by those writing within the British Cultural Studies tradition and by those responsible for the emerging tradition of feminist cultural studies as well. In the sections below, I examine the theoretical tensions between an emphasis on television's hegemonic functions and considerations of viewer resistance, while discussing these traditions more extensively.

The British Cultural Studies Tradition

In Great Britain, theorists associated with the Centre for Contemporary Cultural Studies (CCCS) of the University of Birmingham, sometimes called the Birmingham School (Stuart Hall, Angela McRobbie, Paul Willis, among others), have built upon Gramsci's theory along with Althusserian Marxism to develop a rather distinctive school of qualitative study of media content and cultural influence.[12] Their reliance on both Gramsci and Althusser leads to a tension between a focus on the active subjectivity of the working class, which Gramsci at times stressed, and a belief in the determinative structures of society delineated in the works of Althusser. In general, theorists of the school have used ethnographic and interpretative as well as historical methodologies to search for evidence of both ideological and political resistance to dominant social ideologies, and the colonization of this resistance, among oppressed gender, class, ethnic, and other groups.

Some of those working in the British Cultural Studies tradition have been interested in actual empirical study of the mass media audience. Works of the Birmingham School that treat media audiences specifically include Morley's recent work (1980, 1986) and, in part, the earlier works of Cohen (1973) and Hall et al. (1978). Other Birmingham works treat the operation of culture within consciousness generally, examining in depth the consciousness of specific social groups (working-class youths or women, for example) in order to illuminate in general the ways in which culture does, or does not, determine class, gender, or group consciousness. Among the best of these works are Willis (1977, 1978) and McRobbie (1978a, 1978b, 1981, 1984).

Qualitative methodologies—the in-depth interview, ethnography, and participant observation of small groups and small group discussions—have been used almost exclusively by British Cultural Studies researchers. Such methods have been deemed necessary by members of the school in order to unmask the apparent resistances they seek. Recently, Morley in particular has been interested in using ethnography, and ethnographic interviewing, to replace more traditional interviewing styles, allowing the researcher to pay more attention to the context, rather than merely the content, of informants' remarks (Morley 1981:5, 1986).[13]

There is a tension in Birmingham School work generally in the operant definition of "culture" which members of the school use.[14] As Hall describes, Birmingham researchers tend to investigate both consciousness—the realm of ideas—and, in a more anthropological vein, the social practices of cultural groups. This dual mode of investigation leads to a contradiction in their theoretical orientation. Their investigations of consciousness are primarily informed by a Marxist conception of ideology, which implies that at times the consciousness one investigates is "false," obscuring what is real. Thus Willis (1977), for example, can conclude his study of working-class schoolboys' consciousness, *Learning to Labor,* by making the claim, however indirectly, that the lads he studied do not fully understand their position as members of the working class in capitalist society and that, despite the appearance of resistance, their subjectivity as constituted contributes to their own oppression as members of this class. This judgment, however, for it is a *judgment* of their consciousness, conflicts with the anthropological emphasis in cultural investigation, which urges one to record and understand practices rather than to evaluate them, and particularly urges one to avoid labeling specific forms of consciousness and levels of understanding as "false" or "true."

Such dualities of thought have kept Birmingham researchers, in some respects, ambivalent. They are interested in identifying and describing the practices of subcultures in capitalist society in an anthropological mode; yet their descriptions are always set within a critical Marxist framework, which would lead them to place negative judgments on many of these subcultures. Their respect for the oppression of those they study, however, and their unwillingness to privilege their own position as intellectuals capable of seeing the truth,[15] leaves them many times unwilling to make such judgments and at times seeming to glorify the subjective forms of resistance practiced by oppressed groups, even when these are ineffective. Yet overall, members of the school have a distinct and subtle goal, which they often achieve rather elegantly in their work: to show how active consciousness also contributes to domination in capitalist societies (MacCabe 1986; Willis 1978 is particularly elegant as he achieves this aim). The work of the school has been pioneering for those interested in studying culture and consciousness within capitalist society.

British Cultural Studies as a framework, in accordance with its Marxist heritage, has privileged the concept of social class as a basic category of social analysis. The Cultural Studies paradigm has been used, therefore, primarily to articulate working-class experience with, and appropriation of, dominant cultural forms in capitalist society, again because their Marxist heritage leads Birmingham School researchers to search for resistance by those dominated in society. One of the school's primary terms of analysis, the "subculture," frames cultural use as almost inherently oppositional to the status quo. Cultural groups are categorized as to whether they possess this critical perspective, or lack it. There has also been more of a focus on public groups which are formed according to social class-related criteria, on people who live, work, or go to school together, than there is on the family or the individual as a unit of analysis. In part, this is because the masculinist bias of the school has led its members to concentrate on male expressions of resistance, which are often public, overt, and more easily studied than the characteristically privatized female forms.[16]

The Cultural Studies framework is strongest in its ability to illuminate class-specific responses to mass culture characteristic of the working class, particularly working-class men, but it has not been widely used to investigate the experiences of members of other classes, even in the same society. Gender differences have been particularly difficult for this framework to analyze, therefore, primarily because the genders relate in very different fashions to the subcultural groups that form the basic units of analysis in Cultural Studies. Long (1989) eloquently discusses three main points of feminists' critiques of British Cultural Studies: their public bias, the primacy of class, and the assumption that resistance is rationally expressed. Feminists working in the Cultural Studies tradition have challenged each of these features which dominate most of the school's work. These challenges have led the feminist Cultural Studies researchers in new, somewhat unorthodox directions, spawning a significant body of feminist Cultural Studies in both Britain and the United States.[17]

One of the products of this feminist reaction is Angela McRobbie's remarkable work (1978a, 1978b, 1980, 1982, 1984).[18] In an early piece (1978b), McRobbie notes the virtual absence in the youth culture literature of any discussion pertaining to women.[19] One reason for this, she notes, is the difficulty the observer normally has in gaining access to girls and to female groups. Girls generally spend much more time in private places, such as their homes, or the homes of friends and other family members, than do boys. Girls' groups tend to be smaller—the best-friend dyad is predominant—and again, to gather more often in nonpublic places. Even more important, McRobbie senses that girls' groups exhibit a greater degree of hostility toward the outside questioner than males have shown, perhaps because of the more private, intimate focus of the female social world.

All of these factors contribute to the difficulties the researcher interested in women's cultural experience must face. McRobbie found herself forced to rely more on in-depth interviews (my main tool here as well) and less on participant observation techniques than did Willis in his study of males.[20] Confronting all of these limitations, McRobbie nevertheless produces a fascinating document of the cultural world inhabited by working-class girls. She posits the possibility of a "culture of femininity" which is passed on from mothers to daughters, the content of which differs significantly from the dominant male culture. Interesting for my purposes here is the fact that McRobbie pays close attention to her subjects' creative appropriation of mass media meanings as she describes the content of the "culture of femininity" she has discovered.

McRobbie well notes the masculinist bias of the British Cultural Studies tradition.[21] Effectively, she challenges their privileging of class as the most important culturally organizing category, introducing the variable of gender as at least as important. The integration of these two variables, gender and class, therefore, becomes a major concern for McRobbie and others in her tradition.[22]

Women's Culture and Gender-Based Theories of Media Reception: New Developments in Feminist Cultural Studies

British Cultural Studies articulates the specificity of working-class culture and gives us the theoretical tools with which to begin studying this phenomenon, at least insofar as it occurs among male members of the working class. But in order to flesh out the notion of gender-specific culture and cultural processes, which will also be important in my analysis here, we must extend McRobbie's critique of Birmingham School work to some of the insights of American feminism. In its focus on individual development and processes, American feminism[23] adds to the Cultural Studies' class emphasis a deeper understanding of conscious and unconscious processes governing individual thoughts and behaviors. Viewing, so often practiced by individuals alone in private settings,[24] must be analyzed in part through attention to these aspects of the process.

Feminist Cultural Studies as practiced in the United States has borrowed the American feminist emphasis on individual psychology but has applied this primarily to the analysis of texts (in the tradition of American cultural studies; see note 1). Psychoanalytic theory has figured prominently in the works of this group, particularly in the area of feminist film theory, but again, there have been few attempts to apply this theory to the empirical study of reception processes in actual people.[25]

Radway's (1984b) innovative ethnographic study of female romance readers has helped to pave the way toward a new methodology for studying the female audience. With a background in literary criticism, Radway drew not only from social science research but also from the growing reader-response tradition in literary study as she conceived and executed her study.[26] She identified a group of romance readers in the Midwest and conducted in-depth interviews, group interviews, and surveys with these women in order to investigate the meaning of romance reading for them. Radway employs a feminist interpretation of romance reading, suggesting that the reading activity itself serves the function of claiming personal time for women who might otherwise have very little time to themselves. Radway (1984b:187) also believes that women identify with the active, independent qualities of the romantic heroines they preferred.

Radway's study, with its provocative conclusions, raises many questions. One is particularly left wondering about the tensions between the patriarchal and the feminist aspects of romance content, in conjunction with the possible function of the activity of reading itself.[27] As in the work of the Birmingham School, there is a tension in Radway's book between her desire to respect and simply record the cultural practices of the women she studied, and her feminist political commitments which give her some grounds for making negative judgments regarding the content and ultimate consequences of romance reading.[28]

Radway's sample is predominately middle-class.[29] One cannot help wondering how her readers' discussions of romances were shaded by their class position. Would working-class women have identified so strongly with the female heroines the middle-class women preferred? Or, given that working-class women might have chosen a different set of heroines with different qualities as their favorites, would identification with these fictional characters have been as primary a process for working-class women at all? Radway's study leaves these class-specific questions unanswered, making it difficult to determine whether her findings are generalizable to *all* women, or apply only to this class-specific group.

Radway does offer an interesting discussion of the ambivalent attitude her informants display toward the reality of the romantic stories they read.[30] While almost all of Radway's informants deny that romantic stories are "realistic," and assert that they do not expect their own lives to resemble the lives of romantic heroines, at the same time they insist that romances often instruct them about history and geography, broadening their experience and knowledge of the world. Radway concludes that, at the very least, women display an ambivalent attitude toward the reality of the stories they read. She consequently remains ambivalent in theorizing the real impact of romances: in some respects they are liberating, encouraging women to find their own, independent identity, while in other respects they conservatively encourage women to conform to the dictates of their traditional roles as wives, mothers, and nurturers of men and children.

> The women may in fact believe the stories are only fantasies on one level at the very same time that they take other aspects of them to be real and therefore apply information learned about the fictional world to the events and occurrences of theirs. If they do so utilize some fictional propositions, it may well be the case that the readers also unconsciously take others having to do with the nature of the heroine's fate as generally applicable to the lives of real women. In that case, no matter what the women intend their act of reading to say about their roles as wives and mothers, the ideological force of the reading experience could, finally, be a conservative one. In reading about a woman who manages to find her identity through the care of a nurturant protector and sexual partner, the Smithton readers might well be teaching themselves to believe in the worth of such a route to fulfillment and encouraging the hope that such a route might yet open up for them as it once did for the heroine. (Radway 1984b:187)

Radway relates her informants' belief in the reality of romantic characters and stories to their more general acceptance of the reality of the romantic world created by the romance narrative itself (1984b:186-208). Romance novels, she demonstrates, combine the elements of both myth and novel. They offer a plot that promises to detail the adventures of a unique, individual woman but that actually tells a story which has been told many times before and proceeds in a fashion extremely predictable to its readers, although they are not always aware of these elements of repetition (Radway 1984b:207-208). In this sense, as Radway notes, the narrative conveys the message that in some respects, despite individual differences, women are all the same, that they should and must conform to a generically "female" role, reinforcing our society's traditional sexual division of labor (1984b:208). Thus Radway finds that, although women readers may assert their independence with the act of romance reading, the content of romances actually undermines their independence by affirming that the destiny of all women consists in their filling fundamentally identical social roles.

By focusing on romance novels, Radway chose a cultural product specifically directed at, and consumed by, a female audience. Her study paves the way for the possibility of discussing those aspects of women's reception of culture that are specific to their position in society, a position that has been in great flux in recent years, making generalization all the more problematic. Although focused on middle-class women, Radway's work helps us add to the British Cultural Studies' emphasis on class a deeper understanding of the meaning of gender for women's reception of culture. Other recent American works,[31] in particular Long's (1986, 1987) studies of women's reading groups and the interpretation of books, have helped to extend further the theoretical terms and empirical dimensions of Radway's study, delineating the specific issues involved in women's cultural reception and describing the forms women's reception takes in American society. Among their other concerns, these works address women's responses to popular understandings and representations of feminist ideas deriving from the women's liberation movement and the fluidity of women's social positions it helped initiate.

The intersection of class and gender cultures forms the backdrop for my analysis of women's discussions of television. Although the universe of prime-time television entertainment is of course much broader than that of the romance novels Radway studied and much less narrowly directed toward women, there are some similarities between the assumptions about the reality of that universe made by both romance readers and television viewers alike. Here my study benefits from analyses of television content informed by hegemonic cultural theory (Gitlin 1980, 1983). Regarding audience response, my discussion of differences between women of different social classes adds a new dimension to the analysis Radway presents; this aspect of my study benefits directly from British Cultural Studies works. There are distinctions among women in the degree to which they judge and expect television to be realistic and in the standards they apply to that judgment. There are also social class and generational distinctions concerning women's ability to identify with characters they view and in the form such identifications take. (Do women identify with individual characters? With working women or family women? With family or work situations and groups rather than single characters themselves?) I not only encounter the issue of women's responses to feminism but also must confront women's responses to popular understandings and representations of social class relations, class positions, and social mobility in the United States. Each of these factors comes into play in the comparisons I draw. . . .

Work, Family, and Social Class in Television Images of Women: Prefeminism, Feminism, and Postfeminism on Prime-Time Television

. . . Television's presentation of women has changed considerably over the course of its history.[32] Particularly when we consider the relationship of television women to family and work, we can see marked changes in the type of female character most often seen over time. As the shape of the American family has changed with the rising divorce rate and increased acceptance of alternative family forms, and as more and more women, many of them mothers, have entered the paid labor force, television's depiction of the workplace and the family, and of women's relationship to each, has altered significantly as well.

Changes in television images have not always paralleled actual changes in society. Particularly with regard to the depiction of women, we can see how social ideologies mediate between changes in the real world, the images that become available on television, and viewers' choices of television images to watch. Many of us assume that viewers' choices reflect changes that have occurred in the real world, but this is not always the case. We can point to certain themes of discrepancy between real-world changes and the television images people chose at corresponding moments in history.

Like other forms both of art and mass culture, popular television images represent certain social groups, issues, and institutions systematically and repetitively in a manner that often reflects the position of these groups within our society's hierarchical power structure. In the case of women, some have argued that popular television narratives minimize the problems contemporary American women face as they attempt to carve out new identities for themselves as individuals in the face of social realities and expectations which have altered radically and rapidly. Studies find that television portrayals of women fail to represent the pressures of work and family, finding and paying for child care, balancing home and job responsibilities and stretching the family budget, which many women experience in their lives. On television, all single mothers are middle-class or wealthier and almost half of all families are at least upper-middle-class; there are no poor families. This contrasts with our society, in which 69% of all homes headed by women are poor, and the annual median income for a family with two working parents is just over $30,000. Also more than half of all television children in single-parent families live with their fathers, who experience few financial difficulties in being a single parent; in society, on the other hand, 90% of all children in single-parent families live with their mothers, whose average annual income is under $9,000.[33]

Popular television, of course, cannot be said to reflect society, nor should this be its role. Popular television *does* reflect a desire to simplify terrains of ideological confusion and contradiction within our society. Some argue (Taylor 1989) that television provides us with fantasy-level solutions to some of our most pressing social problems, particularly those relating to the disintegration of our families and the growing instability of our private lives. Other commentators stress the ways television misrepresents our most common social and personal problems, thus proliferating representations of our lives which are systematically distorted in ways that reflect the dominant ideologies in our culture (Gitlin 1980, 1983).

Without taking a conclusive stance on this issue (although I instinctively desire greater overt recognition by television of women's problems in both the family and the workplace and feel critical of television when this recognition is lacking), I nevertheless maintain that it is sociologically interesting to pinpoint precisely those places in which television representation departs most widely and systematically from reality, insofar as the latter is possible to ascertain. I leave it to the women I have interviewed, however, to address, as audience members, competing theories as to television's proper role in our society. . . .

Prefeminist Family Television

Prefeminist fiction television had no shortage of women who were active, insightful, and personally courageous. And indeed there was frequently the suggestion in early programming that women's lives were colored by an injustice that came to their sex. But here, different from later television narratives, there is a sharp dichotomy between women's social roles *as women* and the divergent path they would have to traverse were they to escape their destiny as women and become fully articulated human beings. For the most part, on early television women are depicted primarily *as women*. Rarely (if ever) are early television women shown to be mature, independent individuals. Family women in particular are shown to be women whose existence is closely bound up with, and by, others in their family group, particularly their male partners. In addition, family women on early television are consistently pictured almost exclusively in the domestic or private realm; rarely do they legitimately venture into the male, public world of work. And, unlike the male individuals peopling these shows, early television women are often depicted in inextricable solidarity with one another. . . .

[C]ontrast between images of the working-class and middle-class family raises some interesting questions regarding the ideological dimensions of television images of class, of women, and of the relationship between the two. Most basically, the working class is grossly underrepresented on early television family shows.[34] This is a problem that continues in television's later years. Even more interesting, working-class family structure is stereotyped in a way that displays specific prejudices about sex roles in working-class versus middle-class marriages. The working-class family is seen as "matriarchal" as opposed to the "patriarchal" or "egalitarian" marriages portrayed in the middle-class families. This is interesting since in reality working-class women have even less power than do middle-class women in their marriages, as they do in society, because they have fewer alternatives to their domestic role.[35] . . . [W]orking-class life, and the working-class woman's experience in particular, is glorified on popular television.

"Feminist" Television

Different television genres have taken up different social tasks and followed different developmental histories. Even in the era of "recombinant" programming—that is, where television shows customarily reproduce and repackage the qualities of other, successful shows—we need to distinguish the role of women in the situation comedy from the representation of women in drama. . . . Early television was dominated by variety shows and dramatic anthologies. With the exception of *The Martha Raye Show* (variety) and *The Loretta Young Show* (drama) the most popular shows were hosted by men. As dramatic programs with continuing casts and situations replaced the anthologies in the late fifties and early sixties, women became even more peripheral. Women played only supporting roles in the westerns that supplanted the antholo-

gies in the ratings—as the "love interest," or as the "innocent imperiled." Only in situation comedies did women provide an active center.
Women (and the working class) were ghettoized in the world of canned
(and live) laughter.

The second-wave feminist movement of the late sixties and early
seventies coincided with and helped to produce a marked change in the
television images of women across genres. Where women's exit from
the snug bonds of domesticity had been a cause for amusement, as in
the situation comedies, or a source of danger, as in the dramas, women
were now seen with increasing legitimacy outside the home. By the late
seventies and early eighties, it was no longer unusual to see images of
strong women working in nontraditional positions. I have tentatively
called some of these representations "feminist" because they stress
women's activities in the public, rather than the domestic, realm. I
realize that this is an oversimplification of the term and that it magnifies
what was often a very thin social content; nevertheless, it is useful in
describing what turned out to be a short era in the history of television's
portrayal of women.

In the action-adventure genre, the success of *Charlie's Angels* showed
that women could hold audience attention in active roles traditionally
reserved for men. It also showed that success could be the composite of
quite diverse "viewing pleasures." The *Angels* were both active and
attractive; their collaboration and command could appeal to feminist
sensibilities; their glamour and sex appeal could also appeal to decid-
edly nonfeminist sensibilities, including the action genre's historically
male audience. The three glamorous detectives, after all, worked in the
service of the unseen (and clearly authoritative) Charlie.

> Throughout the run, the Angels got in and out of jeopardy while relying on
> Charlie, their unseen detective boss, to bail them out. It was probably no
> small part of the show's appeal to men that Charlie was heard but never
> seen. Male authority was invisible, and the "girls" kept free of romance.
> Charlie's ambassador on the scene was the sexless Bosley, eunuch to
> Charlie's harem. In the male viewer's fantasy, he could *be* Charlie, ever
> supervising, ever needed, ever returned-to monopolist of Angels. (Gitlin,
> 1983:73)

As Todd Gitlin remarks, the Angels are both independent career
women while remaining distinct sex objects. In a sense, they promised
women it was possible to have the best of both worlds at the same time,

to be sexy (for men) while engaged in exciting work (for themselves, but also for men's admiration). Such dual messages were carried by many representations of women during television's "feminist" era. . . .

Postfeminist Era Television

Since the heyday of the second-wave feminist movement, television images have changed once more, again partly in directions that can be alarming from some feminist perspectives. There is a trend for women to be shown back in the home and for shows to espouse what may be termed postfeminist values, which are often those values concerning women's proper roles regarding work and family that were traditional in the fifties. This is the era of postfeminist television.

Postfeminist television retains some of the aspects characterizing feminist era television, but repackages them with a twist. For the most part, women are attributed some version of a work identity, however superficial, along with their family role but not at the expense of a family role. On postfeminist television, women's family role is normally emphasized; or if it is not, this very fact commands a great deal of narrative attention in the television show. The trend on postfeminist television is to take women out of the workplace-family and put them back in the home, in a revitalization of traditional family values that melds with a superficial acceptance of feminist perspectives concerning women and work. Concomitantly, the theme of women's collective resistance to these families is not nearly as prominent as it was in many prefeminist family shows. Perhaps now that we can no longer take the family for granted, television cannot afford to be so cavalier in offering multiple, comic depictions of women's dissatisfactions and rebellions.

Of course, the term "postfeminist" is itself ambiguous, and often connotes contradictory meanings. Brought to the attention of the public by Betty Friedan in 1981, postfeminism has been used by feminists to mean the recognition that the women's liberation movement of the late sixties and early seventies no longer presents a unified front, that the particular circumstances of race and class are not merely "add-ons" to the central circumstance of being a woman, and that we are in a period where the "fact" of power is felt everywhere, but where the sometimes oversimplified attributions of power, whether to men, "the big bosses," or the Tri-Lateral Commission, no longer seem to offer such immediate and intelligible hoped-for redress.

But postfeminism is often taken to mean something else too—something felt quite bitterly by women who have identified with the women's liberation movement; this sense of its meaning is the closest to mine here. Postfeminism has been used to describe the mindset of a generation of women who have come of age after the heyday of the women's liberation movement and reaped the benefits of the social reforms and changed attitudes that the movement gained—often at the cost of upset and humiliation to the women who fought for them—but who categorically refuse to call themselves feminists, and who cling to symbols of women's traditionally "special" status (these include men opening doors for women and other signs of chivalry).

Ironically, the mass media, primarily television and film, if not the sole determinant of this antifeminist trend among young women, have been a leading cause or at least a leading source of these ideas in our culture. Media representation of this version of postfeminism has occurred in three major forms. First, negative images of the women's movement have proliferated in the major media; their pejorative and caricaturized presentation of "strident feminists" (Tuchman et al. 1978; Baehr 1980; van Zoonen 1988) has become a cliché in both nonfiction and fiction television. The media have provided the environment for this by their symbolic annihilation of feminism from its beginning. Strident feminists are usually seen as loners or disconnected souls. Women as participants in a movement simply are not represented.

Simultaneous with the symbolic annihilation of the women's movement, and again ironically, many of the critical issues that the women's liberation movement raised were incorporated into television narrative. But these issues were raised in a particular, mass-mediated form. The second way television has "posted" feminism has been the tendency to personalize or individualize solutions to the problems of women. This tendency furthers media annihilation of the women's movement, encouraging as it does the lack of any group identity for women. In television, a woman might experience a problem because she is a woman, but she would solve the problem because she is a competent or even superior individual. The solution might occur to her in interaction with others, but in the end it is *private* insight and personal courage—not public or collective action—that offer her a way out. That television would come to this solution in the representation of women's issues, given the deep cultural legacy of utilitarian individualism, is not at all surprising. Fiction and nonfiction television alike are clearly more able to represent politics as a function of personality than as a product of social structure or collective action. It is perhaps ironic that such "collective" productions as are television products take such an individualist bent. . . .

My discussion is offered as a starting point, a way for us to begin to define the shape and dynamic of cultural processes at the individual and social group level in complex societies. Qualitative methodology, as I have employed it, presupposes that events at this individual level, though not the only level we should investigate, are nevertheless meaningful and contribute to our greater understanding of culture.

In interpreting my study, I start from two convictions which are often construed to be contradictory in the literature on mass media reception: first, that the mass media in general and television in particular serve as important mechanisms for disseminating and reinforcing ideology in liberal capitalist societies and, second, that individuals and groups of individuals receive media actively, that to receive television involves the active interpretation of its images and their meaning. Viewers bring their own perspectives, often critical ones, to the viewing experience.

More often than not, these two sets of assumptions are held to be incompatible in our field. It is often assumed that, if one accepts the terms of hegemony theory, then one holds that the mass media audience is passive and that one's attention will focus on media form, content, and control rather than on problems of reception. This assumption unfairly oversimplifies the premises of the notion of hegemony, however, and misrepresents the intentions of those who have adapted this theory to mass media study. The theory of hegemony is, at heart, a theory of human action. Unlike many social theories, hegemony theory highlights the role of the thoughts, beliefs, and practices of human actors in the process of social change.

Marx's dictum that "men [in this case, women] make history, but they do not do so under conditions of their own choosing" may be applied to media scholars' use of hegemony theory as well. While consciousness of—and conscious resistance to—a society's dominant ideas are important motors for the process of social change, we do not always control the conditions which form our consciousness. While it may be human nature to continually seek further knowledge of those conditions, we can never become fully enlightened about the determinants of our consciousness; this point has been made abundantly clear by the works of Marx and Freud and the commentators on them.[36]

The study of media reception, therefore, like the study of all complex processes of thought and action, to be complete must involve considerations of both conscious and unconscious thought processes, of creative and resistant impulses as well as determined and controlled responses. It is a large task. Not surprisingly, most attempts to study media reception emphasize only one small part of the total picture. Hegemonic discussions, unfortunately, have de-emphasized the critical response of audience members; studies of the active audience have de-emphasized media's hegemonic nature. Like most others, my study is also a limited investigation of television reception, but it is one I hope will fill some gaps currently in our literature.

Overall, I take the position that television reception is a complicated process, one that cannot be adequately summarized either by the term "resistance" or by the terms "passivity" and "accommodation." With the open-ended interviewing method I employ in the study, women are able to express elements of both, and often do, in their responses to my questions and in their discussions overall. Theories that cannot account for both are bound to understate the complexity of the problem. It is much too simplistic to argue that women resist domination when they watch and talk about television.[37] Although in many respects television texts are open to competing interpretations, in other respects they bear the unmistakable marks of the hegemonic culture that creates them. It is wishful thinking, I fear, to believe that viewers are unaffected by these ideas as they are present in both mass media texts and concomitantly in our culture at large.

It is also simplistic, however, to argue that television viewers are simply passive recipients of the medium's hegemonic messages, or that members of a culture simply imbibe, passively, the ideological messages of that culture. Individuals and groups show themselves capable of creativity and independence both in thought and in strategies of action in many ways in our culture.[38] People often express, verbally and actively, resistance to dominant ideas and realize the contradictions among competing aspects of our cultural ideologies. Women watching television are no different. Often they find themselves frustrated with their family and/or work situations, and are dissatisfied with the ideas our culture makes available for expression of this frustration. The process of receiving television may include strategies for expressing, as well as for coping with, this frustration. Evidence of this abounds in women's responses to my interviews. In my discussion, however, rather than making an overarching claim as to the ends television watching serves in our society, I emphasize the different forms in which these responses to questions about television occur between class- and age-differentiated groups.

In the course of my study, marked class differences emerged when I compared discussions of television offered by working-class and middle-class women. Working-class women's search for realism on television seems in large part responsible for these differences. Often, working-class women begin their discussion of television characters by assessing their realism. In fact, their search for realism leads working-class women, in the end, to a more distanced, perhaps resistant, stance toward television they like, and to identify with relatively few television characters.[39] More often, they are extremely critical of television characters, and there seems to be little propensity on my informants' part toward identification with these characters, even with characters on shows women told me that they enjoy and watch often. For middle-class women, on the other hand, the realism of situations and even characters is seldom an overtly discussed issue. They often harbor favorable, somewhat personal feelings toward television characters inhabiting shows they describe to be silly or unrealistic.

A convenient way to sum up these differences might be to observe that while middle-class women focus their criticism on television shows in a very general way, they more often respond positively to individual characters on these shows, even characters they may find comic or unrealistic. In fact, middle-class women more often identify with television characters, in particular with their situations and dilemmas vis-à-vis family and other relationships, than do working-class women. Paradoxically, then, middle-class women generally seem to like television less overall but to identify with its characters and situations more than working-class women.

Working-class women, on the other hand, while overall claiming to value television more highly, are often critical both of television shows themselves and of the characters on them, primarily for their lack of realism.[40] Working-class women's lack of identification with television characters is perhaps not surprising when one considers the middle- or upper-class bias of most television content. What is more surprising and disturbing is their judgment that many of television's middle-class shows offer accurate pictures of reality; this suggests that some women learn from television to see middle-class life as "real," and raises alarming possibilities for television's impact on women's consequent interpretation of their own experience.

Working-class women resist television but, paradoxically, the standards of critique they use are not their own. In large part, working-class women criticize television content for its lack of reality; yet the concept of reality used here corresponds to television's portrayal of middle-class life. The potential resistant thrust of their critique of television, therefore, is blunted by television's hegemonic impact itself.

Comparing older with younger women's responses, I find that, at the older extreme of the life cycle, gender-related considerations govern women's responses to television more than class, for both historical and developmental reasons. In younger women's responses, class differences are more prominent. At both ends of the age spectrum, women respond most to what many feel they are missing in their lives. Older women, while critical of television's working women in certain respects, speak longingly of the interesting and different sorts of jobs women are pictured holding on current television. One has the sense that for older women television is an important cultural reminder of many of the experiences not widely available to women in the prefeminist era of their youths; in this respect, television is almost a liberating, or enlarging, force for them.

Younger women focus more on family than on work. Aware of new ideals for women in the workplace that conflict with older prescriptions for women in the famiiy, younger working-class women often view family television with an interesting mixture of criticism and sadness. Children of broken homes are sometimes painfully nostalgic for the intact nuclear families early television depicts. Middle-class women are somewhat less critical of family television, some gratefully acknowledging it as a refuge from unhappy childhoods.

A comparison among women of different ages reveals that, at different points in its history and for different groups of women, television can serve either as a fairly conservative or as a relatively radical repository of cultural ideas. Older women feel that their horizons are broadened by what they see on television, especially by the roles television women play at work. Many younger women find that television encourages their longings for and exacerbates their feelings of loss about traditional family forms. Paradoxically, from a feminist perspective, television can be construed as feminist or progressive for older women, inspiring criticism of sexual mores but drawing their eager attention to depictions of women at work. In younger women, post-feminist television in particular inspires criticism, admiration, and nostalgia, a mix in which resistance blends with an often backward-looking sentiment. Younger women are happy to see images of women successfully combining work and family, but they are skeptical as well. Few see such realities in their own futures. Younger working-class women often split feminist or postfeminist female characters and talk only about their family lives, either not relating to their generally middle-class work situations or not believing that they combine this work happily with their family roles.

In sum, my findings lead me to conclude that the hegemonic aspects of the way television operates are more gender-specific for middle-class women (e.g., in ways related to the organization of the class system in our society). I certainly do not mean to suggest that working-class women are not oppressed by their gender. Rather, I argue that how they interact with television culturally is more a function of their social class membership than their membership in a particular gender group. At either end of the age spectrum, women of both classes tend to respond more to gender-related variables than to those related to social class, with younger women more critically suspicious of television's images picturing women's changing social positions, and older women more hopeful and accepting of the stories these images tell; both trends are tempered, however, by strongly opposite, and contradictory, responses.

In conclusion, women's reception of television is affected by both their position as women in our society and their membership in social class and age groups. In comparing the remarks of women of different social classes, I find that television contributes to their oppression in the family and in the workplace both *as* women and, for working-class women, as members of the working class. While women criticize television and resist much of its impact, it is clear that television contributes to these two dimensions of women's oppression. In addition, women of different age groups experience television's political impact differently; both older and younger women are at once critical of, and compelled by, pictures of television women in the family and at work.

My findings stand in contradiction to those theorists who would argue that viewers use the mass media to resist cultural hegemony all the time, or to hegemony theorists who might argue that the mass media operate as a cultural monolith, presenting the audience with politically determined content that is received uniformly across all groups.[41] Instead, television is both a source of resistance to the status quo for different groups of women and a reinforcer for the patriarchal and capitalist values that characterize the status quo. Mass media in general and television in particular function complexly and paradoxically in our society, simultaneously fostering conformity and encouraging resistance to it among dominated groups.

My research leads me to suggest that, until more conclusive evidence accrues that either capitalist or patriarchal cultural hegemony prevails in our culture, or that resistance to it is widespread, we must look beyond the institution of television for a clearer picture as to how its participation in either trend articulates with our cultural practices as a whole. If women's tendency to resist hegemony through creative interpretations of television truly stops in the kitchen, then this evidence of resistance must be counted as something else. Theorists of resistance must develop some means for assessing the political effectiveness of the resistance they chronicle.

Overall, this maps the terrain of class and generational differences in women's interpretations of television entertainment programming in the United States. My work will serve, I hope, to raise issues involved in investigating women's media reception; further work, of course, will be necessary to refine and deepen our understanding of these issues. Scholars in Europe and the United States have lately attempted ethnographic audience study. As I have discussed [previously] most of these studies have focused on audiences and groups within audiences outside the United States. In some ways, the vast diversity one encounters within American culture makes it a natural laboratory for ethnographic study, yet in other ways, the constant interchange between subcultures in this country makes it difficult, and forbidding, to identify specific subcultures upon which to concentrate. Introducing the variable of gender makes such groupings even more difficult to attain.

The reception of television and the other popular media gives us an important window into the cultural lives of groups within our society. Such studies can help us begin to talk meaningfully about cultural life within a society as vast and complex as our own. I hope that others will build on the work I offer here, and that ultimately we will develop a clearer picture of how cultural processes operate and reproduce themselves for women in our society. . . .

Notes

[Editors' Note: This chapter was constructed from three separate sections of a book and some of the notes have been renumbered for chronological order; this renumbering is indicated with note numbers in brackets in the text and below.]

1. Some might lump together the hegemonic and the British Cultural Studies traditions into one larger "critical" tradition of media study, which stands in contradistinction to less "critical," more mainstream, work, since both the former traditions owe much to Marxist (particularly Althusserian and Gramscian) theoretical roots. When one focuses on the audience, as I do here, the distinction between "critical" and "mainstream," so basic to most characterizations of communication research in the United States and Great Britain, is rather limiting. As some have pointed out, American critical research has often neglected the question of the audience (Fejes 1984); in Britain, however "audience" study (although the notion of audience is more broadly conceived than in the United States, almost as a "cultural" audience) has been a primary theme of critical communication researchers.

Cultural studies as developed by the Birmingham School—particularly in their presumption of an active and resistant audience and their use of qualitative methodology in studying that audience—have begun to exert a wide influence on other contemporary studies of the media audience, both in the United States and abroad. For instance, Tamar Liebes and Elihu Katz (the latter one of the originators of the "dominant paradigm" in mainstream research and once identified solely with this paradigm and with uses and gratifications research) have launched a series of intercultural studies of reception of the television series *Dallas* (Katz and Liebes 1984; Liebes 1984; see also Ang 1985). The *Dallas* studies make use of qualitative research techniques, primarily focused interviews with groups of viewers, often in family or family-like settings. In addition, researchers recorded viewers' conversations and comments made while watching the show. Unlike much earlier American audience research, the focus of the *Dallas* studies has been viewer interpretation of the elements—plot, character, narrative—of the show.

Others in the United States as well have begun to move their studies of their audience out of the "mainstream" by using qualitative methods of study and engaging with some of the same issues and questions traditionally asked by those in the critical tradition (Lull 1987a). For some other examples of this new and exciting direction of communication research, see especially Lull (1978, 1980, 1987a, 1987b); Webster and Wakshlag (1982); Brody and Stoneman (1983); Goodman (1983); Lemish (1985, 1987); Schwartz (1986); Anderson (1987); Bryce (1987); Cantor (1987); Lindlof (1987a, 1987b); Lindlof and Meyer (1987); Messaris (1987); Schwartz and Griffin (1987); Traudt, Anderson, and Meyer (1987); Traudt and Lont (1987); Lindlof and Grodin (1989).

While my use of methodology is often similar to that employed in these studies, theoretically my project is grounded more squarely in the critical traditions I proceed to discuss (although, as I have indicated, the divisions I make here de-emphasize the considerable overlap between groupings).

2. For more extensive definitions of the term "ideology," see especially Hall (1977a, 1983); Gitlin (1980, 1983). Mannheim (1936) offers perhaps the classic sociological definition of ideology as beliefs promoted by ruling elites in order to maintain and perpetuate their position of dominance. Over the past several decades the discussion of ideology in the social sciences has evolved from an emphasis on the forcible imposition of ideas and beliefs "from the top down" to a greater recognition of the participation of those below. The translation of both Gramsci and the writings of the early Marx into English has contributed to this shift in the definition of the concept of ideology.

3. See Antonio Gramsci, *Selections from the Prison Notebooks,* ed. and trans. Quintin Hoare and Geoffrey Nowell Smith (New York: International, 1971). Gramsci's notion of

hegemony has been developed more recently by Williams (1973, 1977c), and has been applied directly to contemporary media study by Gitlin (1980, 1983).

4. See Adorno (1954); Sklar (1980); Gitlin (1980, 1983, 1986); and Bagdikian (1983).

5. The definition of the term "realism" merits some discussion here. What does it mean for a television viewer to speak of a television show or character as realistic? In fact, the answer to this question is far from obvious. Viewers may vary by sex, social class, even individually as to their meaning in labeling a television program or character to be realistic. Even critics cannot agree on the meaning of the label "realism" when this is applied to a work of art or, in this case, to a product of the mass media. In general, while much used in the critical literature, the term is ill-defined and, consequently, is often used idiosyncratically by individual critics within fields and certainly by critics in different fields of analysis.

Auerbach (1953) speaks exhaustively of the vicissitudes in the attempt to define reality throughout the entire history of Western literature. While he remains reluctant to define the term "realism" itself, he limits his project instead to differences in the way "realistic subjects" have been treated from the time of classical antiquity through the modernist literature of the twentieth century. Auerbach traces the rise of subjectivism in twentieth-century writers to the decline of a widely recognized social consensus in our time as to what the real world is all about.

> As recently as the nineteenth century, and even at the beginning of the twentieth, so much clearly formulable and recognized community of thought and feeling remained in those countries that a writer engaged in representing reality had reliable criteria at hand by which to organize it. At least, within the range of contemporary movements, he could discern certain specific trends; he could delimit opposing attitudes and ways of life with a certain degree of clarity. To be sure, this had long since begun to grow increasingly difficult. . . . At the time of the first World War and after—in a Europe unsure of itself, overflowing with unsettled ideologies and ways of life, and pregnant with disaster—certain writers distinguished by instinct and insight find a method which dissolves reality into multiple and multivalent reflections of consciousness. That this method should have been developed at this time is not hard to understand. (Auerbach 1953:550-551)

Raymond Williams (1977b) echoes Auerbach's reluctance to define a specific realistic method, noting that an abstract realistic method does not exist. Rather, the question as to whether a particular work is or is not realistic must be considered within the social and political context of that work, the intentions of its authors, and the conditions of its reception. Put more simply, what is realistic in one context is not necessarily realistic in another context. While he does identify the three essential qualities of the genre of realistic literature and drama which emerged in the late nineteenth century—these are the representation of "the people" or lower classes as well as the upper classes, a movement toward setting actions in the present, and an emphasis on secular, as opposed to religious, action—Williams nevertheless maintains that these works must be contextualized in order to fully ascertain their realistic nature (Williams 1977b:63-64). In his discourse realism, as opposed to the genre of "naturalism," which also emerged at this time and signified the depiction of surface-level reality, connotes the representation of the actual reality behind the mere surface appearance of events. When one refers to a realistic work, therefore, one is not merely referring to the reflection of the world as it appears, but, drawing upon ideas that developed along with the rational scientific attitude, one is actually claiming that the work in question represents some truth about the nature of reality which transcends surface appearances (Williams 1977b:64-65; Watt 1957:32).

Turning to the way realism is defined in discussions of the visual media, we find that what is commonly referred to by critics (although again, there is dissension) as realistic film evolved out of the conventions characterizing the nineteenth-century realistic novel and drama as described by Williams above. When applied to the use of a film camera, realism most often connotes the following conventions: the camera is a single eye, and there is no possibility of an alternative viewpoint; as Williams puts it, "the viewer has to go along or detach him or herself, he or she has no complex seeing within the action. . . . a great deal is taken for granted in knowledge and recognition of the situation" (1977b:69).

This sense that much is taken for granted, as to how the viewer will understand and contextualize the situation depicted, certainly characterizes current television entertainment programming in this country. While much is beginning to be written regarding the possible differences between film and television realism (Ellis 1982; Feuer 1986) from the critics' point of view, in this volume I have investigated the way television is received as realistic from the vantage of television viewers themselves. Whatever critics eventually decide as to the precise definition of television realism in relation to filmic realism, the programs I investigated all follow what are for my purposes very similar conventions with regard to the placement of the camera and the positioning of the spectator.

6. For discussions of the decline of the public sphere, see Habermas (1962) and, more recently, Postman's (1985) interesting discussion of the way television has come to substitute for a true public sphere in our society and the effects this has had on the nature of our public discourse. See also Meyrowitz (1985).

7. Bellah et al. (1985) challenge this assumption, studying the role of public commitment in the lives of Americans from different walks of life. They make a persuasive case for the importance of public life in the contemporary United States which in some ways undercuts the argument about television I make here.

8. See Gitlin (1983:332) for further discussion of these ideas about television and the social world. See also Gerbner's Cultivation Project (Gerbner 1972; Gerbner and Gross 1976; Gerbner et al. 1980; and Hirsch 1981).

9. See Edmundson (1986), who notes the marked success of the television situation comedy formula over all other program formats. He theorizes that the situation comedy is a format uniquely suited to a primarily family medium.

10. Gitlin (1979) presents an excellent discussion of the primary conventions of prime-time television and of their possible effects.

11. See Metz (1982) and Mulvey (1975). Kuhn (1982) offers a good summary of the debate between feminist and Metzian film theorists, and summarizes the debate among feminists about Mulvey's thesis.

12. Fiske (1987b) discusses the tension between Althusser's influence on the work of the Birmingham School and that of Gramsci. The Gramscian emphasis on the active subject at times clashed with the Althusserian focus on ideological structures, which at times implied a more determined view of the subject. This tension in their view of the subject characterizes much of the work the CCCS produced and is in large part responsible for its richness.

13. See Press and Lembo (1989) for a review and critique of current uses of the ethnographic method in audience studies.

14. The concept of culture has been central to theorists of the school (Hall 1977a, 1980b, 1983). As in our society, culture is defined by CCCS members variably to refer in its anthropological sense to overall modes and patterns of actions and beliefs and, more narrowly, to refer to artistic products worthy of study (Williams 1976). The mass media are interesting to those who propose both definitions simultaneously, both as the center of general cultural practices and as examples of artistic consumption in our society. Members of the school have turned their attention to mass media use in both interests.

Members of the Birmingham School have produced theoretical and empirical work focusing on the cultural processes of capitalist society. The mass media have been studied by researchers associated with the school in the context of their role as repositories and disseminators of "cultural" content. Birmingham School theorists have been interested in the content the mass media produce, which they have studied as ideologically constructed texts, and in mass media as one of many institutional complexes that produce ideology. Mass media consumption and the meanings this consumption engenders have been studied as factors that interact with a group's cultural way of being in the world, as a part of the cultural fabric of life in capitalist societies.

15. See Gramsci (1971) on the role of the intellectual in the capitalist social formation. See also Konrad and Szelenyi (1979) and Bourdieu (1984).

16. In his recent work on patterns of television watching, however, Morley (1986) does use the family as the unit of analysis.

17. Willis's (1977, 1978) studies in particular sparked a reaction in the feminist community, since although he includes some infuriating sexist references indicative of the way women figure in the lives of his male subjects, he rarely addresses his informants' sexism directly and virtually omits any study or discussion of women at all.

18. See also McRobbie and Garber (1976), McRobbie and McCabe (1981), and McRobbie and Nava (1984).

19. See also Brake (1980) and McRobbie (1982).

20. There has been much debate about the status of so-called feminist methodologies in the social sciences. Although the possibility of developing a specifically feminist methodology for the study of social processes remains tantalizing, as yet no consensus has been reached, by either feminists or their critics, as to whether this will be possible. See especially Gregg (1978), Belenky et al. (1986), Cook and Fonow (1986), Cirksena (1987), and Harding (1987) for provocative commentary on this question. Feminist theorists agree only that a feminist methodology must overtly address the inevitable power inequities between researcher and informant. See Long's (1989) discussion of Roman's (1987, 1988) interesting, innovative research for a good example of a researcher explicitly attempting to use feminist methodology, and an extremely innovative version of it, in her research.

21. See also McRobbie (1984) for a more recent, and complex, challenge to the rationalist bias of masculinist cultural studies. In two critical review essays, McRobbie (1980, 1982) spells out her criticism of British Cultural Studies more explicitly.

22. In her recent review essay, Long (1989) cites the following works as examples of feminist cultural studies research addressing the integration of class and gender: McRobbie and Garber (1976), Amos and Parmar (1981), Brundson (1981), Hobson (1981, 1982), Parmar (1982), Carter (1984), Nava (1984a, 1984b), as well as the McRobbie works already cited.

23. Here I speak particularly of Chodorow (1978) and the response her work has sparked, as well as of the more broadly popular liberal feminist tradition (Friedan 1963, 1981); see Black (1989) for a good review and history of this tradition.

24. Of course, this assumption that television viewing is primarily solitary is currently being widely challenged. See Lull (1978), Morley (1986), and Lembo 1988).

25. Holland (1975b) offers an interesting exception to this tendency. Working in the tradition of reader-response theory, Holland applies psychoanalytic theory to the analysis of five actual readers interpreting a single text, producing a fascinating document of the personal reasons that might cause readers to interpret the same text differently. Although interesting, the study was limited in its scope by its intensive focus on a few individuals; however, this sharp focus gives the study its unusual explanatory depth.

26. Reader-response criticism is a growing area of literary criticism which attempts to turn critics away from a strictly text-centered emphasis to a focus on readers as well. Those most often identified with the school include Holland (1975a, 1975b), Eco (1979), Fish (1980), Tompkins (1980), and Culler (1981). Unfortunately, few reader-response theorists propose concrete plans for audience study, which is understandable since most are rooted in a literary rather than a social-scientific tradition. The closest the tradition seems to come to actual audience study is in the work of Holland, who adopts a psychoanalytic approach. As I discussed in note 25 above, in *Five Readers Reading,* Holland traces the decodings that five different readers of a single text make to each reader's "identity theme," culled from an investigation of the reader's psychoanalytic profile with the help of interviews and projective tests. This work may be criticized for being too subjective in its explanation of the critical process. While psychoanalytic profiles may certainly be important, one must also take social, political, and economic context into account when assessing the activity of interpretation.

Radway herself mentions that, of the reader-response theorists, Fish (1980) has had the most influence on her project, particularly because of his appreciation for the social context of individual interpretation. She criticizes his ultimately text-centered, rather than reader-centered, emphasis, while noting that the primary goal of the reader-response theorists has been to integrate the two foci.

27. Radway herself mentions the patriarchal content of romances, and the possible ways this content may work against the more feminist interpretation of the act of romance reading which she offers earlier in the book. See especially Radway's concluding chapter (1984b:209-222) for a good summary of her results.

28. See Douglas (1983) for a more explicit feminist condemnation of romances, which does not even attempt to take readers' views into account (see also Douglas 1977). Douglas's work has been widely criticized by feminists; Snitow (1983) offers a reply.

29. Radway herself notes that her sample was almost exclusively middle-class.

30. See especially chapter 6 of Radway's book (1984b:196-208) for her analysis of the significance of this ambivalence toward the realism of romantic novels which she found among her informants.

31. See also Roman (1987, 1988), Rose (1989), and Amesly (1989), again all cited in Long's (1989) excellent review. . . .

[32.] Most empirical studies of women's images in television have used content analysis to focus somewhat narrowly on the problem of where female characters fit in with the larger overall sample of women on television. These studies compare women's images to images of men on television, noting differences and similarities between the two groups. Tedesco (1974), for example, performs content analysis which yields clear differences between male and female television characters. She notes that television women are younger, more likely to be minor than major characters, more likely to be victims of violent crimes, more likely to be married, and much less likely to hold powerful positions when compared with men on television. More recently, Lichter et al. (1986) note that some of these facts have not changed: on prime-time television, female characters are still far outnumbered by males (only one out of five characters on prime-time shows is female), and they are even more outnumbered among relatively powerful characters such as doctors, judges, lawyers, professors, and corporate executives and college graduates generally. In all of these cases, women's representation on television underrepresents their power and presence in the real world. In addition, Lichter et al. (1986) find that women on television are more concerned with sex and marriage than are men.

Studies that discuss and evaluate the specific qualities of female characters on television have been interesting, but rare. Weibel (1977) discusses generally the qualities of specific female characters in the history of television. Mendelsohn (1971) also generalizes about the qualities of television women. Adorno (1954), Gans (1966), and Sklar (1980) offer interesting discussions that focus quite distinctly on working women in television. Lemon (1978), Sklar (1980), and Gray (1986) discuss the black family. Soap opera characters have been widely reviewed, as in the works of Modleski (1979, 1982), Cantor and Pingree (1983), Intintoli (1984), Allen (1985), and Rosen (1986). Some of these studies have taken a specifically feminist perspective, but often the meaning of a feminist critical perspective vis-à-vis television analysis has been unclear.

[33.] One study, "Prime Time Kids: An Analysis of Children and Families on Television," was based on fifteen situation comedies that had children as continuing characters during the 1984-85 prime-time season. The study was reported in the September 2, 1985, issue of *Broadcasting*. The figures reported here are derived from this study. . . .

[34.] When all family shows on early television are considered, the percentage of working-class families is 29 percent of all families depicted.

[35.] See Komarovsky (1967) and Rubin (1976) on this point. . . .

[36.] See Habermas (1974) for an explanation of both Freud and Marx on uncovering and enlightenment; Ricoeur (1970) is also useful for a discussion of the hermeneutic aspects of Freud.

[37.] See Gitlin (1989) and Lembo and Tucker (1990) for critical reviews illustrating how this argument has become widespread in the literature.

[38.] See Swidler (1986) for an interesting description of the way culture operates as a set of practical strategies.

[39.] "Identification," like "realism," is a concept difficult for scholars to define and use precisely. I use the term in this study to refer to cases in which women saw a part or parts of themselves in a particular television character and talked about that character in these terms. Paradoxically, while working-class women judged television to be *more* realistic than did middle-class women, they saw its character images to be *less* realistic *for themselves*—they actually identified *less* with specific characters than did middle-class women. Middle-class women, in contrast, while judging television to be less realistic overall, are much *more* able and likely to identify personally with specific characters and their problems, particularly those related to the family and situated in a family context.

[40.] Of course, women of both classes may be inaccurately representing how much they like and how much they actually watch television. Some women claim to dislike television immensely, yet go on to reveal detailed knowledge of it clearly indicating that they watch it frequently and carefully.

[41.] I realize that both of these positions are in essence ideal types; representatives of neither hold to their position in so extreme a form without qualification. I state them here, however, because there is a tendency in the mass media literature to construe these positions in such dichotomous terms. I respond here more to this tendency than to the positions themselves.

References

[Editors' Note: The following references have been extracted from the larger reference list of the source book in which this chapter originally appeared, and have been adapted slightly in style.]

Adamson, W. L. (1980). *Hegemony and revolution: A study of Antonio Gramsci's political and cultural theory*. Berkeley: University of California Press.

Adorno, T. (1954). Television and the patterns of mass culture. *Quarterly of Film, Radio and Television, 8*, 213-235.

Allen, R. C. (1985). *Speaking of soap operas*. Chapel Hill: University of North Carolina Press.

Althusser, L. (1971). *Lenin and philosophy* (B. Brewster, Trans.). London: Monthly Review Press.

Altman, R. (1986). Television/sound. In T. Modleski (Ed.), *Studies in entertainment: Critical approaches to mass culture*. Bloomington: Indiana University Press.

Amesly, C. (1989). How to watch Star Trek. *Cultural Studies, 3*(3), 323-339.

Amos, V., & Parmar, P. (1981). Resistances and responses: The experiences of black girls in Britain. In A. McRobbie & T. McCabe (Eds.), *Feminism for girls: An adventure story*. London: Routledge & Kegan Paul.

Anderson, J. A. (1987). Commentary on qualitative research and mediated communication in the family. In T. R. Lindlor (Ed.), *Natural audiences*. Norwood, NJ: Ablex.

Ang, I. (1985). *Watching Dallas: Soap opera and the melodramatic imagination* (D. Couling, Trans.). London: Methuen.

Auerbach, E. (1953). *Mimesis: The representation of reality in Western literature* (W. Trask, Trans.). Princeton, NJ: Princeton University Press.

Baehr, H. (Ed.). (1980). *Women and media*. Oxford: Pergamon.

Bagdikian, B. (1983). *The media monopoly*. Boston: Beacon.

Belenky, M. F., Clinchy, B. M., Goldberger, N. R., & Tarule, J. M. (1986). *Women's ways of knowing: The development of self, voice, and mind*. New York: Basic Books.

Bellah, R., Madsen, R., Swidler, A., Sullivan, W. M., & Tipton, S. M. (1985). *Habits of the heart*. Berkeley: University of California Press.

Black, N. (1989). *Social feminism*. Ithaca, NY: Cornell University Press.

Boggs, C. (1976). *Gramsci's Marxism*. London: Pluto.

Bourdieu, P. (1984). *Distinction: A social critique of the judgement of taste* (R. Nice, Trans.). Cambridge, MA: Harvard University Press.

Brake, M. (1980). *The sociology of youth culture and youth subcultures.* London: Routledge & Kegan Paul.

Brody, G. H., & Stoneman, Z. (1983). The influence of television viewing on family interactions. *Journal of Family Issues, 4*(2), 329-348.

Brundson, C. (1981). Crossroads: Notes on soap opera. *Screen, 32*(4), 32-37.

Bryce, J. W. (1987). Family time and television use. In T. R. Lindlor (Ed.), *Natural audiences.* Norwood, NJ: Ablex.

Cammett, J. M. (1967). *Antonio Gramsci and the origins of Italian communism.* Stanford, CA: Stanford University Press.

Cantor, M. G. (1987). Commentary on qualitative research and mediated communication in subcultures and institutions. In T. R. Lindlor (Ed.), *Natural audiences.* Norwood, NJ: Ablex.

Cantor, M., & Pingree, S. (1983). *The soap opera.* Beverly Hills, CA: Sage.

Carter, E. (1984). Alice in the consumer wonderland. In A. McRobbie & M. Nava (Eds.), *Gender and generations.* London: Macmillan.

Chodorow, N. (1978). *The reproduction of mothering: Psychoanalysis and the sociology of gender.* Berkeley: University of California Press.

Cirksena, K. (1987). Politics and difference: Radical feminist epistemological premises for communication studies. *Journal of Communication Inquiry, 11*(1), 19-28.

Cohen, S. (1973). *Folk devils and moral panics.* St. Albans: Paladin.

Cook, J., & Fonow, M. (1986). Knowledge and women's interests: Issues of epistemology and methodology in feminist sociological research. *Sociological Inquiry, 56*(1), 2-29.

Culler, J. (1981). *The pursuit of signs: Semiotics, literature, deconstruction.* Ithaca, NY: Cornell University Press.

Dinnerstein, D. (1976). *The mermaid and the minotaur: Sexual arrangements and human malaise.* New York: Harper Colophon.

Douglas, A. (1977). *The feminization of American culture.* New York: Knopf.

Douglas, A. (1983). Soft-porn culture. *The New Republic, 183*(9), 25-29.

Eco, U. (1979). *The role of the reader: Explorations in the semiotics of texts.* Bloomington: Indiana University Press.

Edmundson, M. (1986). Father still knows best. *Channels, 6*(32), 71-72.

Ellis, J. (1982). *Visible fictions: Cinema, television, video.* London: Methuen.

Fejes, F. (1984). Critical mass communications research and media effects: The problem of the disappearing audience. *Media, Culture and Society, 6,* 219-232.

Feuer, J. (1986). Narrative form in American network television. In C. MacCabe (Ed.), *High theory/low culture.* Manchester: Manchester University Press.

Fish, S. (1980). *Is there a text in this class? The authority of interpretive communities.* Cambridge, MA: Harvard University Press.

Fiske, J. (1986). Television and popular culture: Reflections on British and Australian practice. *Critical Studies in Mass Communication, 3,* 200-216.

Fiske, J. (1987b, March 17). *British and American cultural studies.* Unpublished lecture delivered to the Department of Communication, University of Michigan, Ann Arbor.

Flax, J. (1983). Political philosophy and the patriarchal unconscious: A psychoanalytic perspective on epistemology and metaphysics. In S. Harding & M. B. Hintikka (Eds.), *Discovering reality.* Boston: D. Reidel.

Friedan, B. (1963). *The feminine mystique.* New York: Norton.

Friedan, B. (1981). *The second stage.* New York: Summit.

Gans, H. (1966). Popular culture in America: Social problem in a mass society or social asset in a pluralist society. In H. S. Becker (Ed.), *Social problems: A modern approach*. New York: Wiley.

Gerbner, G. (1972). Violence in television drama: Trends and symbolic functions. In G. S. Comstock & E. A. Rubinstein (Eds.), *Television and social behavior: Vol. 1. Media content and control*. Washington, DC: Government Printing Office.

Gerbner, G., & Gross, L. (1976). Living with television: The violence profile. *Journal of Communication, 26*(2), 173-199.

Gerbner, G., Gross, L., Morgan, M., & Signorielli, N. (1980). The "mainstreaming" of America: Violence profile No. 11. *Journal of Communication, 30*(3), 10-29.

Gitlin, T. (1979). Prime time ideology: The hegemonic process in television entertainment. *Social Problems, 26*(3), 251-266.

Gitlin, T. (1980). *The whole world is watching: Mass media in the making and unmaking of the new left*. Berkeley: University of California Press.

Gitlin, T. (1983). *Inside prime time*. New York: Pantheon.

Gitlin, T. (Ed.). (1986). *Watching television*. New York: Pantheon.

Gitlin, T. (1989). Review of All consuming images by Stuart Ewen. *Tikkun, 4*(4), 110-112.

Goodman, I. F. (1983). Television's role in family interaction: A family systems perspective. *Journal of Family Issues, 4*(2), 405-424.

Gramsci, A. (1971). *Selections from the prison notebooks of Antonio Gramsci* (G. Nowell-Smith & Q. Hoare, Eds. & Trans.). London: Lawrence and Wishart.

Gray, H. (1986). Television and the new black man: Black male images in prime-time situation comedy. *Media, Culture and Society, 8*, 223-242.

Gregg, N. (1978). Reflections on the feminist critique. *Journal of Communication Inquiry, 11*(1), 8-18.

Habermas, J. (1962). *Strukturwandel der Offentlichkeit*. Berlin: Luchterhand Verlag.

Habermas, J. (1974). *Theory and practice* (J. Viertel, Trans.). London: Heinemann.

Hall, S. (1977a). Culture, the media and the "ideological effect." In J. Curran, M. Gurevitch, & J. Woollacott (Eds.), *Mass communication and society*. Beverly Hills, CA: Sage.

Hall, S. (1980b). Cultural studies: Two paradigms. *Media, Culture, and Society, 2*, 57-72.

Hall, S. (1983). The problem of ideology: Marxism without guarantees. In B. Matthews (Ed.), *Marx: A hundred years on*. London: Lawrence and Wishart.

Hall, S., Critcher, C., Jefferson, T., Clarke, J., & Roberts, B. (Eds.). (1978). *Policing the crisis: The state and law and order*. London: Macmillan.

Harding, S. (Ed.). (1987). *Feminism and methodology*. Bloomington: Indiana University Press.

Hirsch, P. (1981). On not learning from one's own mistakes: A reanalysis of Gerbner et al.'s findings on cultivation analysis, Part II. *Communication Research, 8*(1), 3-37.

Hobson, D. (1981). Now that I'm married . . . . In A. McRobbie & T. McCabe (Eds.), *Feminism for girls: An adventure story*. London: Routledge & Kegan Paul.

Hobson, D. (1982). *Crossroads: The drama of a soap opera*. London: Methuen.

Holland, N. (1975a). *The dynamics of literary response*. New York: Norton.

Holland, N. (1975b). *Five readers reading*. New Haven, CT: Yale University Press.

Intintoli, M. J. (1984). *Taking soaps seriously*. New York: Praeger.

Katz, E., & Liebes, T. (1984). Once upon a time in Dallas. *Intermedia, 12*(3), 28-32.

Komarovsky, M. (1967). *Blue-collar marriage*. New York: Random House.

Konrad, G., & Szelenyi, I. (1979). *The intellectuals on the road to class power* (A. Arato & R. E. Allen, Trans.). New York: Harcourt Brace Jovanovich.

Kuhn, A. (1982). *Women's pictures*. London: Routledge & Kegan Paul.

Lembo, R. (1988). *Viewing relations in television culture: Toward an ethnography of the audience*. Paper presented at the American Sociology Association, Atlanta, GA.

Lembo, R., & Tucker, K. H., Jr. (1990). Culture, television, and opposition: Rethinking cultural studies. *Critical Studies in Mass Communication, 7*(2), 97-116.

Lemish, D. (1985). Soap opera viewing in college: A naturalistic inquiry. *Journal of Broadcasting and Electronic Media, 29*(3), 275-293.

Lemish, D. (1987). Viewers in diapers: The early development of television viewing. In T. Lindlog (Ed.), *Natural audiences* (pp. 33-57). Norwood, NJ: Ablex.

Lemon, J. (1978). Dominant or dominated? Women on prime-time television. In G. Tuchman (Ed.), *Hearth and home*. New York: Oxford University Press.

Lichter, R., Lichter, L., & Rothman, S. (1986). The politics of the American dream—From Lucy to Lacy: TV's dream girls. *Public Opinion, 9*(3), 16-19.

Liebes, T. (1984). Ethnocentricism: Israelis of Moroccan ethnicity negotiate the meaning of Dallas. *Studies in Visual Communication, 10*(3), 46-72.

Lindlof, T. R. (Ed.). (1987a). *Natural audiences: Qualitative research of media uses and effects*. Norwood, NJ: Ablex.

Lindlof, T. R. (Ed.). (1987b). Ideology and pragmatics of media access time in prison. In T. R. Lindlof (Ed.), *Natural audiences: Qualitative research of media uses and effects*. Norwood, NJ: Ablex.

Lindlof, T. R., & Grodin, D. (1989, May 29). *When media use can't be observed: Problematic aspects of the researcher-participant relationship*. Paper presented at annual meeting of the International Communication Association, San Francisco.

Lindlof, T. R., & Meyer, T. P. (1987). Mediated communication as ways of seeing, acting, and constructing culture: The tools and foundations of qualitative research. In T. R. Lindlof (Ed.), *Natural audiences: Qualitative research of media uses and effects*. Norwood, NJ: Ablex.

Long, E. (1986). Women, reading, and cultural authority: Some implications of the audience perspective in cultural studies. *American Quarterly, 38,* 591-612.

Long, E. (1987). Reading groups and the crisis of cultural authority. *Cultural Studies, 1*(2), 306-327.

Long, E. (1989). Feminism and cultural studies: Britain and America. *Critical Studies in Mass Communication, 6*(4), 427-435.

Lull, J. (1978). Choosing television programs by family vote. *Communications Quarterly, 26*(4), 53-57.

Lull, J. (1980). Family communication patterns and the social uses of television. *Communication Research, 7*(3), 319-334.

Lull, J. (1987a). Critical response: Audience texts and contexts. *Critical Studies in Mass Communication, 4,* 318-322.

Lull, J. (1987b). Thrashing in the pit: An ethnography of San Francisco punk subculture. In T. R. Lindlof (Ed.), *Natural audiences: Qualitative research of media uses and effects*. Norwood, NJ: Ablex.

MacCabe, C. (Ed.). (1986). *High theory/low culture*. Manchester: Manchester University Press.

Mannheim, K. (1936). *Ideology and utopia*. New York: Harcourt Brace Jovanovich.

Marc, D. (1989). *Comic visions: Television comedy and American culture.* Winchester, MA: Unwin Hyman.

McRobbie, A. (1978a). *Jackie: An ideology of adolescent femininity.* Birmingham: Centre for Contemporary Cultural Studies.

McRobbie, A. (1978b). Working-class girls and the culture of femininity. In Women's Studies Group (Ed.), *Women take issue* (pp. 96-108). London: Hutchison.

McRobbie, A. (1980). Settling accounts with subcultures: A feminist critique. *Screen Education, 34,* 37-49.

McRobbie, A. (1981). Just like a Jackie story. In A. McRobbie & T. McCabe (Eds.), *Feminism for girls: An adventure story.* London: Routledge & Kegan Paul.

McRobbie, A. (1982). The politics of feminist research: Between talk, text and action. *Feminist Review, 12,* 46-57.

McRobbie, A. (1984). Dance and social fantasy. In A. McRobbie & M. Nava (Eds.), *Gender and generation.* New York: Macmillan.

McRobbie, A., & Garber, J. (1976). Girls and subcultures. In S. Hall & T. Jefferson (Eds.), *Resistance through rituals.* London: Hutchinson.

McRobbie, A., & McCabe, T. (Eds.). (1981). *Feminism for girls: An adventure story.* London: Routledge & Kegan Paul.

McRobbie, A., & Nava, M. (Eds.). (1984). *Gender and generation.* New York: Macmillan.

Mendelsohn, H. (1971). *The neglected majority: Mass communications and the working person.* New York: Alfred P. Sloan Foundation.

Messaris, P. (1987). Mothers' comments to their children about the relationship between television and reality. In T. R. Lindlof (Ed.), *Natural audiences: Qualitative research of media uses and effects.* Norwood, NJ: Ablex.

Metz, C. (1982). *The imaginary signifier: Psychoanalysis and the cinema.* Bloomington: Indiana University Press.

Meyrowitz, J. (1985). *No sense of place: The impact of electronic media on social behavior.* Oxford: Oxford University Press.

Modleski, T. (1979). The search for tomorrow in today's soap operas. *Film Quarterly, 33*(1), 12-21.

Modleski, T. (1982). *Loving with a vengence: Mass-produced fantasies for women.* New York: Methuen.

Morley, D. (1980). *The Nationwide audience: Structure and decoding* (Monograph No. 11). London: BFI.

Morley, D. (1981). The Nationwide audience: A critical postscript. *Screen Education, 39,* 3-14.

Morley, D. (1986). *Family television.* London: Comedia.

Mulvey, L. (1975). Visual pleasure and narrative cinema. *Screen, 16*(3), 6-18.

Nava, M. (1984a). Drawing the line. In A. McRobbie & M. Nava (Eds.), *Gender and generation.* New York: Macmillan.

Nava, M. (1984b). Youth service provision, social order and the question of girls. In A. McRobbie & M. Nava (Eds.), *Gender and generation.* New York: Macmillan.

Parmar, P. (1982). Gender, race, and class: Asian women in resistance. In Centre for Contemporary Cultural Studies (Ed.), *The empire strikes back.* London: Hutchinson.

Postman, N. (1985). *Amusing ourselves to death.* New York: Penguin.

Press, A., & Lembo, R. (1989, May). *The hegemony of the text: A critique of text-centered conceptions of television viewing.* Paper presented at the meetings of the International Communication Association, San Francisco.

Radway, J. (1984b). Interpretive communities and variable literacies: The functions of romance reading. *Daedalus, 113*(3), 49-73.

Ricoeur, P. (1970). *Freud and philosophy: An essay on interpretation* (D. Savage, Trans.). New Haven, CT: Yale University Press.

Roman, L. (1987). *Punk femininity: The formation of young women's gender identities and class relations in the extramural curriculum within a contemporary subculture.* Unpublished doctoral dissertation, University of Wisconsin—Madison.

Roman, L. (1988). Intimacy, labor, and class: Ideologies of feminine sexuality in the punk slam dance. In L. Roman, L. Christian-Smith, & E. Ellsworth (Eds.), *Becoming feminine: The politics of popular culture.* London: Falmer.

Rose, T. (1989, October). *"Hit the road Sam": Black women rappers and sexual difference.* Paper delivered at the meetings of the American Studies Association, Toronto.

Rosen, R. (1986). Search for yesterday. In T. Gitlin (Ed.), *Watching television.* New York: Pantheon.

Rubin, L. (1976). *Worlds of pain: Life in the working-class family.* New York: Basic Books.

Schiller, H. I. (1985). Breaking the West's media monopoly. *The Nation, 241*(8), 248-251.

Schudson, M. (1978). *Discovering the news.* New York: Basic Books.

Schwartz, D. (1986). Camera clubs and fine art photography. *Urban Life, 15*(2), 165-195.

Schwartz, D., & Griffin, M. (1987). Amateur photography: The organizational maintenance of an aesthetic code. In T. R. Lindlof (Ed.), *Natural audiences: Qualitative research of media uses and effects.* Norwood, NJ: Ablex.

Sklar, R. (1980). *Prime-time America: Life on and behind the television screen.* Oxford: Oxford University Press.

Snitow, A. B. (1983). Mass market romance: Pornography for women is different. In A. B. Snitow, C. Stansell, & S. Thompson (Eds.), *Powers of desire: The politics of sexuality.* New York: Monthly Review Press.

Swidler, A. (1986). Culture in action: Symbols and strategies. *American Sociological Review, 51,* 273-286.

Taylor, E. (1989). *Prime time families: Television culture in postwar America.* Berkeley: University of California Press.

Tedesco, N. S. (1974). Patterns in prime time. *Journal of Communication, 24*(2), 119-124.

Tompkins, J. P. (Ed.). (1980). *Reader-response criticism.* Baltimore: Johns Hopkins University Press.

Traudt, P. J., Anderson, J. A., & Meyer, T. P. (1987). Phenomenology, empiricism, and media experience. *Critical Studies in Mass Communication, 4*(3), 302-310.

Traudt, P. J., & Lont, C. M. (1987). Media-logic-in-use: The family as locus of study. In T. R. Lindlof (Ed.), *Natural audiences: Qualitative research of media uses and effects.* Norwood, NJ: Ablex.

Tuchman, G., Daniels, A. K., & Benet, J. (Eds.). (1978). *Hearth and home: Images of women in the mass media.* New York: Oxford University Press.

van Zoonen, L. (1988). Rethinking women and the news. *European Journal of Communication, 3,* 35-53.

Watt, I. (1957). *The rise of the novel.* Berkeley: University of California Press.

Webster, J. H., & Wakshlag, J. J. (1982). The impact of group viewing on patterns of television program choice. *Journal of Broadcasting, 26*(1), 445-455.

Weibel, K. (1977). *Mirror, mirror.* New York: Anchor.

Williams, R. (1960). *Culture and society.* New York: Columbia University Press.

Williams, R. (1973). *The country and the city.* New York: Oxford University Press.

Williams, R. (1974). *Television: Technology and cultural form.* London: Fontana.

Williams, R. (1976). *Keywords.* London: Fontana.

Williams, R. (1977b). A lecture on realism. *Screen, 18*(1), 61-74.

Williams, R. (1977c). *Marxism and literature.* Oxford: Oxford University Press.

Willis, P. (1977). *Learning to labor: How working-class kids get working-class jobs.* New York: Columbia University Press.

Willis, P. (1978). *Profane culture.* London: Routledge & Kegan Paul.

Of all the institutions of daily life, the media specialize in orchestrating everyday consciousness—by virtue of their pervasiveness, their accessibility, their centralized symbolic capacity. They name the world's parts, they certify reality as reality—and when their certifications are doubted and opposed, as they surely are, it is those same certifications that limit the terms of effective opposition. To put it simply: The mass media have become core systems for the distribution of ideology.

4

The Whole World Is Watching

TODD GITLIN

Since the advent of radio broadcasting half a century ago, social movements have organized, campaigned, and formed their social identities on a floodlit social terrain. The economic concentration of the media and their speed and efficiency in spreading news and telling stories have combined to produce a new situation for movements seeking to change the order of society. Yet movements, media, and sociology alike have been slow to explore the meanings of modern cultural surroundings.

People directly know only tiny regions of social life; their beliefs and loyalties lack deep tradition. The modern situation is precisely the common vulnerability to rumor, news, trend, and fashion: lacking the assurances of tradition, or of shared political power, people are pressed to rely on mass media for bearings in an obscure and shifting world. And the process is reciprocal; pervasive mass media help pulverize political community, thereby deepening popular dependence on the media themselves. The media bring a manufactured public world into private space. From within their private crevices, people find themselves relying on the media for concepts, for images of their heroes, for guiding information, for emotional charges, for a recognition of public values, for symbols in general, even for language. Of all the institutions of daily life, the media specialize in orchestrating everyday consciousness—by virtue of their pervasiveness, their accessibility, their centralized symbolic capacity. They name the world's parts, they certify reality as reality—and when their certifications are doubted and opposed, as they surely are, it is those same certifications that limit the terms of effective opposition. To put it simply: The mass media have become core systems for the distribution of ideology.

That is to say, every day, directly or indirectly, by statement and omission, in pictures and words, in entertainment and news and advertisement, the mass media produce fields of definition and association, symbol and rhetoric, through which ideology becomes manifest and concrete. One important task for ideology is to define—also define away—its opposition. This has always been true, of course. But the omnipresence and centralization of the mass media, and their integration into the dominant economic sector and the web of the State, create new conditions for opposition. The New Left of the 1960s, facing nightly television news, wire service reports, and a journalistic ideology of "objectivity," inhabited a cultural world vastly different than that of the Populist small farmers' movement of the 1890s, with its 1,500 autonomous weekly newspapers, or that of the worker-based Socialist party of the early 1900s, with its own newspapers circulating in the millions. By the 1960s, American society was dominated by a *consolidated* corporate economy, no longer by a *nascent* one. The dream of Manifest Destiny had become realized in a missile-brandishing national security state. And astonishingly, America was now the first society in the history of the world with more college students than farmers. The social base of radical opposition, accordingly, had shifted from small farmers and immigrant workers to blacks, students, youth, and women. What was transformed was not only the dominant *structures* of capitalist society but its *textures*. The whole quality of political movements, their procedures and tones, their cultural commitments, had changed. There was now a mass market culture industry, and opposition movements had to reckon with it—had to operate on its edges, in its interstices, and against it. The New Left, like its Populist and Socialist party predecessors, had its own scatter of "underground" newspapers, with hundreds of thousands of readers, but every night some 20 million Americans watched Walter Cronkite's news, an almost equal number watched Chet Huntley's and David Brinkley's, and over 60 million bought daily newspapers that purchased most of their news from one of two international wire services. In a floodlit society, it becomes extremely difficult, perhaps unimaginable, for an opposition movement to define itself and its worldview, to build up an infrastructure of self-generated cultural institutions, outside the dominant culture.[1] Truly, the process of making meanings in the world of centralized commercial culture has become comparable to the process of making value in the world through labor. Just as people *as workers* have no voice in what they make, how they make it, or how the product is distributed and used, so do people *as producers of meaning* have no voice in what the media make of what they say or do or in the context within which the media frame their activity. The resulting meanings, now mediated, acquire an eery substance in the real world, standing outside their ostensible makers and confronting them as an alien force. The social meanings of intentional action have been deformed beyond recognition.

In the late twentieth century, political movements feel called upon to rely on large-scale communications in order to *matter,* to say who they are and what they intend to publics they want to sway; but in the process they become "newsworthy" only by submitting to the implicit rules of newsmaking, by conforming to journalistic notions (themselves embedded in history) of what a "story" is, what an "event" is, what a "protest" is. The processed image then tends to *become* "the movement" for wider publics and institutions who have few alternative sources of information, or none at all, about it; that image has its impact on public policy, and when the movement is being opposed, what is being opposed is in large part a set of mass-mediated images. Mass media define the public significance of movement events or, by blanking them out, actively deprive them of larger significance. Media images also become implicated in a movement's self-image; media certify leaders and officially noteworthy "personalities"; indeed, they are able to convert leadership into *celebrity,* something quite different. The forms of coverage accrete into systematic framing, and this framing, much amplified, helps determine the movement's fate.

For what defines a movement as "good copy" is often flamboyance, often the presence of a media-certified celebrity-leader, and usually a certain fit with whatever frame the newsmakers have construed to be "the story" at a given time; but these qualities of the image are not what movements intend to be their projects, their identities, their goals. Yet while they constrict and deform movements, the media do amplify the issues that fuel these same movements; they expose scandal in the State and in the corporations, while reserving to duly constituted authority the legitimate right to remedy evils. The liberal media quietly invoke the need for reform—while disparaging movements radically opposed to the system that needs reforming.

The routines of journalism, set within the economic and political interests of news organizations, normally and regularly combine to select certain versions of reality over others. Day by day, *normal* organizational procedures define "the story," identify the protagonists and the issues, and suggest appropriate attitudes toward them. Only episodically, in moments of political crisis and large-scale shifts in the overarching hegemonic ideology, do political and economic managers and owners intervene directly to regear or reinforce the prevailing journalistic routines. But most of the time the taken-for-granted code of "objectivity" and "balance" presses reporters to seek out scruffy-looking, chanting, "Viet Cong" flag-waving demonstrators and to counterpose them to reasonable-sounding, fact-brandishing authorities. Calm and cautionary tones of voice affirm that all "disturbance" is or should be under control by rational authority; code words like *disturbance* commend the established order. Hotheads carry on, the message connotes, while wiser heads, officials and reporters both, with superb self-control, watch the unenlightened ones make trouble.

Yet these conventions originate, persist, and shift in historical time. The world of news production is not self-enclosed; for commercial as well as professional reasons, it cannot afford to ignore big ideological changes. Yesterday's ignored or ridiculed kook becomes today's respected "consumer activist," while at the same time the mediated image of the wild 1960s yields to the image of laid-back, apathetic, self-satisfied 1970s. Yesterday's revolutionary John Froines of the Chicago Seven, who went to Washington in 1971 to shut down the government, goes to work for it in 1977 at a high salary; in 1977 Mark Rudd surfaces from the Weather Underground, and the sturdy metafather Walter Cronkite chuckles approvingly as he reports that Mark's father thinks the age of 30 is "too old to be a revolutionary"—these are widely publicized signs of presumable calmer, saner times. Meanwhile, movements for utility rate reform, for unionization in the South, for full employment, for disarmament, and against nuclear power—movements that are not led by "recognized leaders" (those whom the media selectively acknowledged as celebrities in the first place) and that fall outside the prevailing frames ("the New Left is dead," "America is moving to the right")—are routinely neglected or denigrated—until the prevailing frame changes (as it did after the accident at Three Mile Island). An activist against nuclear weapons, released from jail in May 1978 after a series of demonstrations at the Rocky Flats, Colorado, factory that manufactures plutonium triggers for all American H-bombs, telephoned an editor he knew in the *New York Times*'s Washington bureau to ask whether the *Times* had been covering these demonstrations and arrests. No, the editor said, adding: "America is tired of protest. America is tired of Daniel Ellsberg." Blackouts do take place; the editorial or executive censor rationalized his expurgation, condescendingly and disingenuously, as the good shepherd's fair-minded act of professional news judgment, as his service to the benighted, homogenized, presumable sovereign audience. The closer an issue is to the core interests of national political elites, the more likely is a blackout of news that effectively challenges that interest. That there is safety in the country's nuclear weapons program is, to date, a core principle; and so news of its menace is extremely difficult to get reported—far more difficult, for example, than news about the dangers of nuclear power after Three Mile Island. But if the issue is contested at an elite level, or if an elite position has not yet crystallized, journalism's more regular approach is to *process* social opposition, to control its image and to diffuse it at the same time, to absorb what can be absorbed into the dominant structure of definitions and images and to push the rest to the margins of social life.

The processed message becomes complex. To take a single example of a news item: On the *CBS Evening News* of May 8, 1976, Dan Rather reported that the FBI's burglaries and wiretaps began in the 1930s and continued through World War Il and the cold war; and he concluded the piece by saying that these activities reached a peak "during the civil disturbances of the sixties." In this piece we can see some of the contradictory workings of broadcast journalism—and the limits within which contradictory forces play themselves out. First of all, Rather was conveying the information that a once sacrosanct sector of the State had been violating the law for decades. Second, and more subtly—with a clipped, no-nonsense manner and a tough-but-gentle, trustworthy, Watergate-certified voice of technocracy—he was deploring this law-breaking, lending support to those institutions within the State that brought it to the surface and now proposed to stop it, and affirming that the media are integral to this self-correcting system as a whole. Third, he was defining a onetime political opposition *outside* the State as "civil disturbance." The black and student opposition movements of the 1960s, which would look different if they were called, say, "movements for peace and justice," were reduced to nasty little things. Through his language, Rather was inviting the audience to identify with forces of reason within the State: with the very source of the story, most likely. In a single news item, with (I imagine) no deliberate forethought, Rather was (a) identifying an abuse of government, (b) legitimating reform within the existing institutions, and (c) rendering illegitimate popular or radical opposition outside the State. The news that man has bitten dog carries an unspoken morality: It proposes to coax men to stop biting those particular dogs, so that the world can be restored to its essential soundness. In such quiet fashion, not deliberately, and without calling attention to this spotlighting process, the media divide movements into legitimate main acts and illegitimate sideshows, so that these distinctions appear "natural," matters of "common sense."[2]

What makes the world beyond direct experience look natural is a media *frame*.[3] Certainly we cannot take for granted that the world depicted is simply the world that exists. Many things exist. At each moment the world is rife with events. Even within a given event there is an infinity of noticeable details. Frames are principles of selection, emphasis, and presentation composed of little tacit theories about what exists, what happens, and what matters. In everyday life, as Erving Goffman (1974, pp. 10-11 and passim) has amply demonstrated, we frame reality so as to negotiate it, manage it, comprehend it, and choose appropriate repertories of cognition and action. *Media* frames, largely unspoken and unacknowledged, organize the world both for journalists who report it and, in some important degree, for us who rely on their reports. *Media frames are persistent patterns of cognition, interpretation, and presentation, of selection, emphasis, and exclusion, by which symbol-handlers routinely organize discourse, whether verbal or visual.* Frames enable journalists to process large amounts of information quickly and routinely: to recognize it as information, to assign it to cognitive categories, and to package it for efficient relay to their audiences. Thus, for organizational reasons alone, frames are unavoidable, and journalism is organized to regulate their production. Any analytic approach to journalism—indeed, to the production of any mass-mediated content—must ask: What is the frame here? Why this frame and not another? What patterns are shared by the frames clamped over this event and the frames clamped over that one, by frames in different media in different places at different moments? And how does the news-reporting institution regulate these regularities?

And then: What difference do the frames make for the larger world?

The issue of the influence of mass media on larger political currents does not, of course, emerge only with the rise of broadcasting. In the Paris of a century and a half ago, when the commercial press was young, a journalistic novice and littérateur-around-town named Honoré de Balzac was already fascinated by the force of commercialized images. Central to his vivid semiautobiographical novel, *Lost Illusions,* was the giddy, corroded career of the journalist. Balzac saw that the press degraded writers into purveyors of commodities. Writing in 1839 about the wild and miserable spectacle of "A Provincial Great Man in Paris," Balzac (1898) in one snatch of dinner-party dialogue picked up the dispute aborning over political consequences of a mass press; he was alert to the fears of reactionaries and the hopes of Enlightenment liberals alike:

> "The power and influence of the press are only at their dawn," said Finot. "Journalism is in its infancy, it will grow and grow. Ten years hence everything will be subjected to publicity. Thought will enlighten everything, it—."
>
> "Will blight everything," interposed Blondet.
>
> "That's a *bon mot*," said Claude Vignon.
>
> "It will make kings," said Lousteau.
>
> "It will unmake monarchies," said the diplomat.
>
> "If the press did not exist," said Blondet, "we could get along without it; but it's here, so we live on it."
>
> "You will die of it," said the diplomat. "Don't you see that the superiority of the masses, assuming that you enlighten them, would make individual greatness the more difficult of attainment; that, if you sow reasoning power in the heart of the lower classes, you will reap revolution, and that you will be the first victims?" (p. 112)

Balzac's ear for hopes and fears and new social tensions was acute; he was present at the making of a new institution in a new social era. Since then, of course, radio and now television have become standard home furnishings. And in considerable measure broadcast content has become part of the popular ideological furniture as well. But while researchers debate the exact "effects" of mass media on the popularity of presidential candidates and presidents, or the "effects" on specific patterns of voting or the salience of issues, evidence quietly accumulates that the texture of political life has changed since broadcasting became a central feature of American life. Media certainly help set the agendas for political discourse; although they are far from autonomous, they do not passively reflect the agendas of the State, the parties, the corporations, or "public opinion."[4] The centralization and commercialization of the mass media of communication make them instruments of cultural dominance on a scale unimagined even by Balzac. In some ways the very ubiquity of the mass media removes media *as a whole system* from the scope of positivist social analysis; for how may we "measure" the "impact" of a social force that is omnipresent within social life and that has a great deal to do with constituting it? I work

from the assumption that the mass media are, to say the least, a significant social force in the forming and delimiting of public assumptions,
attitudes, and moods—of ideology, in short. They sometimes generate,
sometimes amplify, a field of legitimate discourse that shapes the
public's "definitions of its situations," and they work through selections
and omissions, through emphases and tones, through all their forms of
treatment.

Such ideological force is central to the continuation of the established
order. I take it for now that the central command structures of this order
are an oligopalized, privately controlled corporate economy and its
intimate ally, the bureaucratic national security state, together embedded within a capitalist world complex of nation-states. But the economic
and political powers of twentieth-century capitalist society, while formidable, do not by themselves account for the society's persistence, do
not secure the dominant institutions against the radical consequences
of the system's deep and enduring conflicts. In the language of present-
day social theory, why does the population accord legitimacy to the
prevailing institutions? The goods are delivered, true; but why do
citizens agree to identify themselves and to behave as consumers,
devoting themselves to labor in a deteriorating environment so as to
acquire private possessions and services as emblems of satisfaction?
The answers are by no means self-evident. But however we approach
these questions, the answers will have to be found in the realm of
ideology, of culture in the broadest sense. Society is not a machine or
a thing; it is a coexistence of human beings who do what they do
(including maintaining or changing a social structure) as sentient,
reasoning, moral, and active beings who experience the world, who are
not simply "caused" by it. The patterned experiencing of the world takes
place in the realm of what we call ideology. And any social theory of
ideology asks two interlocking questions: How and where are ideas
generated in society? And why are certain ideas accepted or rejected in
varying degrees at different times?

In the version of Marxist theory inaugurated by Antonio Gramsci
(1971), *hegemony* is the name given to a ruling class's domination
through ideology, through the shaping of popular consent. More recently, Raymond Williams has transcended the classical Marxist base-
superstructure dichotomy (in which the "material base" of "forces and
relations of production" "gives rise" to the ideological "superstructure"). Williams has proposed a notion of hegemony as "not only the
articulate upper level of 'ideology,' " but "a whole body of practices

and expectations" that "constitutes a sense of reality for most people in the society" (Williams, 1973; see also Williams, 1977, especially pp. 108-114). The main economic structures, or "relations of production," set limits on the ideologies and commonsense understandings that circulate as ways of making sense of the world—without mechanically "determining" them. The fact that the networks are capitalist corporations, for example, does not automatically decree the precise frame of a report on socialism, but it does preclude continuing, emphatic reports that would embrace socialism as the most reasonable framework for the solution of social problems. One need not accept all of Gramsci's analytic baggage to see the penetrating importance of the notion of hegemony—uniting persuasion from above with consent from below—for comprehending the endurance of advanced capitalist society. In particular, one need not accept a strictly Marxist premise that the "material base" of "forces of production" in *any* sense (even "ultimately") precedes cultures.[5] But I retain Gramsci's core conception: Those who rule the dominant institutions secure their power in large measure directly and *indirectly,* by impressing their definitions of the situation upon those they rule and, if not usurping the whole of ideological space, still significantly limiting what is thought throughout the society. The notion of hegemony that I am working with is an active one: hegemony operating through a complex web of social activities and institutional procedures. Hegemony is done by the dominant and collaborated in by the dominated.

Hegemonic ideology enters into everything people do and think is "natural"—making a living, loving, playing, believing, knowing, even rebelling. In every sphere of social activity, it meshes with the "common sense" through which people make the world seem intelligible; it tries to *become* that common sense. Yet, at the same time, people only partially and unevenly accept the hegemonic terms; they stretch, dispute, and sometimes struggle to transform the hegemonic ideology. Indeed, its contents shift to a certain degree, as the desires and strategies of the top institutions shift, and as different coalitions form among the dominant social groups; in turn, these desires and strategies are modified, moderated by popular currents. In corporate capitalist society (and in state socialism as well), the schools and the mass media specialize in formulating and conveying national ideology. At the same time, indirectly, the media—at least in liberal capitalist society—take account of certain popular currents and pressures, symbolically incorporating them, repackaging and distributing them throughout the society.

That is to say, groups out of power—radical students, farmworkers, feminists, environmentalists, or homeowners groaning under the property tax—can contest the prevailing structures of power and definitions of reality. One strategy that insurgent social movements adopt is to make "news events."

The media create and relay images of order. Yet the social reality is enormously complex, fluid, and self-contradictory, even in its own terms. Movements constantly boil up out of the everyday suffering and grievance of dominated groups. From their sense of injury and their desire for justice, movements assert their interests, mobilize their resources, make their demands for reform, and try to find space to live their alternative "lifestyles." These *alternative* visions are not yet *oppositional*—not until they challenge the main structures and ideas of the existing order: the preeminence of the corporate economy, the militarized State, and authoritarian social relations as a whole. In liberal capitalist society, movements embody and exploit the fact that the dominant ideology enfolds contradictory values: liberty versus equality, democracy versus hierarchy, public rights versus property rights, rational claims to truth versus the arrogations and mystifications of power.[6] Then how does enduring ideology find its way into the news, absorbing and ironing out contradictions with relative consistency? How, in particular, are rather standardized frames clamped onto the reporting of insurgent movements? For the most part, through journalists' routines.

These routines are structured in the ways journalists are socialized from childhood and then trained, recruited, assigned, edited, rewarded, and promoted on the job; they decisively shape ways in which news is defined, events are considered newsworthy, and "objectivity" is secured. News is managed routinely, automatically, as reporters import definitions of newsworthiness from editors and institutional beats, as they accept the analytical frameworks of officials even while taking up adversary positions. When reporters make decisions about what to cover and how, rarely do they deliberate about ideological assumptions or political consequences.[7] Simply by doing their jobs, journalists tend to serve the political and economic elite definitions of reality.

But there are disruptive moments, critical times when the routines no longer serve a coherent hegemonic interest. The routines produce news that no longer harmonizes with the hegemonic ideology or with important elite interests as the elites construe them; or the elites are themselves so divided as to quarrel over the content of the news. (In the extreme case, as in Chile in 1973, the hegemonic ideology is pushed to the extremity of its self-contradiction, and snaps; the dominant frame then shifts dramatically, in that case toward the Right.) At these critical moments, political and economic elites (including owners and executives of media corporations) are more likely to intervene directly in journalistic routine, attempting to keep journalism within harness. To put it another way, the cultural apparatus normally maintains its own momentum, its own standards and procedures, which grant it a certain independence from top political and economic elites. In a liberal capitalistic society, this bounded but real independence helps legitimate the institutional order as a whole and the news in particular. But the elites prefer not to let such independence stretch "too far." It serves the interests of the elites as long as it is "relative," as long as it does not violate core hegemonic values or contribute too heavily to radical critique or social unrest. (It is the elites who determine, or establish routines to determine, what goes "too far.") Yet when elites are themselves at odds in important ways, and when core values are deeply disputed—as happened in the 1960s—journalism itself becomes contested. Opposition groups pressing for social and political change can exploit self-contradictions in hegemonic ideology, including its journalistic codes. Societywide conflict is then carried into the cultural institutions, though in muted and sanitized forms. And then ideological domestication plays an important part—along with the less visible activities of the police[8]—in taming and isolating ideological threats to the system.

News is one component of popular culture; the study of news should ultimately be enfolded within a more ample study of all the forms of cultural production and their ideology. Television entertainment is also an ideological field, and must have played a part in formulating and crystallizing the cultural tendencies of the 1960s; surely it deserves extensive treatment of its own.[9] So do other cultural forms, including popular songs, popular fiction (genre novels as well as magazine stories), jokes, and popular films (which are not necessarily the acclaimed films that critics prefer to see and to analyze); so do the careers of pop stars like Bob Dylan and Joan Baez, the San Francisco bands, and hip heroes who stood somewhere on the thin and fluid boundary between the New Left and the counterculture. Let popular culture have its analytic due: We live in it.

Notes

1. This point is made by Adamson (1978).

2. For further analysis of the meaning of this and other television news items, see Gitlin (1977a).

3. On media frames, see Tuchman (1978) and Hall (1973).

4. Least of all, public opinion: Evidence is accumulating that the priorities conveyed by the media in their treatment of political issues lead public opinion rather than following it. See McCombs and Shaw (1972); McLeod, Becker, and Byrnes (1974); Baker, McCombs, and McLeod (1975, especially pp. 38-53); and Blumler and McQuail (1968).

5. For a brilliant demonstration of ways in which culture helps *constitute* a given society's "material base," and in particular the way in which the bourgeois concept of utility conditions capitalism's claims to efficiency, see Sahlins (1976, Part 2).

6. I adapt this argument from my "Prime Time Ideology" (1979).

7. As Gaye Tuchman (1978) writes, "News both draws upon and reproduces institutional structures" (p. 210). For particulars, see Sigal (1973), Roshco (1975), and most fully, Gans (1979).

8. Very little has been written on direct relations between police agencies and mass media. Gans (1979) makes the valuable point that "perhaps the most able sources are organizations that carry out the equivalent of investigative reporting, offer the results of their work as 'exclusives,' and can afford to do so anonymously, foregoing the rewards of publicity" (p. 121). For a survey of the FBI's COINTELPRO media operations, especially in New York, Chicago, Los Angeles, and Milwaukee, at least between 1956 and 1971, and a few extant details of direct cooperation between the FBI and reporters, see Berlet (1978). I know of no evidence of cooperation between the FBI and either CBS News or the *New York Times,* but this entire field is terra incognita.

9. Considering the great amount of time Americans and others spend watching TV entertainment, there is a great imbalance in sociological attention: many more studies have been done on the production and meanings of news, which is more transparently available for political understandings, than of everyday fiction. I have sketched some preliminary categories for the analysis of TV entertainment conventions in "Prime Time Ideology" (1979). On TV entertainment and its evolution in general, there is abundant material in Barnouw's *The Image Empire* (1970), *Tube of Plenty* (1975), and *The Sponsor* (1978); in Fiske and Hartley, *Reading Television* (1978); and in Goldsen, *The Show and Tell Machine* (1977), though many analytic questions remain. On the content and history of specific shows and types of shows, see Czitrom (1977); Gitlin (1977b); Knutson (1974); Real, (1977, pp. 118-139, on medical shows); and Schneider (1977, on police shows). On soap operas, see Porter (1977). On the production process, see Cantor (1971), Brown (1971), and Tuchman (1974).

References

Adamson, W. (1978). Beyond reform and revolution: Notes on political education in Gramsci, Habermas and Arendt. *Theory and Society, 6,* 429-460.

Baker, L. B., McCombs, M. E., & McLeod, J. M. (1975). The development of political cognitions. In S. H. Chaffee (Ed.), *Political communication* (pp. 21-63). Beverly Hills, CA: Sage.

Balzac, H. de. (1898). *Lost illusions* (Vol. 2; G. B. Ives, Trans.). Philadelphia: George Barrie.

Barnouw, E. (1970). *The image empire*. New York: Oxford University Press.

Barnouw, E. (1975). *Tube of plenty*. New York: Oxford University Press.

Barnouw, E. (1978). *The sponsor*. New York: Oxford University Press.

Berlet, C. (1978). COINTELPRO: What the (deleted) was it? Media op. *The Public Eye, 1*, 28-38.

Blumler, J. G., & McQuail, D. (1968). *Television in politics: Its uses and influence*. London: Faber.

Brown, L. (1971). *Television: The business behind the box*. New York: Harcourt Brace Jovanovich.

Cantor, M. G. (1971). *The Hollywood TV producer*. New York: Basic Books.

Czitrom, D. (1977). Bilko: A sitcom for all seasons. *Cultural Correspondence, 4*, 16-19.

Fiske, J., & Hartley, J. (1978). *Reading television*. London: Methuen.

Gans, H. (1979). *Deciding what's news*. New York: Pantheon.

Gitlin, T. (1977a). Spotlights and shadows: Television and the culture of politics. *College English, 38*, 791-796.

Gitlin, T. (1977b, November-December). The televised professional. *Social Policy*, pp. 94-99.

Gitlin, T. (1979). Prime time ideology: The hegemonic process in television entertainment. *Social Problems, 26*, 264-265.

Goffman, E. (1974). *Frame analysis: An essay on the organization of experience*. New York: Harper & Row.

Goldsen, R. K. (1977). *The show and tell machine*. New York: Dial.

Gramsci, A. (1971). *Selections from the prison notebooks* (Q. Hoare & G. Nowell Smith, Eds. and Trans.). New York: International.

Hall, S. (1973). *Encoding and decoding in the television discourse* (mimeo). Birmingham, England: University of Birmingham, Centre for Contemporary Cultural Studies.

Knutson, P. (1974). Dragnet: The perfect crime? *Liberation, 18*, 28-31.

McCombs, M. E., & Shaw, D. I. (1972). The agenda-setting function of mass media. *Public Opinion Quarterly, 36*, 176-187.

McLeod, J. M., Becker, L. B., & Byrnes, J. E. (1974). Another look at the agenda-setting function of the press. *Communication Research, 1*, 131-166.

Porter, D. (1977). Soap time: Thoughts on a commodity art form. *College English, 38*, 782-788.

Real, M. R. (1977). *Mass-mediated culture*. Englewood Cliffs, NJ: Prentice-Hall.

Roshco, B. (1975). *Newsmaking*. Chicago: University of Chicago Press.

Sahlins, M. (1976). *Culture and practical reason*. Chicago: University of Chicago Press.

Schneider, B. (1977). Spelling's salvation armies. *Cultural Correspondence, 4*, 27-36.

Sigal, L. V. (1973). *Reporters and officials: The organization and politics of newsmaking*. Lexington, MA: D. C. Heath.

Tuchman, G. (1974). Assembling a network talk-shaw. In G. Tuchman (Ed.), *The TV establishment* (pp. 119-135). Englewood Cliffs, NJ: Prentice-Hall.

Tuchman, G. (1978). *Making news*. New York: Free Press.

Williams, R. (1973). Base and superstructure in Marxist cultural theory. *New Left Review, 82*, 3-16.

Williams, R. (1977). *Marxism and literature*. New York: Oxford University Press.

TV is always watching, always in or subjected to monitoring and surveillance when it has two eyes, one of which can be the eye donated by video.

Video is what is watching television . . .

5

Video/Television/Rodney King:
Twelve Steps Beyond
The Pleasure Principle

AVITAL RONELL

Headline News

My contention (and others have argued this according to different impulses and grammars) is that television has always been related to the law, which it locates at the site of crucial trauma. Even when it is not performing metonymies of law it is producing some cognition around its traumatic diffusions: thus even the laugh track, programming the traumatic experience of laughter, can be understood to function as a shock absorber. It signals the obsessive distraction that links laughter to history, within which Baudelaire located the loss of balance and, indeed, "mankind's universal fallen condition" ("Essence"). With loss of balance and the condition of falling, we are back to that unreadable blur that is said to project the step—or the charge—taken by Mr. Rodney King on March 3, 1991.

Headline News

One would have to bring to bear a critique of violence à la Benjamin, if it were not that TV were itself trying to tell us something about the status of legal and social fictions. TV does not know what it knows. In the idiom of Heideggerian insight, TV cannot think the essence of TV which, however, it is constantly marking and remarking. Television's principal compulsion and major attraction comes to us as the relation to law. As that which is thematized compulsively, the relation to law is at once there and not there, canceling its program by producing it. (Hence the proliferation of police shows, from *Dragnet* to *Perry Mason, 911, Hard Copy, Top Cops, FBI,* and courtroom dramas; even westerns with their lone law enforcers and sheriffs belong to this topos.) This relation to law, which television compulsively repeats as its theme, is simultaneously presented as the unthematizable par excellence—that is to say, this is a relation that cannot be presented as such but can only be appealed to or offered up as metonymic citation. Television is summoned before the law, but every attempt to produce the relation to law on a merely thematic level produces instead a narrative which is itself metonymic; the narrative is metonymic not because it is narrative, but because it depends on metonymic substitution from the start. In other words, television cannot say the continuity of its relation to itself or its premier "object" which I am calling force. This is why Rodney King's show, *Cops on Trial,* is about television watching the law watch video, its call to order, a figure of order that tries to find the language with which to measure out an ethical dosage of force. (On the subject of dosage, Television, as a drug, is also a tranquilizing force, regularly absorbing and administering hits of violence. Alfred Hitchcock would doze off in front of TV after a hard day's work on *Psycho,* claiming that TV, unlike film, was soporiferous.) Alternately stimulating and tranquilizing, ever anxiety-producing, television belongs to the domain of drugs, which is why, once again, the Rodney King event has to start its narrative engine with a false start, acknowledged by all: everyone involved in the chase had to start by assuming that they were pursuing a PCP suspect. Without this—technology's relation to the asserted effects of drugs, hallucination, and supernatural force—there would be no act of television reading itself, which is to say a "self" pumped up on the supposition of drugs but without any substance behind it, which is to say a "self" pumped up on the supposition of hallucination and exteriority but without any substance behind it.

Channel Twelve

The defense team takedown involved approaching George Holiday's video tape by replicating the violence that had been done to Mr. Rodney King. The unquestioned premise upon which the team of lawyers based its defense of the police called for an interpretation of video in terms of a "frame by frame" procedure. No one questioned this act of framing; and the verdict which ensued unleashed the violence that would explode the frames set up by the Court. In the blow by blow account, counting and recounting the event of the beating, the defense presented the sequentiality of photographs whose rhythm of articulation was beat into the Court records. The chilling effects of warping video into freeze frame photography cannot be underestimated, and teaches us that video requires a *reading*—something having little to do with immediate sense perception. The temporization that reading video entails was halted by both sides of the case (the prosecution appeared to believe that the video "spoke for itself" and did nothing to produce a reading of the idiom of video). The profound ignorance with which video was apprehended by the prosecution and by the defense was bound to refigure the violence to which Mr. King was submitted. No one needs to read Jacques Derrida's work on framing (*Truth*) in order to know that justice was not served in Simi Valley, California. But, possibly, if one had concerned oneself with the entire problematic of the frame, its installation and effects of violence—indeed the *excessive force* that acts of framing always imply—then it would have been something of an imperative to understand what it means to convert in a court of law a video tape into a photograph. For the photograph has been developed, in the readings of Walter Benjamin ("Work," *Berliner*), Roland Barthes (*Camera*), Derrida (Interview), and a number of others, as that which draws upon phantomal anxieties as well as the subject's inexorable arrest. I need not stress the extent to which the black body in the history of racist phantasms has been associated with the ghost or zombie. Perhaps we ought to begin, then, with the astonishing remark of Jacques Lacan when he was on "Television":

> —*From another direction, what gives you the confidence to prophesy the rise of racism? And why the devil do you have to speak of it?*
> —Because it doesn't strike me as funny and yet, it's true.
>
> With our *jouissance* going off the track, only the Other is able to mark its position, but only insofar as we are separated from this Other. Whence certain fantasies—unheard of before the melting pot.
>
> Leaving this Other to his own mode of *jouissance,* that would only be possible by not imposing our own on him, by not thinking of him as underdeveloped. (36)

It would appear that, in "Television," the incompletion of our *jouissance* is marked, or at least its off-track predicament is marking off a boundary that exposes the Other to the projections of racist fantasies. One of the fantasies that set off the necessity of mutilating the body of Rodney King involved precisely the *jouissance* of the Other, or the second degree of self that emerges with destructive *jouissance*: drugs. In order to get in gear, the police force had to imagine that its suspect was on PCP. What does it mean to say that the police force was hallucinating drugs? In the first place, the force was watching the phantom of television, racist television. In order to break Rodney King, the phantasm of the other on drugs—beside himself, not himself, a zombie—had to reach a consensus. Which was immediately reached. The Rodney King event was articulated as a metonymy of the war on drugs; this war, I have argued elsewhere (*Crack Wars*), constitutes an act of ethnocide by hallucinating mainstreamers. But the Rodney King event is also an eruption of the effaced Gulf War. When television collapsed into a blank stare, whiting out the Gulf War, nomadic video flashed a metonymy of police action perpetrated upon a black body. I would like to argue these points with as much clarity as the blurs, the static, allow.

The empirical gesture that opened the violence on March 3, 1991, was linked to Rodney King's legs. Did he take a step or was he charging the police? The footage seemed unclear. The defense team charged that King had in fact charged the police. "Gehen wir darum einen Schritt weiter" ("Let's therefore take a further step"), writes Freud in *Beyond the Pleasure Principle*—a text that brings together the topoi of charges, repetition compulsion, violence, and phantasms. Let us take another step, and another, and as many as it takes, in order to read the charges that are electrifying our derelict community.

Channel Eleven

Unlike telephony, cinema, or locomotion, television emerged as a prominent figure of our time only after the Second World War. There are many reasons for this (the Nazis voted in radio as the transferential agency par excellence; television was canceled out of the secret service of fascisoid transfixion). The mass invasion of television occurred after the war; it was served on the cold war platter, which is to say that in one way or another TV is not so much the beginning of something new, but is instead the residue of an unassimilable history. Television is linked crucially to the enigma of survival. It inhabits the contiguous neighborhoods of broken experience and rerouted memory. Refusing in its discourse and values to record, but preferring instead to play out the myths of liveness, living color, being there, television will have produced a counterphobic perspective to an interrupted history. I hope to scan the way TV acts as a shock absorber to the incomprehension of survival: the critical enigma of our time.

Channel Ten

Benjamin theorized the difference between *Überleben* and *Weiterleben*—surviving and living on ("Goethes"). Television plays out the tensions between these modalities of being by producing narratives that compulsively turn around crime. These narratives, traveling between real and fictive reference, allow for no loose ends but suture and resolve the enigmas they name. Television produces corpses that need not be mourned because, in part, of the status of surviving that is shown. Still, television itself is cut up, lacerated, seriated, commercial broken, so that its heterogeneous corpus can let something other than itself leak out. I would like to explore in slowmo, though scheduling always rushes us, the status of crime time which has saturated television if only to name an unreadable relation to the incomprehensibility of survival and its relation to law.

Channel Nine

The death of God has left us with a lot of appliances. Indeed, the historical event we call the death of God is inscribed within the last metaphysical spasm of our history as it continues to be interrogated by the question of technology. The event of the death of God, which dispersed and channeled the sacred according to altogether new protocols, is circuited through much of technology, occasionally giving rise to electric shocks. I am referring to God because, despite everything, He in part was the guarantor of absolute representability and of the transparent rendering of truth. In an era of constitutive opaqueness—there is no transcendental light shining upon us, we dwell in the shadows of mediation and withdrawal, there will be no revelation, can be no manifestation as such—things have to be tuned in, adjusted, subjected to double takes, and are dominated by amnesia. Without recourse to any dialectic of incarnation, something yet beams through, as though the interruption itself were the thing to watch.

Channel Eight

Among the things that TV has insisted upon, little is more prevalent than interruption or the hiatus for which it speaks and of which it is a part. The hiatus persists in a permanent state of urgency, whence the necessity of the series. The series, or seriature, extradites television to a mode of reading in which interruption insists, even if it does so as an interrupted discourse whose aim is to recapture its own rupture.

Channel Seven

So, in the space of interruption (an atopy or interruption that used to be called "television land"), there exists a muted injunction to read the hiatus and let oneself be marked by the hiatus—a necessity of negotiating the lineage of the net. Granted, I am displacing the focus from television as totality to the seriality of derangement, a place deranged, dislocated, disarticulated, a "place" where seriality always involves the possibility of serial killing. If TV has taught us anything—and I think it is helpful to locate it somewhere between Kansas and Oz, an internal spread of exteriority, an interruption precisely of the phantasmatic difference between interiority and exteriority—this principally concerns, I think, the *impossibility of staying at home.* In fact, the more local it gets, the more uncanny, not-at-home it appears. Television, which Heidegger, when he was on, once associated with the essence of his thinking, chaining you and fascinating you by its neutral gleam, is about being-not-at-home, telling you that you are chained to the deracinating grid of being-in-the-world. Perhaps this explains why, during his broadcast season, Lacan spoke of *homme*-sickness. We miss being-at-home in the world, which never happened anyway, and missing home, Lacan suggests, has everything to do with being sick of *homme.* So where were we? asks the scholar.

Channel Six

We have no way of stabilizing or locating with certainty the "in" of being-in-the-world, no matter how much channel surfing you are capable of sustaining. Television exposes that constitutive outside that you have let into the house of being, inundating and saturating you, even when it is "off." While television, regardless of its content or signified, tends toward an ontologization of its status—no matter what's on, I dare say, it is emptied of any signified, it is a site of evacuation, the hemorrhaging of meaning, ever disrupting its semantic fields and phenomenal activities of showing—television participates as a trace in the articulation of sheer uncanniness. This is what Heidegger understands as our fundamental predicament of being-not-at-home in this world (which we have yet to locate and which technology helps to map in terms of teletopies, which is of no help). While television's tendential urge guides it toward ontology, there are, however, internal limits that freeze frame the ontological urge into an ethical compulsion. One of these internal limits that is at once lodged outside and inside TV is a certain type of monitoring—the nomadic, aleatory, unpredictable eruption we sometimes call video.

Channel Five

TV has always been under surveillance. From credit attributions to ratings, television swerves from the ontological tendency to the establishment of legitimacy, which places it under the pressures of an entirely other obligation. It is no wonder that television keeps on interrupting itself and replaying to itself the serial crime stories that establish some provisional adjudication between what can be seen and an ethico-legal resolution to the programs of showing. Oedipus has never stopped running through television, which obligates us to read the violence of legitimation and patricidal shooting that back it up. At any rate, the crime stories that TV compulsively tells itself have been charged with possession of a mimetic trigger; in other words, where TV allegorizes its interrupted relation to law, it is charged with producing a contagion of violence. A perpetual matter of dispute, the relation of television to violence is, however, neither contingent nor arbitrary but zooms in on the absent, evacuated center of televisual seriature. At the core of a hiatus that pulses television, I am placing the mutism of video, the strategy of its silence and concealment. Though I recognize the radically different usages to which they have been put and the divergent syntaxes that govern their behavior, I am more interested in the interpellation that takes place between television and video, the way the one calls the other to order, which is one way of calling the other to itself: In fact, where nomadic or testimonial video practices a strategy of silence, concealment, and unrehearsed semantics, installed as it is in television as bug or parasite, watching (out) (for) television, it at times produces the *Ethical Scream* that television has massively interrupted.

This ethical scream that interrupts a discourse of effacement (even if that effacement should indeed thematize crime and its legal, moral, or police resolutions), this ethical scream—and video means for us "I saw it"—perforates television from an inner periphery, instituting a break in the compulsive effacement that in fact engages television (I am not speaking of the politically correct gestures that TV has produced by star trekking interracial and interspecial specials: these are on the order of thematic considerations which have been sufficiently interpreted elsewhere). When testimonial video breaks out of concealment and into the television programming which it occasionally supersedes, it is acting as the call of conscience of television. This is why, also, when television wants to simulate a call of conscience (the call of conscience [*Gewissensruf*] is the aphonic call discussed in Heidegger's *Being and Time,* sect. 62), it itself reverts to video. The abyssal inclusion of video as call of conscience offers no easy transparency but requires a reading; it calls for a discourse. As we have been shown with singular clarity in the Rodney King case and, in particular, with the trial, what is called for when video acts as the call of conscience is not so much a viewing of a spectacle, but a reading; and, instead of voyeurism, an exegesis. On both sides of the showing of this video, we are confronted with the image of condemned and deserted bodies—what I describe in *Crack Wars* as the "trash bodies," dejected and wasted—and this is why, when you're an television, as its spectral subject on either side of the screen, you've been trashed, even if watching television is only a metonymy of being wasted in the form, for instance, of "wasting time." To the extent that we, like Rodney King, are shown being wasted by the deregulation of force, and are left crumpled by the wayside, we know we are dealing with a spectral experience and the memory of the phantom.

Channel Four

Haunted TV: the phantom of the Gulf War, bleeding through the body of King. Haunted TV: showing by not showing what lay at our feet, the step out of line. Haunted TV: focusing the limitless figure of the police, this index of a phantom-like violence because they are everywhere. The police aren't just the police "today more or less than ever," writes Derrida; "they are the figure sans figure" ("Force" 1009). They cut a faceless figure, a violence without a form as Benjamin puts it: *gestaltlos* ("Critique"). This formless, ungraspable figure of the police, even as it is metonymized, spectralized, and even if it installs its haunting presence everywhere would remain, if Benjamin had his way, a determinable figure proper to the civilized states.

Channel Three

The Rodney King event not only forces a reading of force and enforcement of law, but requires citation and the reading precisely of the phantom body of the police. The police become hallucinatory and spectral because they haunt everything. They are everywhere even where they are not. Their present is not presence: *they are television.* But when they come after you and beat you they are like those televisions that explode into a human Dasein and break into a heterotopy that stings. Always on, they are on your case, in your face.

What video teaches, something that television knows but cannot as such articulate, is that every medium is related in some crucial way to spectres. This ghostly relationship that the image produces between phenomenal and referential effects of language and image is what makes ethical phrasing as precarious as it is necessary.

Because of its transmission of ghostly figures, interruption, and seriature, television would be hard to assimilate to the Frankfurt School's vision of it, where the regime of the visual is associated with mass media and the threat of a culture of fascism. This threat always exists, but I would like to read the way television in its couple with video offers a picture of numbed resistance to the unlacerated regimes of fascist media as it mutates into forms of video and cybernetic technology, electronic reproduction, and cybervisual technologies.

Channel Two

Television is being switched on out of a number of considerations. Despite and beside itself, TV has become the atopical locus of the ethical implant. Not when it is itself, if that should ever occur or stabilize, but when it jumps up and down on the static machine, interfering as an alterity of a constant disbandment.

One problem with television is that it exists in trauma, or rather trauma is on television. This presents us with considerable technical difficulty, to be extent that trauma can be experienced in at least two ways: as a memory that one cannot integrate into one's own experience, and as a catastrophic knowledge that one cannot communicate to others. If television cannot be hooked up to what we commonly understand by experience, and if it cannot communicate, even telecommunicate, a catastrophic knowledge but can only—perhaps—signal the transmission of a gap (at times a yawn), a dark abyss, or the black box of talking survival—then what is it doing? Also, why does it at once induce the response of non-response and get strapped with charges of violent inducement?

Channel One

I have to admit that initially, when adjusting myself to technology, I was more seriously drawn in by the umbilicus of the telephone, whose speculative logic kept me on a rather short leash. On first sight, television seemed like a corruption, as in the case of supercessions, of telephony; it seemed like a low grade transferential apparatus, and I felt television and telephone fight it out as in the battle in *Robocop* between mere robot (his majesty the ego) and the highly complex cyborg (who came equipped with memory traces, superego, id, and—ever displacing the ego—a crypt). In yet another idiom, telephony was for me linked to the Old Testament (the polite relation to God, as Nietzsche says [*Genealogy*]), where television seemed like the image-laden New Testament (where one rudely assumes an intimacy with God and makes one of His images appear on the screen of our historical memory). Needless to say, I was on the side of the more remote, less controlled, audible sacred, to the extent that its technical mutation can be figured as the telephone. The Old Testament unfolds a drama of listening and inscription of law; the New Testament produces a kind of videodrome revision of some of the themes, topoi, and localities of its ancestral text. Now, I am not referring us to these texts in order to expose a conversion of any sort, but merely for the purpose of turning the dial and switching the ways in which our being has been modalized by a technology that works according to a different protocol of ethical attunement. If I refer us to the twin Testaments, this is in part to explore with you the site of testimony that television, despite and beside itself, initiates. It is no accident that television, for the dramas we have come to associate with the names of Lacan, Elvis, Heidegger, Anita Hill, Rodney King, Lee Harvey Oswald, Viet Nam—fill in the blanks—and Desert Storm, has become the locus of testimony, even if we are faced with false testimony, rhetorical deceit, or resolute non-coverage. In a moment I will try to show, to the extent that anything can be shown, why the Gulf War was presented to us as a discourse of effacement; in other words, why at moments of referential need, *the experience of the image is left behind.* This has everything to do with the interruptive status of death but also, equally down to earth, with the problematic of thematization. In other words, I believe there is a concurrent mark of an invisible channel in television that says the problematic of thematization, which makes the rhetoricity of the televisual image collapse into a blank stare.

At moment such as these—most manifestly, the seriated nothing that was "on" during the Gulf War—television is not merely performing an allegory of the impossibility of reading, because this would still be a thematizing activity (the problematic activity of thematizing will be taken up again in the Rodney King case). During the Gulf War, television, as a production system of narrative, image, information flow, and so forth, took a major commercial break as it ran interference with its semantic and thematic dimensions. This interference that television ran with itself, and continues to rerun on a secret track, points us to something like the essence of television. I would like to argue that the Rodney King event, which forced an image, though not as stabilized narration, back on the screen, presented that which was unpresentable during the war—Rodney King, the black body under attack by a massive show of force, showed what would not be shown in its generalized form: the American police force attacking helpless brown bodies in Iraq. Now it so happens that the Rodney King trial is about force itself. Thematically, what is being measured, tested, and judged in the televised trial is the question of force, one of excessive police force. And there's the catch; we saw it blown up and cut down in the Anita Hill case: force can never be perceived. This is a persistent question circulating in the more or less robust corpus of philosophical inquiry. The question now is, how can philosophy talk about force?

The question par excellence in the Rodney King trial treats the regulation of force, its constitution and performance, in terms of an ethics of dosage. While TV was under the covers, nomadic video captured the images of brute force committed by the LAPD. Now, anyone who has watched the trial knows that the referential stability of the images has been blown out of the water. Witnesses were reading blurs and blurring images. The status of the image as a semantic shooting range has been severely undermined as TV conducts an interrogation of force. This interrogation was forced upon TV—it involves an interrogation, I would submit, about its own textual performance in the production of force. What comes out provisionally, at least, is the fact that video, nomadic video—aleatory, unpredictable vigilant, testimonial video—emerges as the call of conscience of broadcast TV, including CNN, C-SPAN, etc.

Channel Zero

What interests me provisionally, here, concerns the two eyes of television. TV is always watching, always in or subjected to monitoring and surveillance when it has two eyes, one of which can be the eye donated by video. I am not saying that video is the truth of television, nor its essence; it is what is watching television: it is the place of the testimonial that cannot speak with referential assurance but does assert the truth of what it says. This is why I want to focus it as the call of conscience, which is to say that video responds in some crucial sense to the call of television. Now, you have seen me play with the contrast and wave TV into the realm, or rather logic, of telephony. How can TV make a call, or more precisely, respond a call? The way we call it is crucial. (At the same time as TV is being watched by video and called to order, football has decided to dispense with instant replay. This decision, while made by team owners and not by media technologists, theorists, or media activists, nonetheless asserts that when it comes to calling it, TV withdraws its bid for claims made on behalf of referential stability.)

Let me try to unfold some of these points briefly. On one level, television calls for a theory of distraction which appears to be rooted in the trauma that it is always telling, yet is unable to fix. This suggests a complicated economy of visual playback and shock absorption, for trauma essentially involves an image without internalization. Recently, Cathy Caruth has argued that trauma

> . . . does not simply serve as a record of the past but precisely registers the force of an experience that is not yet fully owned. . . . This paradoxical experience . . . both urgently demands historical awareness and yet denies our usual modes of access to it. . . . While the images of traumatic reenactment remain absolutely accurate and precise, they are largely inaccessible to conscious recall and control. (9)

Let me bring some of these strands into contact with one another. TV is irremissible; it is always on, even when it is off. Its voice of conscience is that internal alterity that runs interference with television in order to bring it closer to itself, but this close circuit surveillance can be experienced only in the mode of a disjunction. Television presents itself as being there only when it is other than itself: when it mimes police work or when, during the Gulf War, blanking out in a phobic response to the call of reference, it became a radio. And yet, it's not that simple: in this case it *showed* itself not showing, and becoming the closed, knotted eye of blindness. Within this act of showing itself not showing, posing itself as exposed, which is to say, showing that its rapport to the promise of reference is essentially one of phobia, it produced a dead gaze—what Blanchot would call "a gaze become the ghost of eternal vision." There is something in and from television that allows sight to be blinded into a neutral, directionless gleam. Yet, "blindness is vision still," "a vision which is no longer the possibility of seeing" (32).

In a sense, TV doubled for our blindness and in fact performed this rhetoric of blindness that guided the Gulf War. Television entered us into the realm of the eternal diurnal, night vision, and twenty-four-hour operational engagement, TV-guided missiles that exploded sight at the point of contact. Television showed precisely a *tele*vision, that is, a vision which is no longer the possibility of seeing, and if it taught us anything, it was this: what fascinates us robs us of our power to give sense; drawing back from the world, it draws us along. Despite the propaganda contracts which it had taken out, television produced a neutral gleam that tells us the relation between fascination and not seeing. If it showed anything, television showed a television without image, a site of trauma in which the experience of immediate proximity involves absolute distance. But it was through video, intervening as the call of conscience of TV, as foreign body and parasitical inclusion in broadcast television, that a rhetoricity of television blindness emerged. Marking the incommensurate proximity of the same, testimonial video split television from its willed blindness and forced it so see what it would not show. Something was apprehended.

A monument to that which cannot be stabilized, television captures the disruption, seriature, the effraction of cognition, breaks—whether commercial or constitutive—and is prompted by the need to play out the difference between reference and phenomenality. On this score, there is one more thing to be said about the relation of television to trauma. This has everything to do with the essential character of traumatism as a nonsymbolizable wound that comes before any other effraction: this would be TV's guide—how to symbolize the wound that will not be shown. Of the perspectives in television that are most perplexing, one is the alternation marked between hypermnesia and amnesia. What is the relation between amnesia and the image? We have observed in films such as *Total Recall* that acts of remembering are somehow prompted by mnemonic devices along the lines of video implants. In fact, video has consistently attracted thematizations of internalized memory (*Erinnerung* in Hegel's vocabulary[1]) that are nothing if not the literalization of *Gedächtnis,* an external memory prompter, a cue, or memo-padding. While these video implants are often accompanied by nightmarish hues, they somehow remain external to the subject who needs these prompters to supplement an absence of memory. The image comes to infuse an amnesiac subject. Total recall is not the same as memory or recollection, and it is only total to the extent that it names the need for a prosthetic technology that would produce a memory track. In such films the video transport—these are always pointing to a modality of transport: getting higher, they combine the idioms of drugs and electronics—the technochip induces some sort of trip, memory as lapsus, as the transmission of the slip. The video transport coexists with a condition of amnesia. It is to this amnesia, and as this amnesia, channel surfing through blank zones of trauma, that television, as that which operates on screen memories and forgetting, secretly measures the force of an unbearable history.

Note

1. See in particular Derrida's treatment of Hegel's *Erinnerung* in *Mémoires.*

References

Barthes, Roland. *Cameria Lucida: Reflections on Photography.* Trans. Richard Howard. New York: Farrar, 1981.
Baudelaire, Charles. "De l'essence du rire et généralement du comique dans les arts plastiques." *Oeuvres complètes.* Ed. Claude Pichois. Vol. 2 Paris: Gallimard, 1976. 525-43. 2 vols. 1975-76.
Benjamin, Walter. *Berliner Kindheit um Neunzehnhundert. Gesammelte Schriften* 4: 235-304.

Benjamin, Walter. "Critique of Violence." *Reflections: Essays, Aphorisms, Autobiographical Writings.* Trans. Edmund Jephcott. Ed. and intro. Peter Demetz. New York: Harcourt, 1978. 277-300.

Benjamin, Walter. *Gesammelte Schriften.* Ed. Rolf Tiedemann and Hermann Schweppenhäuser. 7 vols. Frankfurt a.M.: Suhrkamp, 1972-89.

Benjamin, Walter. "Goethes *Wahlverwandtschaften*" ("Goethe's *Elective Affinities*"). *Gesammelte Schriften* 1: 123-201.

Benjamin, Walter. "The Work of Art in the Age of Mechanical Reproduction." *Illuminations: Essays and Reflections.* Trans. Harry Zohn. Ed. and intro. Hannah Arendt. New York: Schocken, 1969. 217-43.

Blanchot, Maurice. "The Essential Solitude." *The Space of Literature.* Trans. and intro. Ann Smock. Lincoln: University of Nebraska Press, 1982. 19-34.

Caruth, Cathy. "Introduction." *American Imago* 48.1 (1991): 1-12.

Derrida, Jacques. "The Force of Law: The 'Mystical Foundation of Authority.' " Trans. Mary Quaintance. "Deconstruction and the Possibility of Justice." *Cardozo Law Review* 11.5-6 (1990): 919-1045.

Derrida, Jacques. Interview. *Droit de regards.* by Marie-Françoise Plissart. Paris: Minuit, 1985. i-xxxvi.

Derrida, Jacques. *Mémoires for Paul de Man.* Trans. Cecile Lindsay, Jonathan Culler, and Eduardo Cadava. New York: Columbia UP, 1986.

Derrida, Jacques. *The Truth in Painting.* Trans. Geoff Bennington and Ian McLeod. Chicago: University of Chicago Press, 1987.

Freud, Sigmund. *Beyond the Pleasure Principle.* 1920. *The Standard Edition of the Complete Psychological Works of Sigmund Freud.* Trans. and ed. James Strachey. Vol. 18. London: Hogarth, 1955. 1-64. 24 vols. 1953-74.

Heidegger. *Being and Time.* Trans. John Macquarrie and Edward Robinson. New York: Harper, 1962.

Lacan, Jacques. "Television." Trans. Denis Hollier, Rosalind Krauss, and Annette Michelson. *October* 40 (1987): 5-50.

Nietzsche, Friedrich. *On the Genealogy of Morals.* Trans. and ed. Walter Kaufmann and R. J. Hollingdale. New York: Vintage, 1967.

Robocop. Dir. Paul Verhoeven. Orion, 1987.

Ronell, Avital. *Crack Wars: Literature, Addiction, Mania.* Lincoln: University of Nebraska Press, 1992.

Total Recall. Dir. Paul Verhoeven. Tri-Star Pictures, 1990.

HIROSHIMA-NAGASAKI, AUGUST 1945—
NOT FOR SENSITIVE U.S. EYES.

6

The Case of the A-Bomb Footage

ERIK BARNOUW

It was in 1970, a quarter of a century after the footage was shot, that the documentary film *Hiroshima-Nagasaki, August 1945* had its premiere and won an audience, an international one, as it turned out. In recounting the origin and history of this film I want to emphasize the extraordinary 25-year hiatus. It seems to me to have implications for filmmakers and film scholars and perhaps for the democratic process.[1]

I became involved in this story in its later stages, as producer of the 1970 compilation documentary, and this involvement came about almost by accident. Before I explain how this happened, let me go back to the beginning of the story, as I have been able to piece it together over the years.

In August 1945, after the two atom bombs had been dropped on Hiroshima and Nagasaki, a Japanese film unit named Nippon Eiga Sha was commissioned by its government to make a film record of the effects of the devastating new weapon. Nippon Eiga Sha was a wartime amalgamation of the several newsreel and documentary units that had existed before the war. They had been nationalized for war purposes.

The man entrusted with the making of the film was Akira Iwasaki, a film critic, historian, and occasional producer. The choice of Iwasaki for the assignment was significant. During the 1930s he had been the leader of a leftist film group called Prokino or Proletarian Film League, similar to the Workers Film and Photo Leagues in the United States. Being antimilitarist, Prokino had been outlawed shortly before the war, and some of its members had been jailed under a preventive-detention law. Iwasaki himself had spent part of the war in prison. The fact that he had regained standing and was given the film assignment reflected the turbulent situation in the final days of the war, and the extent to which the military had already lost status.[2]

Because of the breakdown of transport and the difficulty of obtaining adequate supplies, it took the Nippon Eiga Sha film crews some time to reach their locations, but they were at work in Hiroshima and Nagasaki when the American occupation forces arrived. What happened then has been described by Iwasaki. "In the middle of the shooting one of my cameramen was arrested in Nagasaki by American military police. . . . I was summoned to the GHQ and told to discontinue the shooting." The filming was halted, but Iwasaki says he remonstrated, and "made arguments" with the occupation authorities. "Then" he writes,

> came the group of the Strategic Bombing Survey from Washington and they wanted to have a film of Hiroshima and Nagasaki. Therefore the U.S. Army wanted to utilize my film for the purpose, and changed its mind. Now they allowed me or better ordered me to continue and complete the film.[3]

During the following weeks, under close U.S. control, much additional footage was shot. All was in black and white; there was no color film in Japan at this time. As the shooting progressed, the material was edited into sequences under the overall title "Effects of the Atomic Bomb." There were sequences showing effects on concrete, effects on wood, effects on vegetation, and so on. The emphasis was on detailed scientific observation. Effects on human beings were included, but sparsely. Survivors on the outer fringes of the havoc were photographed in improvised treatment centers, but here too the guiding supervisory principle was scientific data gathering rather than human interest. The interests of the camera teams were to some extent at variance with this.

The edited material had reached a length of somewhat less than 3 hours when the saga entered a new phase. Occupation authorities suddenly took possession of the film—negative, positive, and outtakes—and shipped it to Washington. Film and all related documents were classified SECRET and locked away, disappearing from view for almost a quarter of a century. Most people, including those in the film world, remained unaware of its existence. Apparently a few feet were released for Army-approved uses, and the project was briefly mentioned in *Films Beget Films*, by Jay Leyda, published in 1964, a book that began as a memorandum for the Chinese government on the values of film archives. But whether the earliest Hiroshima and Nagasaki footage still existed was an American military secret. With later color footage of the ruins making an appearance and to some extent satisfying curiosity, the missing footage did not become an issue in the United States.

Until 1968 I was oblivious to its existence. But early that year a friend, Mrs. Lucy Lemann, sent me a newspaper clipping she had received from Japan, which excited my interest. It was from the English-language *Asahi Evening News* (January 26, 1968) and reported that the footage shot in Hiroshima and Nagasaki in 1945 by Japanese cameramen had been returned to Japan from the United States and that the government would arrange a television screening "after certain scenes showing victims' disfiguring burns are deleted." The item also stated that the film would later be made available on loan to "research institutions" but it added: "In order to avoid the film being utilized for political purposes, applications for loan of the film from labor unions and political organizations will be turned down."

I was at this time chairman of the film, radio, and television division of the Columbia University School of the Arts, and had organized a related unit called the Center for Mass Communication, division of Columbia University Press, producing and distributing documentary films and recordings. Naturally the clipping seemed to demand some investigation or action. Mrs. Lemann was a contributor to the World Law Fund, and at her suggestion I wrote for further information to Professor Yoshikazu Sakamoto, Professor of International Politics at the University of Tokyo, an associate of the Fund. His prompt reply said that the Japanese had negotiated with the U.S. Department of State for the return of the film but the Department of Defense was thought to control it. The material sent to Japan was not the original nitrate film but a safety-film copy.

Somewhat impulsively, I wrote a letter on Columbia University stationery, signed "Chairman, Film, Radio, Television," addressed to "The Honorable Clark M. Clifford, Secretary of Defense," with the notations that "cc" should go to the Secretary of State Dean Rusk and to Dr. Grayson Kirk, President of Columbia University. The letter asked whether Columbia's Center for Mass Communication might have the privilege of releasing in the United States the material recently made available for showing in Japan.[4] I felt a bit flamboyant in this, but sensed I had nothing to lose. I scarcely expected results. But to my amazement, a letter arrived within days from Daniel Z. Henkin, Deputy

Assistant Secretary of Defense, stating that the Department of Defense had turned the material over to the National Archives and that we could have access to it there.[5] So it was that early in April 1968 I found myself with a few associates in the auditorium of the National Archives in Washington, looking at some 2 hours and 40 minutes of Hiroshima and Nagasaki footage. We also examined voluminous shot lists in which the location of every shot was identified and its content summarized and indexed. Every sheet bore the classification stamp SECRET but this had been crossed out and another stamp substituted: "NOT TO BE RE-LEASED WITHOUT APPROVAL OF THE D.O.D." There was no indication of the date of this partial declassification. We guessed that some routine declassification timetable had taken effect, but without public announcement. Perhaps we were merely the first to have inquired about the material.[6]

Some in our group were dismayed by the marginal quality of much of the film, a result, perhaps, of the circumstances under which it had been shot and the fact that we were looking at material some generations away from the original. But this quality also seemed a mark of authenticity, and it seemed to me that enough of the footage was extraordinary in its power, unforgettable in its implications, and historic in its importance to warrant our duplicating all of it. A grant from Mrs. Lemann to Columbia University Press made it possible to order a duplicate negative and workprint of the full 2 hours and 40 minutes, along with photostats of the priceless shot lists. During the summer of 1968 all this material arrived at Columbia University from the National Archives, and we began incessant study and experimentation with the footage, with constant reference to the shot lists and other available background information.[7]

The footage contained ruins in grotesque formations, and endless shots of rubble. At first we were inclined to discard many of the less striking rubble sequences, but when we learned that one had been a school (where most of the children had died at their desks), and one had been a prison (where 140 prisoners had died in their cells), and another had been a trolley car (whose passengers had evaporated, leaving in the rubble a row of their skulls and bones), even the less dramatic shots acquired new meaning. Eventually a montage of such rubble shots, linked with statistics about the people annihilated or injured, and the distance of each location from the center of the blast, became a key sequence in the film.

The paucity of what we called "human-effects footage" troubled us deeply. We felt that we would have to cluster this limited material near the end of our film for maximum effect, but meanwhile we resolved on a sweeping search for additional "human-effects footage." We wrote to the Defense Department asking whether additional material of this sort had perhaps been held back. The Pentagon's staff historian answered, assuring us nothing was being held back, and adding: "Out-takes from the original production no longer exist, having probably been destroyed during the conversion from acetate [*sic*] to safety film—if they ever were turned over to the US Government at all."[8] This curious reply made us wonder whether footage such as we hoped to find might still exist in Japan or might be held by people in the United States who were in Japan during the Occupation. Barbara Van Dyke, who became associate producer for our film, began writing letters to a long list of people, asking for information on any additional footage. In the end this search proved fruitless; we found we had to proceed without additional "human-effects footage."

One of those to whom she wrote was the Japanese film critic and historian Akira Iwasaki, the original producer. His name was not mentioned in documents received from the Defense Department or from the National Archives but was suggested by the writer Donald Richie, a leading authority on Japanese cinema, as a likely source of information.[9] Iwasaki did not reply to our inquiry; he explained later that he had doubted the "sincerity" of our project.

Her search did produce one extraordinary find. One of the occupants of the observation plane that followed the Enola Gay, the bomb-dropping plane, to Hiroshima was Harold Agnew, who later became head of the Los Alamos laboratory. As a personal venture he had taken with him a 16 mm camera. The very brief sequence he brought back provides an unforgettable glimpse of the historic explosion, and the shuddering impact of the blast on the observation plane itself, which seems likely for a moment to be blown to perdition. From Mr. Agnew we acquired a copy of this short sequence.

Our first rough assembly was some 40 minutes long, but we kept reducing it in quest of sharper impact. What finally emerged, after more than a year of experimentation, was a quiet 16 minute film with a factual, eloquently understated narration written by Paul Ronder and spoken by him and Kazuko Oshima. Ronder and Geoffrey Bartz did the editing, with musical effects by Linea Johnson and Terrill Schukraft.

We consulted at various stages with Albert W. Hilberg, M.D., and historian Henry F. Graff. We were not sure the film would have the effect we hoped for, but our doubts were soon resolved.

After several small screenings, we arranged a major preview at the Museum of Modern Art in February 1970, to which the press was invited. The auditorium was jammed, and at the end of the showing the audience sat in total silence for several seconds. We were at first unsure what this meant, but the comments soon made clear what it meant. Later that day the UPI ticker carried a highly favorable report that treated the film as a major news event, mentioning the address of the Center for Mass Communication and the print sale price, $96. Two days later checks and orders began arriving in the mail and continued without promotional effort on our part, at the rate of 100 a month. In 5 months almost 500 prints were sold to film libraries, colleges, school systems, clubs, community groups, and churches. Every screening seemed to bring a surge of letters and orders. Foreign sales came quickly.

Two things amazed us: (a) the electric effect on audiences everywhere and (b) the massive silence of the American networks. All had been invited to the press preview; none had attended. Early in the morning after the resounding UPI dispatch, all three commercial networks phoned to ask for preview prints and sent motorcycle couriers to collect them, but this was followed by another silence. By making follow-up phone calls we learned that CBS and ABC were "not interested." Only NBC thought it might use the film, if it could find a "news hook." We dared not speculate what kind of event this might call for.

The networks' attitude was, of course, in line with a policy all three had pursued for over a decade, of not broadcasting documentaries other than their own. We at Columbia University were outraged at the network policy.[10] We had half expected that the historic nature of the material would in this case thrust the policy aside. But we were for the moment too busy filling nontelevision orders to consider any particular protest or action.

Then a curious chain of media phenomena changed the situation. On April 5, 1970, the Sunday supplement *Parade,* which generally gave its chief attention to the romantic aberrations of the mighty, carried a prominent item about *Hiroshima-Nagasaki, August 1945,* calling it unforgettable, and necessary viewing for the people of any nation possessing the bomb. This apparently caused the editors of the Boston *Globe,* which carried *Parade,* to wonder why television was ignoring the film. They made phone calls to nuclear scientists and others, asking their opinions on the matter, and reached several who had attended our previews. The result was a lead editorial in the Sunday *Globe* (April 5, 1970) headed: "HIROSHIMA-NAGASAKI, AUGUST 1945—NOT FOR SENSITIVE U.S. EYES." It quoted Dr. S. E. Luria, Sedgwick Professor of Biology at Massachusetts Institute of Technology, describing the film as "a very remarkable document" and adding, "I wish every American could see it, and particularly, every Congressman." Norman Cousins described himself as "deeply impressed." The *Globe* ended its editorial with a blast at the networks for ignoring the film. *Variety* (April 22, 1970), the show-business weekly, was interested in the *Globe*'s "needling" of the networks, and featured the issue in a special box in its next edition. This brought sudden action from National Educational Television, which a few days later signed a contract to broadcast the film in early August, 25 years after the dropping of the bombs. No sooner had the contract been signed than NBC announced that it wanted the film for use on its monthly magazine series, *First Tuesday*. When Sumner Glimcher, manager of the Center for Mass Communication, explained that the film was committed to NET, he was asked if we could "buy out" NET so that NBC could have the film, but we declined to try.

As the issue of a U.S. telecast was moving to a resolution, we were aware of parallel, and apparently more feverish, developments in Japan. Our first inkling of what was happening in Japan came at the Museum of Modern Art preview, at which we were approached by a representative of TBS (Tokyo Broadcasting System) one of Japan's commercial systems, with an offer to purchase Japanese television rights. To be negotiating such a matter seemed strange, in view of the Japanese government's announced plans for a television screening, but the TBS man was persistent and eager, and we finally signed an agreement authorizing a telecast, with an option to repeat. The telecast took place March 18, 1970, and the option to repeat was promptly exercised. We gradually became aware, through bulletins from Japan, of the enormous impact made by these telecasts. The government-arranged showing had taken place earlier over NHK, the government network, but had included little except rubble. Human beings had been excised "in deference to the relatives of the victims," but this action had brought a storm of protest. It was against this background that TBS had negotiated for our film. It also gave our film, which made use of everything that the NHK telecast had eliminated, an added impact. Professor Sakamoto of the University of Tokyo began sending us voluminous translations of favorable reviews and articles, one of which paid special tribute to Columbia University for showing the Japanese people "what our own government tried to withhold from us." The reviews included major coverage in a picture magazine of the *Life* format. Viewing statistics were provided. The *Mainichi Shimbun* (March 20 and 22, 1970) reported that the film "caused a sensation throughout the country," while in Hiroshima "the viewing rate soared to four times the normal rate." The *Chugoku Shimbun* (March 19, 1970) reported:

> At the atomic injury hospital in Hiroshima last night, nine o'clock being curfew time, all was quiet. Only in one room on the second floor of the west wing, the television diffidently continued its program. . . . They had obtained special permission from the doctors. . . . The first scene was of ruins. "That's the Aioi Bridge." "That's the Bengaku Dome." The women follow the scenes. Even the Chinese woman who had not wanted to see is leaning from her bed and watching intently. . . . The scene of victims which has elicited so much comment is now on. "That's exactly how it was," they nod to each other. However, when the film was over they contradicted their words and said, "It was much, much worse."

A letter came from the mayor of Hiroshima. The city would mark the 25th anniversary of the bomb with a major observance, including a long television program, and wanted to include material from our film.

The most gratifying response came from Akira Iwasaki, who, after a lapse of almost 25 years, had seen his footage on television. His role in the project was not credited, and he might have been expected to resent this, but no sign of resentment appeared. He wrote us a long letter expressing his gratitude and appreciation for how we had used the material. He also published a long review in a leading Japanese magazine, describing his reaction.

> I was lost in thought for a long time, deeply moved by this film. . . . I was the producer of the original long film which offered the basic material for this short film. That is, I knew every cut of it . . . yet I was speechless. . . . It was not the kind of film the Japanese thought Americans would produce. The film is an appeal or warning from man to man for peaceful reflection— to prevent the use of the bomb ever again. I like the narration, in which the emotion is well controlled and the voice is never raised. . . . That made me cry. In this part, the producers are no longer Americans. Their feelings are completely identical to our feelings. (Iwasaki, 1970)

The impact of the film was further illuminated by a bizarre incident. At my Columbia University office a delegation of three Japanese gentlemen was announced, and ushered in, all impeccably dressed. One member, introducing the leader, identified him as a member or former member of the Japanese Parliament, representing the Socialists. The leader himself then explained that he came on behalf of an organization called the Japan Congress Against A and H Bombs, also known as Gensuikin. In this capacity, he had three requests to make. First, as a token of appreciation for what we had achieved with our film *Hiroshima-Nagasaki, August 1945,* would I accept a small brooch as a gift to my wife? Puzzled and curious, I accepted.

Second, would I consider an invitation to speak in Hiroshima on the 25th anniversary of the dropping of the bomb, in the course of the scheduled observances? I hesitated—the suggestion raised endless questions in my mind, but I said I would consider. The leader seemed reassured and said I would receive a letter.

Then came the third request. Would he be permitted to purchase six prints of *Hiroshima-Nagasaki, August 1945*? I explained that we sold prints at $96, for nonprofit use, making no discrimination among buyers; anyone could buy. With an audible sigh of relief, he suddenly unbuttoned his shirt, ripped out a money belt, and produced six pristine $100 bills. Accustomed to dealing with checks and money orders, it took the office a while to round up the $24 "change." We handed him the six prints. One member of the delegation had a camera ready; photographs were taken and the group departed. But a few days later we received a letter from another organization with a very similar name—the Japan Council Against Atomic and Hydrogen Bombs, or Gensuikyo. It wished the right to translate our film into Japanese, without editing change. Again we wrote to Professor Sakamoto of the University of Tokyo for enlightenment. Again he responded promptly.

The movement against atomic bombs has been split into two groups since early in the 1960s, the immediate cause being the difference in attitude toward the nuclear tests carried on by the Soviet Union. The Japan Congress Against A and H bombs, which politically is close to the Social Democrats, is against all nuclear tests, regardless of nation. The Council Against Atomic and Hydrogen Bombs, the other body, is close to the Communist Party, and is opposed to nuclear tests by the United States, but considers tests by the Socialist countries undesirable but necessary. . . . The

Council is a somewhat larger organization than the other. Many efforts have been made in the past to merge the two bodies but none have been successful to date.[11]

In the following weeks we were bombarded by both Congress and Council with cabled requests about prints, translation rights, and 8 mm rights. To our relief the issue was resolved, or apparently resolved, by another news item from Professor Sakamoto. He reported the revelation that in 1945 a Nippon Eiga Sha technician, fearing that the American military would seize and remove the footage, had secreted a duplicate set in a laboratory ceiling. He had now made this known.[12] From then on we referred Japanese inquirers to this "newly available" resource. Apparently the Defense Department's suspicion, expressed in the letter from the Pentagon historian, had had some validity.

On August 3, 1970, *Hiroshima-Nagasaki, August 1945* had its American television premiere over National Educational Television, giving the system one of its largest audiences to date. "Hiroshima Film Gets Numbers," *Variety* (August 5, 1970) reported. NBC's *Today* program and CBS *Evening News With Walter Cronkite* had decided, at the last moment, to carry news items about the event, using short clips and crediting NET and Columbia University. NET's Tampa Bay outlet did a delayed telecast via tape, after deleting some of the "human-effects footage." So far as we could learn, all other stations carried the full film. The telecast won favorable reviews across the nation, acclaiming NET's decision to show it.

To my disappointment, NET coupled the film with a panel discussion on the subject, "Should we have dropped the bomb?" It was an issue I had resolutely kept out of the film, even though most members of our group wanted the film to condemn Truman's actions. I did not myself see how President Truman, in the situation existing at that time, could have refused a go-ahead. But this seemed to me irrelevant to our film, a bygone issue, already endlessly discussed. To center on it now seemed to me an escape into the past. To me the Hiroshima-Nagasaki footage was meaningful for today and tomorrow, rather than for yesterday.

During the research for my books on the history of American broadcasting, especially *The Image Empire,* I became chillingly aware of how often in recent years men in high position have urged use of atomic weapons. French Foreign Minister Georges Bidault has said that Secretary of State John Foster Dulles, during the Dien Bien Phu crisis, twice offered him atom bombs to use against the beleaguering Vietnamese forces, but he demurred.[13] Oral histories on file at the Dulles Collection in Princeton make clear that Dulles made the offer on advice received from the Joint Chiefs of Staff. Apparently Bidault's refusal (not President Eisenhower's as some writers have assumed) averted another holocaust. During the Quemoy-Matsu confrontation, use of an atom bomb was again discussed.[14] In 1964 Barry Goldwater felt that use of a "low-yield atomic device" to defoliate Vietnamese forests should be considered.[15] (He later emphasized that he had not actually recommended it.) More recently there has been widespread discussion of proposed world strategies based on *tactical* nuclear weapons—a term meant to suggest a modest sort of holocaust, but actually designating bombs equivalent in destructive power to the Hiroshima bomb. A more advanced bomb now equals 2,500 Hiroshima bombs, as our film makes clear. Victory with such weapons would apparently win an uninhabitable world.

Such proposals can only be made by people who have not fully realized what an atomic war can be. When I first saw the Hiroshima-Nagasaki footage, I became aware how little I had comprehended it. Yet this footage gives only the faintest glimpse of future possibilities.

Why, and by what right, was the footage declared SECRET? It contains no military information, the supposed basis for such a classification. Then why the suppression? Why the misuse of the classification device? The reason most probably was the fear that wide showing of such a film might make Congress less ready to appropriate billions of dollars for ever more destructive weapons.

I produced the short film *Hiroshima-Nagasaki, August 1945* with the hope that it would be seen by as many people as possible on all sides of every iron curtain. If a film can have the slightest deterrent effect, it may be needed now more than ever. Fortunately, it is achieving a widening distribution.

Although I did not accept the invitation to the 1970 Hiroshima observances, I have visited Japan twice since then, had long talks with Akira Iwasaki, met one of the cameramen in his 1945 unit, and visited the generously helpful Professor Sakamoto. I continued to correspond with Iwasaki until his death on September 16, 1981.

Notes

1. *Hiroshima-Nagasaki, August 1945* is now widely available. Primary distributor is the Museum of Modern Art, 11 West 53, New York, 10019, which offers prints for life-of-the-print lease or per-day rental. Per-day rentals are also offered by many film libraries—more than 1,000 prints are in circulation. The film's history was discussed by the author in a public lecture in Philadelphia, February 11, 1980, at the Walnut Street Theater; the present report is based on that lecture.

2. Interviews with Akira Iwasaki, Fumio Kamei, Ryuchi Kano, in Tokyo, February 1972; Iwasaki (1978).

3. Letter, Iwasaki to Barbara Van Dyke, March 15, 1970, Hiroshima-Nagasaki file, Barnouw Papers. All letters, memoranda, and press excerpts quoted in the present report are available in a file of some 300 items deposited with the Barnouw Papers in Special Collections, Columbia University Library. Photocopies of the entire file have also been deposited at the Museum of Modern Art, primary distributor of the film, at the Motion Picture, Broadcasting and Recorded Sound Division of the Library of Congress, Washington, DC, and Imperial War Museum, London. The file will be referred to hereafter as "HN file."

4. Letter March 8, 1968, HN file.

5. Letter March 19, 1968, HN file.

6. The lists were on large file cards, cross-referenced for such topics as "Atomic: physical aspect," "Shadow effects," "Shrine," "Debris," "Civilians: Jap." Copies of 53 such cards are in the HN file.

7. The 2 hours, 40 minutes, of *Effects of the Atomic Bomb* held in the National Archives were in the form of 35 mm acetate preservation material made from the original, which was on unstable nitrate and no longer existed. We worked from 16 mm material made from the National Archives holdings.

8. Letter, R. A. Winnacker to author, June 27, 1968. The word *acetate,* used in error, should have been *nitrate,* HN file.

9. Donald Richie, coauthor with Joseph L. Anderson of the 1959 *The Japanese Cinema* and longtime film critic in Tokyo, with occasional service as visiting film curator at the Museum of Modern Art, New York.

10. For genesis of the policy, see Barnouw (1975, pp. 269-270).

11. Letter, Professor Yoshikazu Sakamoto to author, May 4, 1970, HN file.

12. Letter, Sakamoto to author, June 8, 1970, HN file.

13. The Bidault statement is in Drummond and Coblentz (1960, pp. 121-122). Bidault repeated the statement in the Peter Davis documentary film *Hearts and Minds.*

14. Statements by Nathan Twining and George V. Allen in Dulles Oral History Collection, Princeton University, re Dien Bein Phu and Quemoy-Matsu deliberations.

15. The Goldwater statement was in a 1964 ABC-TV interview with Howard K. Smith and became a major focus of the 1964 presidential campaign won by Lyndon B. Johnson.

References

Barnouw, E. (1975). *Tube of plenty.* New York: Oxford University Press.

Drummond, R., & Coblentz, G. (1960). *Duel at the brink: John Foster Dulles' command of American power.* Garden City, NY: Doubleday.

Iwasaki, A. (1970, April 3). It all started with a letter. *Asahi-Graph.*

Iwasaki, A. (1978, July-September). The occupied screen. *Japan Quarterly, 25,* 3.

Leyda, J. (1964). *Films beget films.* New York.

The way in which a war is remembered by a nation through the cultural apparatuses that construct its history is directly related to how that nation further propagates war.

7

The Television Image and Collective Amnesia: Dis(re)membering the Persian Gulf War

MARITA STURKEN

"CNN is live and alive as our humanity is about to die."

An unnamed Turkish writer
(Aksoy & Robins, 1992)

In the codes by which collective remembrance is constructed in American culture, wars are, if nothing else, remembered. The history of national and local memorials in the United States, for instance, is for the most part a history of war memorials. Wars represent moments when citizens are asked to sacrifice for the abstract cause of the nation, and their memorialization in both popular culture and memorials is a reaffirmation of the reasons for that sacrifice and a justification for the loss exacted. Increasingly, wars are memorialized through images and historicized instantly through television.

Because the remembrance of wars is critical to national memory, those wars that have been difficult to memorialize have stood out as ruptures in nationalist narratives. The Vietnam War, for instance, has been memorialized as the war with the difficult memory, whereas the Korean War has simply been forgotten. The specter of World War II, with its insistent and ongoing memorialization in American popular culture, looms over these subsequent wars. The Vietnam War has been the war that popular culture needed to rewrite and restage in order to remember, yet, as the Vietnam Veterans Memorial has demonstrated, it is also a war for which memories continue to erupt and to disrupt simple narratives. The Persian Gulf War is, on the other hand, a war for which Americans have a collective amnesia, a war defined, in a sense, by its television images.

The way in which a war is remembered by a nation through the cultural apparatuses that construct its history is directly related to how that nation further propagates war. Hence the rewriting of the Vietnam War in American popular culture had a direct effect on the manufactured "need" for U.S. involvement in the Persian Gulf War. Attempts to give the Persian Gulf War a simple and neat narrative reinscribing master narratives of World War II—in which, for example, the United States liberates a desperate and weak country imperiled by a dangerous tyrant[1]—are attempts to chart the lineage of war directly from 1945 to 1991 to establish the Vietnam War (and its shadow, the Korean War) as aberrations. The Persian Gulf War will not need to be rescripted in cinematic spectacle, because it was already an event manufactured for the screen and a global audience, complete with a premier date (January 15, 1991) and a cast of familiar characters (the evil, dark tyrant, the fearless newsman, the patriotic weaponry). The history of the Persian Gulf War was written before it began; it was, indeed, a spectacular orchestration of a new ending for the Vietnam War.

Yet, it is almost a cliché at this point to refer to the collective amnesia that has taken place around the Persian Gulf War. This is an amnesia fueled by the war's lack of outcome (Hussein's insistent existence), the rescripting in public discourse of the war as a mere example of a president not tending to domestic issues (hence Bush's loss, reflecting the public's forgetting of his "victory"), and, I would argue, because of the very experience of war via television images that constituted the war's representation. The Gulf War is so forgotten in public discourse that it needed to be restaged rather than remembered on its second-year anniversary, as President Bush bombed Iraq yet again, producing exactly the same generic images of missiles in the night sky.

The merging of war, image/spectacle, and reenactment is a critical aspect of the Persian Gulf War. The camera image has a long history in both the propagation of wars and their documentation and memorialization. Since World War I, camera technology has been integral to the battlefield, with image surveillance of the enemy an essential strategic device. As Paul Virilio (1989) has written:

> Thus, alongside the 'war machine,' there has always existed an ocular (and later optical and electro-optical) 'watching machine' capable of providing soldiers, and particularly commanders, with a visual perspective on the military action under way. From the original watch-tower, through the anchored balloon to the reconnaissance aircraft and remote-sensing satellites, one and the same function has been indefinitely repeated, the eye's function being the function of a weapon. (p. 3)

These two roles of the camera—as a device for constructing cultural memory and history and as a device for waging warfare—were inseparable in the production of images of the Persian Gulf War.

The Television Image:
The Immediate and the Virtual

Phenomenologically, the Persian Gulf War was the first television war of the United States. While the Vietnam War is called the first "living room war," images of the Vietnam War were almost exclusively shot on film and hence subject to the delays the film-developing process requires. There was always at least a 24-hour delay for images of the Vietnam War to reach the United States. The Persian Gulf War, on the other hand, took place in the era of satellite technology and highly portable video technology. It was technologically possible for the world to watch the Persian Gulf War live as it happened, which is precisely why military censorship was instituted in such a stringent fashion to make sure that it was not watched live. Still, notions of the "immediate" and the "live" reigned. Reporters in the Persian Gulf have noted that many of their stories were never aired when they were delayed for a day or two by military censors. Hence any information that was not "immediate" was considered too out of date to have relevance. The illusion of live coverage given by the 24-hour coverage of Cable News Network (CNN) thus worked in consort with military censorship to mark coverage as useless unless it was instantaneous. One of the ironies of the imagery generated by the Persian Gulf War is that, while the war could have been copiously and immediately documented, it was, in fact, depicted in sterile coverage that yielded very few images. Most of what we saw were maps, with still photographs of reporters, and images of reporters in Israel. The round-the-clock television coverage of the war on CNN only offered the illusion that it was a heavily televised war. The few images that were produced did not, in a sense, accumulate but rushed past as they were repeated again and again. Ernest Larsen (1991) writes:

> This was the first war in history that everyone could turn off at night in order to sleep . . . and then switch on again in the morning to know if the world had yet fallen to pieces. The knowledge that such television produces tends not to accumulate, in part because each new moment literally cancels,

without a trace, what we have just seen. This experience of non-accumulation that TV affords us is of course the negation of the otherwise universal process occurring around us everyday, the otherwise inescapable process of capital accumulation. (p. 8)

That the Persian Gulf War was fought in the era of satellite technology affected not only the images that were disseminated (or not) in the media and the surveillance and weapons technology of the war, but the site of the war itself. In the world of electronic and satellite communication, the actual site of the war can become unclear. As McKenzie Wark (1991) writes:

Did the Gulf War take place in Kuwait, Baghdad or Washington? Was the site the Middle East or the whole globe? This is a particularly vexing point. If Iraqi commanders order a SCUD missile launch via radio-telephone from Baghdad, the signal may be intercepted by orbiting US satellites. Another satellite detects the launch using infra-red sensors. Information from both will be relayed to the Pentagon, then again to US command HQ in Saudi Arabia and to Patriot missile bases in Saudi Arabia and Israel. (pp. 6-7)

Wark describes the common notion of the Gulf War as a site of virtual space, one in which the expanded "theater" of the war takes place in electronic space. This notion contributes to the illusion that only those watching CNN really knew what was "really" happening in the war. Scott Simon of National Public Radio has said:

People around the world often had the sensation of being wired into that war. During the first week, the telephone rang in our workroom in Dhahran. "Get down to the bomb shelter," said an editor on the foreign desk who was watching television. "They've just launched a SCUD at you." And a minute later in eastern Saudi Arabia, the air raid sirens sounded. Weeks later, I stood in line with some soldiers waiting to make phone calls back to the United States. "Calling home before the ground war begins?" I asked. And a paratrooper answered, "Calling to find out what's happening in this war. My folks can really see it." . . . Sometimes I have to remind myself that when I say, "I was there—I saw that," I saw that only on television, just like the people watching the war in Kansas or Kenosha. (January 18, 1992)[2]

Yet, it is too simple for us to allow the Gulf War to be historicized as the war that was a computer game, one that reaffirmed our postmodern existence in virtual space. The Gulf War did take place among human bodies and communities. Our ability to render it in retrospect as a high-tech war screens out the level at which it was a conventional war in which the body of the Other was obliterated and made invisible. Implicit in many of these statements is the notion that the "real" war is one that is visually recorded, that is taking place before the camera. When "I was there" connotes watching something on the video screen, the situation of the subject becomes highly problematic.

Image Icons and Spectator Pleasures

In the context of military and media censorship coupled with notions of virtual participation, the few images of the war that did filter through took on tremendous significance in defining its narratives. The two images that have emerged as most iconic of the Persian Gulf War—the night sky of bombs over Baghdad and the point-of-view approach of the "smart" bomb to its target—contrast sharply with the iconic images of the Vietnam War. The fiery night sky over Baghdad is an image of both spectacle and the "unseen." Shot by an ABC cameraman with a special "night sight" heat-sensor lens, it is a surreal, other-worldly image that easily evokes the facile images of missiles chasing targets in video games. The "beauty" of war is shown here at its most extreme, formally and aesthetically riveting. One pilot said, "I could see the outline of Baghdad lit up like a giant Christmas tree. The entire city was just sparkling" (quoted in Friedrich & the editors of *Time,* 1991, pp. 37-38). The Vietnam War never produced images of war as spectacle like this one, perhaps because the nighttime spectacle is, in its sanitized nondepiction of the bombs' destruction in the darkness, the most fantastical and only recently recordable.[3]

This image of the night sky over Baghdad was initially mythologized in the media as the images of Patriot missiles shooting down SCUD missiles headed for Israel and Saudi Arabia. However, since the Gulf War, it has been revealed that what looked like Patriot missiles shooting down SCUDS was in fact the SCUDS coming apart at the end of their flight and falling into pieces onto the Patriots.[4] Yet, none of these qualifying explanations will have any effect on changing the meaning of this image as it has achieved historical status. As an image icon, it signifies the myth of the war as a clean technowar.

The other image icons of the Persian Gulf War also emphasized the predominating narrative of the war as a battle of technology: the electronic "missile-cam" images taken from aircraft and bombs. These are images of targeted buildings seen through crosshairs and then exploding, and point-of-view images of a bomb's approach to a site, flashing off the instant before impact. They carry power not only as the first popular images of their kind but also as images that allow the viewer a voyeuristic and vicarious experience. Watching these images, the viewer can imagine being in the bomber, imagine being the bomb itself, blasting forward and exploding in an orgasmic finale, the spectator and the weapon merged. It is in these images that the technology of the media and war merge to the point where they are inseparable. It can be said, however, that these technologies have always been inseparable, because the research on television technology has always been derived from military research. As McKenzie Wark (1991) notes, the military are specialists in the development of communication vectors. Indeed, most of the technologies now accessible to television, including the portable satellite news-gatherers (SNG), are the civilian progeny of equipment developed for military applications.

These missile-cam images are "secret" images, shown to us in the closed camaraderie of the military briefing room, usually seen on a smaller screen with a military spokesman using a pointer to brief us, the American public, on the interpretive codes to understand "our" weaponry.[5] The implied shared secrecy of these images is also the result of their visual coding as images of surveillance. Framed with the crosshairs of a weapon's lens, these images of bombs exploding on their "targets" thus afforded the viewer the feeling of a special kind of sight, a privileged view. They are, paradoxically, both panoptic images of surveillance and expansive images of spectacle.

These images did not originate with the Persian Gulf War in 1991; as images of surveillance, they are part of a long history of war images. Even in World War I, aerial photographs played an important role in trench warfare. What distinguishes the Persian Gulf War images from previous surveillance images is not only their technological proficiency but, most important, that they became the primary public images of the war. The well-orchestrated public relations campaign and censorship of the war presented these images as a means to screen out other, untaken (and unshown) images.[6] These surveillance missile-cam images play a central role in the cultural memory of the war. Hence the American viewing public, and, by extension, the rest of the world watching CNN, were given the illusion not only that they were welcomed into the military briefing room but also that they were situated as spectators within the frame of reference of the bomb. The camera's point of view was the bomb's point of view was our point of view. We became the bomb's vector. Ironically, this did not seem to implicate us as viewers. Rather, the bombs took on agency, absolving us as distanced spectators.

The war in the Persian Gulf did, indeed, signal a new kind of television spectator. Despite the popular notion that television makes us passive and isolated spectators, there is a sense of shared audience with television, one that was heightened during the Gulf War with the sense of the global reach of CNN's "live" coverage—the whole world watching, along with George Bush and Saddam Hussein, the same channel. The pleasures of television spectatorship during the Gulf War were derived not only from this sense of global technocommunity (with the United States and the Soviet Union joined on the same side in this post-cold-war war) but also through the highly structured identification process set up between spectator and weapon. Television's voyeuristic qualities were here brought to an extreme—not only were we seeing without being seen, we were seeing the act itself, the moment of impact. Robert Stam (1992) writes:

> During the Gulf War, television spectatorship became deeply imbricated with personal and national narcissism. . . . Quite apart from any specific voyeuristic content in the news itself, our situation as protected witnesses itself has voyeuristic overtones, triggering a fictitious sense of superiority. In an atomized and hierarchical society where individuals are prodded to dreams of differential status and success, the recital of others' misfortunes inevitably elicits an ambivalent reaction—mingling sincere empathy with mildly sadistic condescension. . . . This diversionary-sadistic effect was brought to its paroxysm by the Gulf War, as Americans were distracted from the humdrum realities of a declining economy, from the collapsing bank system, from racial tension and discrimination, by the dubious pleasures of a spectacular war. (p. 106)

The pleasures of spectatorship of the Gulf War for Americans were thus integral to this tension of immediacy, sadism, and a slight tinge of complicity. We saw, we were "there," yet the technology kept us (and the cameras that extended our sight) at a safe distance.

Metaphors of sight were prevalent during the Gulf War; struggles over who had access to and control over the power to see dominated the Gulf War. At press briefings, General Schwartzkopf talked initially of blinding Saddam Hussein—"We took out his eyes"—by destroying his air force, and American weaponry was consistently referred to as having vision. For instance, the "thermal night sight" employed by American tanks was described as allowing tanks to fight at night or in bad weather when "Iraqi tanks were virtually blind." Thus the notion of "smart" weapons meant weapons that could "see." This emphasis on sight was equaled by a concern with concealment through the use of stealth bombers and other stealth technology.

This preoccupation with establishing the ability of American technology to see can be directly traced to the representations of American technology in the Vietnam War. The "impenetrable" jungle foliage of Vietnam has been consistently blamed for the inability of American military technology to win the war (hence the campaign of massive defoliation by Agent Orange perpetrated by the United States in Vietnam). Not coincidentally, the desert terrain of the Middle East provided the ideal terrain for the American military to see its own technology at work. These "smart" weapons (only 70% of which, we were told after the war, hit their targets) were awarded intelligence, sight, and even memory—they were said to "hold the characteristics of enemy vehicles in their memory."[7]

Dis-re-membering Bodies

The contrast between these Persian Gulf War images and the iconic images of the Vietnam War—the young girl, Kim Phuc, fleeing naked from napalm, the point-blank killing of a Viet Cong suspect by General Loan, the victims of the My Lai massacre—are obvious. The image icons of the Persian Gulf War are of weapons and targets, not of human beings. Military censorship kept reporters and their cameras where they often only had access to bombers taking off and to distant images of weapons in the sky. Images of the dead, of incinerated bodies on the road to Basra, the scene of the "turkey shoot" by U.S. planes on retreating Iraqis, were shown only selectively by the U.S. media. At that point, they clearly did not fit into the script, a script that was crafted to have the weaponry be the subjects of the war and to cast the bodies of American, Allied, Kuwaiti, and Iraqi soldiers and civilians as extras in the background.

The "bloodless" coverage of the war erased the effects of this weaponry on the sentient bodies of civilians. The iconic images of the Vietnam War gained their power as images of the graphic damage of war to the human body—the torn flesh of Kim Phuc, the piles of dead at My Lai, the graphic images of wounded American soldiers. While the

Vietnam War images show the terror at the moment of death, the images of the Gulf War depicted the moment before the bomb's impact. Body counts (a central focus of government and media reports of the Vietnam War) were replaced by weapon counts. This was clearly a strategy devised in reaction to the bodies of the Vietnam War, the bodies of the war dead listed relentlessly on the walls of the Vietnam Veterans Memorial, and the problematic bodies of the Vietnam veterans, bodies that have resisted simple narratives of history.

In the Gulf War, bodies and weapons were reified in the media. Dead civilians were referred to as "collateral damage" and Iraqi soldiers as "targets," while weapons were given the human characteristics of sight and memory. The media thus acquired without irony the technospeak of the military. The only time an image of the destruction caused by American bombs was shown was when an Iraqi bomb shelter was destroyed, killing several hundred people. This image was shown all over the world, but only in very limited and sanitized form in the United States amidst assertions that it had been faked or that Hussein had placed innocent civilians at a strategic military site. This absence erased from the screen and the American psyche the specter of the war victims' bodies, coded already as the dark bodies of the Other. Even the graphic images of the "highway of death" concentrated on the mangled and burned corpses of cars and trucks rather than the dead who had been killed inside. The desert landscape of the Persian Gulf also contributed to this absence of bodies; the desert is mythologized in American culture as an uninhabited site. The image of the desert landscape as both postapocalyptic (already inscribed as a site of war) and unpeopled is reinforced by the fact that most of the desert in the United States is occupied by the military and the Nevada desert is the site of nuclear tests. Hence, not only is the desert the perfect site for testing weapons, it is also a place where bodies are perceived to be absent.

The only bodies that emerged as central in the coverage of the war were the bodies of reporters and the single, sanitized body of the American military. The vast majority of the footage from the Gulf War showed reporters standing before the camera on the outskirts of the war. A significant amount of airtime chatter concerned the safety of reporters who were evacuated by force from Baghdad so that they couldn't witness the war, and who were photographed wearing gas masks in Tel Aviv. These reporters were the surrogate bodies under peril, standing in for the American soldiers and Iraqi people whose moments of danger went unrecorded.

Unlike the fragmented body of the American military during guerrilla war in Vietnam, the body of the military in the Persian Gulf War was perceived as a whole, moving forward in a single mass. Elaine Scarry (1985) writes that the convention of imaging an army as a singular body "assists the disappearance of the human body from accounts of the very event that is the most radically embodying event in which human beings ever participate" (p. 71).[8] Thus the depiction of the American forces as a singular mass also allowed for an effacement of the actual sentient bodies of men and women at risk. In addition, the bodies of Iraqi soldiers were subsumed into a single unit and obliterated from view by American officials' consistent use of Saddam Hussein as their surrogate. These officials talked of "bombing Saddam," which, Hugh Gusterson (1991) notes, "submerged individual Iraqi soldiers into the single unloved figure of Saddam Hussein" (p. 51).

The bodies that are rendered invisible in this war discourse are clearly the bodies marked by race and gender on whose flesh this war was inscribed. The Arab body, marked as Other, was subsumed into the Orientalist portrayals of Saddam Hussein as the quintessential terrorist, Iraqi forces as fanatic followers, and the Middle East as a place of dark chaos. In addition, the presence of many women among U.S. forces did not offset a reinscription of the masculinity of American male soldier, one that is historicized as "lost" in the Vietnam War. American masculinity was reinscribed in the Gulf War through the hypermasculinity of the weaponry, standing in for the American soldier and also for a president (fighting his image as a "wimp").[9] This body, the racially marked and gendered body, could not be rendered visible in the spectacular images of the Gulf War. Spectacle masks the presence of bodies and flesh, and the pleasures of viewing spectacle necessitate the absence of its consequences. The bodies of the Gulf War needed to be dis-remembered for the narrative of technological prowess to be told.

The Image Becomes History

What emerged from the sterile and highly orchestrated images of the Gulf War was a discourse of heroes, in particular weapons as heroes, one that had been conspicuously lacking in the aftermath of the Vietnam War. In media depictions, these were men and women who arrived home untraumatized and pristine, their bodies intact. They were greeted by huge welcome home parades, including the largest (and most expensive) ticker tape parade (with fake ticker tape in the era of computers) in the history of New York City. Clearly, these were not parades about celebrating the end of a 6-week war but were celebrations meant to wipe out the legacy of Vietnam—the stain of defeat and the loss in Vietnam of America's image as a technologically superior world power. The message was baldly put, as a gleeful President Bush declared, "The Vietnam Syndrome is over!" Wasn't all this boyish excitement a backlash against the intense expression of sorrow displayed at the Vietnam Veterans Memorial, an attempt to change the message—war is not about loss and pain, it is about smart weapons and fiery night spectacles; it is not about dead Americans.

Yet, the forgetting of the Gulf War cannot be reduced to its role in rescripting the Vietnam War. Its dis-remembering is both a function of its quick, sound-bite effect, its apparent lack of long-lasting outcome, the minimal number of American casualties, and the narcissism of American national discourse. I would also argue that the collective amnesia of the Gulf War, a kind of strategic forgetting, is also directly connected to the kinds of images it produced.

As electronic images, the images of the Gulf War carry with them the problematic relationship of television to history. In its connotation of immediacy and instant information, the television image evokes the present rather than the past. However, since the early 1980s, many images of "history" have been created on television screens. Ironically, the image icons of the Gulf War are not moving images but stills of television images. The still thus retains a capacity for iconic status, unlike the moving image, in its ability to connote completeness and time captured. Hence, because of channels of distribution for still images and their phenomenological capacity to evoke the past, they take on an iconic status that moving images rarely attain.

The images of the Gulf War are not forgettable because of their phenomenology as television images. They are forgettable in their empty spectacle. These images left no indelible impression precisely because of the way that the phenomenology of these television images intersected with the politics of military and media censorship to create cold, high-tech images that produce no emotions, pain, guilt, or empathy. In comparison to the iconic images of the Vietnam War, images that implicate the viewer and expose the human suffering and brutality of war, these images do not ask the spectator to feel complicity.

The Gulf War would appear then to have a very monolithic historical narrative that exists in the absence of any production of cultural memory to counter that singular history. Yet, I do not think that we can dismiss the degree to which the American public felt it was participating in producing memories of the Gulf War. While the rituals of burying the dead, or even photographing the arrival of casualties in the United States, were carried out with extreme secrecy by the military, for fear of evoking images of Vietnam, many Americans participated in rituals of remembering those at war.[10]

The most obvious among these was, of course, the yellow ribbon. A symbol taken from an old Tony Orlando song, "Tie a Yellow Ribbon 'Round the Old Oak Tree," about an ex-convict returning home from prison, the yellow ribbon first became widely popular during the Iran hostage crisis of 1979, when the families and home towns of the hostages decorated their homes with yellow ribbons to signal their hopes for the hostages' safe release. Since then, the ribbons have cropped up in other situations, including the disappearance of children in Atlanta in the early 1980s. However, with the Gulf War, the yellow ribbons suddenly became a national symbol, not simply signaling an individual far away but the commercialized yellow-ribboning of a nation to display its patriotism. Of course, the occasional personalized yellow ribbon was offered solely as a talisman for the safe passage of someone at war, but these were lost in the proliferation of mass-produced yellow ribbons amidst spectacles such as the jingoistic Super Bowl halftime ceremony in January 1991. The yellow ribbon as a personal activity thus became subsumed into a renewal of faith in what Benedict Anderson has called the "imagined community" of the nation, a means by which consent was created. The yellow ribbon as a reminder of an individual at risk became instead a symbol of a nation's renewal of confidence in itself and its role as a world power.

The yellow ribbons were, of course, delivered to us endlessly via television. In fact, for the imagined community of the nation, it is impossible to separate the "real" war in the Persian Gulf from the television war we experienced. Once shown on television, these yellow ribbons were co-opted by the nationalist narratives created in the television theater of the war. On television, this war had a monolithic meaning, an unchallenged narrative, so simple and so easily forgotten. The challenge, then, is to look beyond this characterization, to see what the illusion of real-time coverage and the iconic images of the Gulf War screen out, to see beyond the image of the Gulf War as war in which television gave us the capacity to see the "real" event. We are complicit in television's spectacle and the pleasures of its spectatorship and, if the Persian Gulf War is forgotten, we the spectators are the ones who are allowing it to be erased without memory.

Notes

1. For an in-depth discussion of the central metaphors of the Gulf War, see Lakoff (1991).

2. © Copyright National Public Radio ® 1992. The news report by NPR's Scott Simon was originally broadcast on National Public Radio's "Weekend Edition/Saturday" on January 18, 1992, and is used with the permission of National Public Radio. Any unauthorized duplication is strictly prohibited.

3. The image of the Baghdad night has commonly been referred to as a kind of Fourth of July spectacle. Indeed, at the Fourth of July celebration in New York in 1991, only a month after the huge welcome home parade for veterans of the Persian Gulf War, fireworks displays in the East River reenacted this image of bombs exploding over Baghdad, the metaphor complete.

4. Journalist Philip Knightly told Simon that "what we were seeing was actually the SCUD missile breaking up of its own volition or under the control of the Iraqi controllers because they realized that if they split the SCUD before the Patriot was able to hone in on it, the Patriot would become confused over which part of the SCUD it should attack. So although it looked like marvelous pyrotechnics in the sky over both Israel and Saudi Arabia, what we were seeing was not what we were told we were seeing" (from National Public Radio, January 18, 1992, © Copyright National Public Radio ® 1992. See note 2.).

5. In her essay, "From Secrets of Life to Secrets of Death," Evelyn Fox Keller (1990) discusses how "life has traditionally been seen as the secret of women, a secret from men" (p. 178). Keller suggests that the secrets of men can be seen most clearly in the well-guarded secrets of nuclear war technology—the secrets of men as the secrets of death. The military briefing room for the press during the Gulf War was the site, despite the presence of several woman reporters, of a male collectivity that was deliberately constructed by the military as secretive and exclusive. The good-humored inside jokes and comradeship of word jockeying in these press conferences made clear the clubby relationship between the press and the military, and the illusion of camaraderie masked the fact that many questions went unasked and unanswered.

6. The censorship of the war worked to prevent images from being taken and to exclude those images that violated the narrative being constructed by the government. For instance, well-known documentary videomaker Jon Alpert, who had been producing segments on Central America and other subjects for NBC's *Today Show* for 15 years, produced a piece in Iraq with Ramsey Clark about the deaths of civilians and damage caused by U.S. bombing. Not only did NBC refuse to run the footage (it was shown on WNET, the New York public television station, where it was framed by hostile commentary, and, ironically, on MTV), but Alpert lost his job as a stringer for NBC as a

consequence. NBC is owned by General Electric, which is one of the largest defense contractors in the country. See Schechter (1992, p. 28).

7. Since the war, it has been revealed that the "smart" weapons were in fact a very small percentage of the bombs dropped on Iraq, about 8.8% (see Schechter, 1992, p. 31). According to Scott Simon, "More than ninety percent of the bombs dropped onto Iraq were huge, blunt, lumbering percussion bombs, fuel air bombs, which burn the air in a man's lungs; or Bouncing Betties, those diabolical basketball-shaped bombs that bounce up to explode at a height that will shatter an average man's spine" (National Public Radio, January 18, 1992, © Copyright National Public Radio ® 1992. See note 2.).

8. The illusion of a single mass did not offer any reduction in the confusion about who the enemy was that characterized the Vietnam War. Of the 148 casualties from the Gulf War, 35 were officially attributed to "friendly fire" or what the military calls "fratricide." Many people die from friendly fire in all wars. However, despite the low number of casualties, the figure for the Gulf War is a relatively high percentage.

9. The media preoccupation with the presence of significant numbers of American women serving in the Gulf points to the way in which sexual equality emerged as a redeeming narrative of the war. In media coverage, the women serving in the Gulf were almost exclusively portrayed as mothers and pictured with photographs of their children. This phenomenon worked to negate their role as soldiers, revealing a deep ambivalence about their participation in the war machine; if they were mothers, they were not threatening to the gendered military status quo. As Cynthia Enloe (1983) has written, women have always participated in warfare, yet the front has always been defined as the place where women are not.

10. At Dover Air Force base, where the dead arrived, the military prohibited any photographs or admittance of the press. This marked a significant change of policy. Dover Air Force base has meaning as a site of national mourning. The crew of the *Challenger,* the Marines who died in Lebanon, and the dead from U.S. incursions into Panama and Grenada were all ritually mourned at Dover. This restriction with the Gulf War was an obvious attempt to negate the presence of American dead and also to avoid the historical connotations of the rituals of mourning the dead from the Vietnam War.

References

Aksoy, A., & Robins, K. (1992). Exterminating angels: Morality, violence, and technology in the Gulf War. In H. Mowlana, G. Gerbner, & H. Schiller (Eds.), *Triumph of the image: The media's war in the Persian Gulf—A global perspective* (pp. 322-336). Boulder, CO: Westview.

Enloe, C. (1983). *Does khaki become you? The militarization of women's lives.* Boston: Pandora.

Friedrich, O., & the editors of *Time.* (Eds.). (1991). *Desert Storm: The war in the Persian Gulf.* Boston: Little, Brown.

Gusterson, H. (1991). Nuclear war, the Gulf War, and the disappearing body. *Journal of Urban and Cultural Studies, 2*(1), 45-56.

Keller, E. F. (1990). From secrets of life to secrets of death. In M. Jacobus, E. F. Keller, & S. Shuttleworth (Eds.), *Body/politics* (pp. 177-191). New York: Routledge.

Lakoff, G. (1991). Metaphor and war: The metaphor system used to justify war in the Gulf. *Journal of Urban and Cultural Studies, 2*(1), 59-72.

Larsen, E. (1991). Gulf War TV. *Jump Cut, 36,* 3-10.

Scarry, E. (1985). *The body in pain.* New York: Oxford University Press.

Schechter, D. (1992, January/February). The Gulf War and the death of the TV news. *The Independent,* pp. 28-31.

Stam, R. (1992). Mobilizing fictions: The Gulf War, the media, and the recruitment of the spectator. *Public Culture, 4*(2), 101-126.

Virilio, P. (1989). *War and cinema* (P. Camiller, Trans.). New York: Verso.

Wark, M. (1991). News bites: War TV in the Gulf. *Meanjin, 50*(1), 5-18.

Video represented a new frontier—a chance to create an alternative to what many considered the slickly civilized, commercially corrupt, and aesthetically bankrupt world of television. Video offered the dream of creating something new, of staking out a claim to a virgin territory where no one could tell you what to do or how to do it, where you could invent your own rules and build your own forms.

8

Guerrilla Television

DEIRDRE BOYLE

Video pioneers didn't use covered wagons; they built media vans for their cross-country journeys colonizing the vast wasteland of American television. It was the late 1960s, and Sony's introduction of the half-inch video Portapak in the United States was like a media version of the Land Grant Act, inspiring a heterogeneous mass of American hippies, avant-garde artists, student-intellectuals, lost souls, budding feminists, militant blacks, flower children, and jaded journalists to take to the streets if not the road, Portapak in hand, to stake out the new territory of alternative television.

In those early days everyone with a Portapak was called a "video artist." Practitioners of the new medium moved freely within the worlds of conceptual, performance, and imagist art as well as documentary. Skip Sweeney of Video Free America, once called the "King of Video Feedback," also designed video environments for avant-garde theater (*AC/DC, Kaddish*) and collaborated with Arthur Ginsberg on a fascinating multimonitor documentary portrait of the lives of a porn queen and her bisexual, drug addict husband, *The Continuing Story of Carel and Ferd*. Although some artists arrived at video having already established reputations in painting, sculpture, or music, many video pioneers came with no formal art training, attracted to the medium because it had neither history nor hierarchy nor strictures, because one was free to try anything and everything, whether it was interviewing a street bum (one of the first such tapes was made by artist Les Levine in 1965) or exploring the infinite variety of a feedback image. Gradually the practitioners divided into two camps: the video artists and the video documentarists. The reasons for this fissure were complex, involving the competition for funding and exhibition, a changing political and cultural climate, and a certain disdain for nonfiction work as less creative than "art"—an attitude also found in the worlds of film, photography, and literature. But in video's early years, guerrilla television embraced art as documentary and stressed innovation, alternative approaches, and a critical relationship to television.

Just as the invention of movable type in the fifteenth century made books portable and private, video did the same for the televised image; and just as the development of offset printing launched the alternative press movement in the 1960s, video's advent launched an alternative television movement in the 1970s. Guerrilla television was actually part of that larger alternative media tide that swept over the country during the 1960s, affecting radio, newspapers, magazines, publishing, as well as the fine and performing arts. Molded by the insights of Marshall McLuhan, Buckminster Fuller, Norbert Wiener, and Teilhard de Chardin; influenced by the style of New Journalism forged by Tom Wolfe and Hunter Thompson; and inspired by the content of the agonizing issues of the day; video guerrillas set out to "tell it like it is"—not from the lofty, "objective" viewpoint of TV cameras poised to survey an event but from within the crowd, subjective, and involved.

Video Gangs

For baby boomers who had grown up on TV, having the tools to make your own was heady stuff. Most early videomakers banded together into media groups; it was an era for collective action and communal living, where pooling equipment, energy, and ideas was more than good sense. But for kids raised on "The Mickey Mouse Club," belonging to a media gang also conferred membership in an extended family that unconsciously imitated the television models of their youth. Some admitted they were attracted by the imagined "outlaw" status of belonging to a video collective, less dangerous than being a member of the Dalton gang—or the Weather Underground—and probably more glamorous. As video collectives sprouted up all over the country, the media gave them considerable play in such magazines as *Time, Newsweek, TV Guide, New York*, and *The New Yorker,* to name a few. They celebrated the exploits of the video pioneers in mythic terms curiously reminiscent of the opening narrations of TV westerns.

Video represented a new frontier—a chance to create an alternative to what many considered the slickly civilized, commercially corrupt, and aesthetically bankrupt world of television. Video offered the dream of creating something new, of staking out a claim to a virgin territory where no one could tell you what to do or how to do it, where you could invent your own rules and build your own forms. Stated in terms that evoke the characteristic American restlessness, boldness, vision, and enterprise that pioneered the West—part adolescent arrogance and part courage and imagination—one discovers a fundamental American ethos behind this radical media movement.

Guerrilla Television Defined

The term *guerrilla television* came from the 1971 book of the same title by Michael Shamberg. The manifesto outlined a technological radicalism that claimed that commercial television, with its mass audiences, was a conditioning agent rather than a source of enlightenment. Video offered the means to "decentralize" television so that a Whitmanesque democracy of ideas, opinions, and cultural expressions—made both by and for the people—could then be "narrowcast" on cable television. Shamberg, a former *Time* correspondent, had discovered video was a medium more potent than print while reporting on the historic "TV as a Creative Medium" show at the Howard Wise Gallery in 1969. Banding together with Frank Gillette, Paul Ryan, and Ira Schneider (three of the artists in the show), among others, they formed Raindance Corporation, video's self-proclaimed think-tank equivalent to the RAND Corporation. Raindance produced several volumes of a magazine called *Radical Software,* the video underground's bible, gossip sheet, and chief networking tool during the early 1970s. It was in the pages of *Radical Software* and *Guerrilla Television* that a radical media philosophy was articulated, but it was in the documentary tapes that were first shown closed-circuit, then cablecast, and finally broadcast that guerrilla television was practiced and revised.

Virtuous Limitations

Before the federal mandate required local origination programming on cable and opened the wires to public access, the only way to see guerrilla television was in "video theaters"—lofts or galleries or a monitor off the back end of a van where videotapes were shown closed-circuit to an "in" crowd of friends, community members, or video enthusiasts. In New York, People's Video Theater, Global Village, the Videofreex, and Raindance showed tapes at their lofts. People's Video Theater was probably the most politically and socially radical of the foursome, regularly screening "street tapes" that might include the philosophic musings of an aging, black, shoe-shine man or a video intervention to avert street violence between angry blacks and whites in Harlem. These gritty, black-and-white tapes were generally edited in the camera, because editing was as yet a primitive matter of cut-and-paste or else a maddeningly imprecise back space method of cuing scenes for "crash" edits. The technological limitations of early video equipment were merely incorporated in the style, thus "real-time video"—whether criticized for being boring and inept or praised for its fidelity to the cinema vérité ethic—was in fact an aesthetic largely dictated by the equipment. Video pioneers of necessity were adept at making a virtue of their limitations. Real-time video became a conscious style praised for being honest in presenting an unreconstructed reality and opposed to conventional television "reality," with its quick, highly edited scenes and narration—whether stand-up or voice over—by a typically white, male figure of authority. When electronic editing and color video became available later, the aesthetic adapted to the changing technology, but these fundamental stylistic expectations laid down in video's primitive past lingered on through the decade. What these early works may have lacked in terms of technical polish or visual sophistication they frequently made up for in sheer energy and raw immediacy of content matter.

With cable's rise in the early 1970s came a new stage in guerrilla television's growth. The prospect of using cable to reach larger audiences and create an alternative to network TV proved a catalytic agent. Video groups sprang up across the country, from rural Appalachia to wealthy Marin County, even to cities like New Orleans, where it would be years before cable was laid. TVTV, guerrilla television's most mediagenic and controversial group, was formed during this time. Founded by *Guerrilla Television*'s Michael Shamberg, TVTV produced its first tapes for cable, then went on to public television, and, finally, to network TV. TVTV's rise and fall traces a major arc in guerrilla television's history.

Shamberg had been thinking about getting together a group of "video freaks" to go to Miami to cover the 1972 presidential nominating conventions. The name came to him one February morning while doing yoga at the McBurney Y in New York. He realized instantly that Top Value Television ("you know, like in Top Value stamps") would also read as TVTV. He and Megan Williams joined with Allen Rucker and members of Ant Farm, the Videofreex, and Raindance to form TVTV's first production crew. Shamberg got a commitment from two cable stations and raised $15,000 to do two, hour-long tapes. The first, a video scrapbook of the Democratic convention titled *The World's Largest TV Studio,* played on cable and would have been the last of TVTV were it not for an unprecedented review in the *New York Times* by TV critic John O'Connor, who pronounced it "distinctive and valuable." With that validation, Shamberg was able to raise more money and hold the cable companies to their agreement, going on to cover the Republican convention the following month. *Four More Years* was the result; it is one of TVTV's best works, demonstrating the hallmarks of their iconoclastic, intimate New Journalism style.

Unlike the Democratic convention, chaotic and diffuse, the Republicans had a clear, if uninspired scenario to reelect Richard Nixon. Instead of pointing their cameras at the podium, TVTV's crew of 19 threaded their way through delegate caucuses, Young Republican rallies, cocktail parties, antiwar demonstrations, and the frenzy of the convention floor. Capturing the hysteria of political zealots, they focused on the sharp differences between the Young Voters for Nixon and Vietnam Vets Against the War, all the while entertaining viewers with foibles of politicians, press, and camp followers alike. One Republican organizer's remark to her staff—"The balloons alone will give us the fun we need"—epitomizes the zany, real-life comedy TVTV captured on tape.

Interviewed on the quality of convention coverage are press personalities whose off-the-cuff remarks ("I'm not a big fan of advocacy reporting"—Dan Rather. "What's news? Things that happen"—Herb Kaplow. "Introspection isn't good for a journalist"—Walter Cronkite.) culminate with Roger Mudd declining to answer Skip Blumberg's futile questions.

Punctuating the carnival atmosphere are venomous verbal attacks on the antiwar vets by onlookers and delegates who charge them with being hopheads, draft dodgers, and unpatriotic—a chilling reminder of the hostility and tragic confrontations of the Vietnam era.

TVTV follows the convention chaos, editing simultaneous events into a dramatic shape that climaxes when delegates and demonstrators alike are gassed by the police. Leavened with humor, irony, and iconoclasm, *Four More Years* is a unique documentary of the Nixon years. In it TVTV demonstrated journalistic freshness, a sardonic view of our political process and the media that covers it, and a sure feel for the clichés of an American ritual.

Forging a Distinctive Style

In forging their distinctive style, TVTV shunned voice-overs; they experimented with graphics, using campaign buttons to punctuate the tape and give it a certain thematic unity; and they deployed a wide-angle lens, which distorted faces as editorial commentary. The fish-eye look, used at first out of practical necessity, because the Portapak lens often didn't let in enough light and went out of focus in many shooting situations, became a TVTV signature that led to later charges of exploitation of unsuspecting subjects. But in the beginning, it was all new and fresh and exciting. The critics pronounced that TVTV had covered the conventions better than all the networks combined, proving the alternate media could beat the networks at their own game and, as one pundit quipped, "for the money CBS spent on coffee."

Although the networks had ENG (electronic news gathering) units at the convention, the contrast was striking. Only a beefy cameraman could withstand the enormous apparatus, including scuba-style backpack to transport so-called portable television cameras. Fully equipped, they looked more like moon men. Compared with this, the lightweight, black-and-white Portapak and recorder in the hands of slim Nancy Cain of the Videofreex looked like a child's toy, which was part of the charm because no one took seriously these low-tech hippies. In video's early days, many didn't believe the tape was rolling because it didn't make the whirring sound of the TV film cameras, and much unguarded dialogue was captured because the medium was new and unfamiliar.

Television Enters the Picture

Thus established, TVTV went on to make their next "event" tape, but this one would be for the TV Lab at PBS's WNET in New York. TVTV, however, were not the first to flirt with "Television." After the Wood-stock Nation caught the networks' attention in 1969, the Videofreex were hired by CBS to produce a pilot that failed spectacularly in winning network approval. In 1970 the May Day Collective shot video-tape at week-long antiwar demonstrations in Washington for NBC News although none of it was ever broadcast. The networks did air some news-breaking Portapak tapes, such as Bill Stephens's 1971 interview with Eldridge Cleaver over the split in the Black Panther party, shown on Walter Cronkite's *Evening News.* They were willing to overlook the primitive quality of tape that had to be shot off a monitor with a studio camera if it meant scooping their competitors, but the 1960 network ban on airing independently produced news and public affairs productions remained in force, and any small-format tapes broadcast were usually excerpted and narrated by network commentators, beyond the editorial reach of their makers.

The introduction of the stand-alone time base corrector in 1973, a black box that stabilized helical scan tapes and made them broadcas-table, changed everything. It was finally possible for small-format video to become a stable television production medium, which not only paved the way for guerrilla television to reach the masses but also for the rise of ENG and, eventually, all-video television production. Given TVTV's unprecedented success with *Four More Years,* it was only logical that they produce the first half-inch video documentary for airing on national public television.

The tape was *Lord of the Universe,* and its subject was the 15-year-old guru Maharaj Ji. Millennium '73, a gathering of the guru's faded flower children followers, was scheduled for the Houston Astrodome, which the guru promised would levitate at the close (like the Yippies at the Pentagon in 1967, the guru knew how to create a media event). Elon Soltes, whose brother-in-law was a would-be believer, followed him with Portapak from Boston to Houston while other TVTV crew members gathered in Houston to tape the mahatmas and the "premies" (followers), getting embroiled in what was to be the most successful TVTV tape but also the most shattering for its makers. Fearful of mind control and violence (a prankish reporter had been brained by a guru body guard not long before) and stricken by the sight of so many of their own generation lost and foundering in the arms of this spiritual Sven-gali, TVTV was determined to expose the sham and get out unscathed. The tape was the zenith of TVTV's guerrilla TV style.

Switching back and forth between the preparation for the actual onstage "performances" of the guru, cameras focused on "blissed out" devotees seeking stability and guidance in the guru's fold. Neon light, glitter, and rock music furnished by the guru's brother (a rotund rip-off of Elvis Presley) on a Las Vegas-style stage was the unlikely backdrop for the guru's *satsang*, or preaching to his followers. Outside, angry arguments between premies and Hare Krishna followers and one bible-spouting militant fundamentalist expose the undercurrent of violence, repression, and control in any extremist religion. TVTV cleverly played off two 1960s radicals against each other. Having traded in his role of countercultural political leader for that of spokesman for an improbable religion, Rennie Davis sings the guru's praises as Abbie Hoffman, one of guerrilla TV's superstars, watches Davis on tape and comments on his former colleague's arrogance and skills as a propagandist. "It's different saying you've found God than saying you know his address and credit card number," Hoffman quips.

Much in evidence is TVTV's creative use of graphics, live music, and wide-angle lens shots. As always there is humor leavening what was for TVTV a tragic situation. At one point our Boston guide to the "gurunoids" innocently remarks, "I don't know whether it's the air conditioning, but you can really feel something." The humor is a black humor, rife with an irony that dangerously borders on mockery but is checked by an underlying compassion for the desperation of lost souls. At home in the world of spectacle and carnival, ever agile in debunking power seekers, TVTV admirably succeeded in producing a document of the times that remains a classic.

Film's Hidden Impact

Paul Goldsmith, a well-known 16 mm vérité cameraman, had joined TVTV along with Wendy Appel and was the principal cameraman on this and subsequent tapes, shooting one-inch color for the time in the Astrodome. Appel, also trained in film but an accomplished videomaker herself, would become TVTV's most versatile editor. Not surprising, some of the most critical people in creating the TVTV style came out of film: Stanton Kaye and Ira Schneider, who worked on the convention tapes, were both filmmakers, as were Goldsmith and Appel. TVTV's raw vitality was a video and cultural by-product, but its keen visual sense and editing was borrowed, in large measure, from film.

TVTV won the DuPont-Columbia Journalism Award for *Lord of the Universe* and, not long after, a lucrative contract with PBS to produce a series of documentaries for the TV Lab. *Gerald Ford's America, In Hiding: Abbie Hoffman, The Good Times Are Killing Us, Superbowl,* and *TVTV Looks at the Oscars* were made in the next 2 years. Some were equal to the TVTV name, such as "Chic to Sheik," the second of the four-part *Gerald Ford's America.* But others showed a decline as the diverse group of video freaks who had once converged to make TVTV a reality—all donating time, equipment, and talent to make a program that would show the world what guerrilla television could do—began to stray in their own directions, no longer willing to be subsumed in an egalitarian mass, no longer able to support themselves on good cheer and beer. With the broadcast of *Lord of the Universe,* some of the best minds in guerrilla television unwittingly abandoned their utopian dream of creating an alternative to network television. Their hasty marriage with cable was on the rocks when TV—albeit public television—seduced them with the fickle affection of its mass audience.

The Beginning of the End

In 1975 TVTV left San Francisco, which had been its home base during its halcyon days, for Los Angeles. This move proved pivotal. They had a contract to develop a fiction idea for the PBS series *Visions.* This was not so much a departure from TVTV's orientation as it might seem. They had been mixing fictional elements in their documentary tapes all along, the most notable being the Lily Tomlin character in the *Oscars* show. TVTV's style had been modeled on New Journalism and the flamboyant approaches of such writers as Hunter Thompson, of Gonzo Journalism fame, who wrote nonfiction like it was fiction.

Supervision consisted of a number of short tapes, "filler" to round off the *Visions* series' hour. It traced the history of television from its early days in the labs of Philo T. Farnsworth to the year 2000 and an imagined guerrilla takeover of a station not unlike CNN. Forsaking the video documentary form that they had pioneered caused some internal battles, but it wasn't until their pilot for NBC, *The TVTV Show,* that the end was in sight.

Part of the problem was that TVTV knew how to make a video documentary—in a way, they had invented it—but they didn't know about producing comedy for "Television." In documentary shooting, improvisation on location was TVTV's trademark; the primitive and evolving nature of portable video equipment and the unpredictable power centers that were TVTV's main targets demanded an adaptive and creative attitude toward all new situations, something TVTV excelled at. But shooting actors in a studio with a set script that never equaled the humor of their documentary "real people" demanded a whole new expertise that TVTV realized too late they couldn't afford to invent as they went along.

Another part of the problem was that, as long as TVTV was making documentaries, the group had its original focus. Once they began making entertainment for mass audiences, their once-radical identity and purpose were gone. For some, the evolution was a gradual and acceptable one. After charges of "checkbook journalism" over the ill-fated interview with Abbie Hoffman, who was then a fugitive, Shamberg lost some of his journalistic zeal. Harsh criticism of the treatment of Cajuns in *The Good Times Are Killing Me* further tarnished TVTV's reputation. With people like Bill Murray and Harold Ramis (who would later become celebrities on *Saturday Night Live*) eager to work with TVTV, the lure of collaborating with talented actors in an area removed from journalistic criticism, funding battles, and the pressures of producing documentaries for public TV was certainly appealing. But for others who still believed in the dream of changing television, the decision proved a hard one because it meant the dream was dead. And with it went the all-for-one spirit that knitted together their disparate egos: TVTV no longer had the fire and purpose it needed to weather the rough storm of a mid-1970s transition.

It took a few years, as TVTV paid off their debts, for their official demise. In the meantime, Shamberg, who had seen the end coming, was already preparing his next venture. He bought the rights to the Neal and Carolyn Cassady story and produced the film *Heartbeat*. It was a box office flop but convinced him to go on. In 1983, two films later, he produced the Academy Award nominee *The Big Chill*, a reunion film about a group of late 1960s hippies who meet at the funeral of one of their own and reflect on how they've changed and been affected by "the big chill."

Changing Times

The fact that TVTV changed along with their times should come as no surprise. TVTV wasn't the only group to pull apart during the late

1970s. The media revolutionaries were growing older and changing—assuming responsibilities for marriages, homes, and families—living in a different world than the one that once celebrated the brash goals and idealistic dreams of guerrilla television. The promise that cable TV would serve as a democratic alternative to corporately owned television was betrayed by federal deregulation and footloose franchise agreements. Public television's early support for experimental documentary and artistic work in video slowed to a virtual halt—the sad demise of WNET's TV Lab in recent months, its latest instance. And funding sources that had once lavished support and enthusiasm on guerrilla TV groups now turned a cold shoulder, preferring to support individuals rather than groups and work that stressed art and experimentation rather than controversy and community.

Once the possibility of reaching a mass audience opened up, the very nature of guerrilla television changed. No longer out to create an alternative to television, guerrilla TV was competing on the same airwaves for viewers and sponsors. As the technical evolution speeded up, video freaks needed access to more expensive production and postproduction equipment if they were to make "broadcastable," state-of-the-art tapes. Although some continued making television their own way, pioneering what has since become the world of low-power TV and the terrain of public access cable, many others yearned to see their work reach a wide audience. Without anyone's noticing it, the rough vitality of guerrilla TV's early days was shed for a slicker, TV look. The "voice of God" narrator, which had been anathema to TVTV and other video pioneers, was heard again. Gone were the innovations—the graphics, the funky style and subjects, the jousting at power centers and scrutiny of the media. Gone was the intimate, amiable cameraperson/interviewer, which was a hallmark of alternative video style. Increasingly, video documentaries began looking more and more like "television" documentaries, with stand-up reporters and slide-lecture approaches that skimmed over an issue and took no stance.

Where one could see the impact of guerrilla television was in its parody. Sincere documentaries about ordinary people had been absorbed and transformed into mock-u-entertainments like *Real People* and *That's Incredible!* The video vérité of the 1976 award-winning *The Police Tapes,* by Alan and Susan Raymond, had become the template for the popular TV series *Hill Street Blues.* In the 1960s, Raindance's Paul Ryan proclaimed, "VT is not TV," but, by the 1980s, VT *was* TV.

Today, in an era of creeping conservatism, the ideals of guerrilla television are more in need of champions than in its heyday when it was easier to stand up for a democratic media that would "tell it like it is" for ordinary people living in late twentieth-century America. Few have come along to take up the challenge of guerrilla television's more radical and innovative past. Although the collectives with names like rock groups—Amazing Grace, April Video, and the Underground Vegetables—have long since disappeared, many notable pioneers continue to keep alive their ideals, some working in public access cable, like DeeDee Halleck (of Paper Tiger Television), or from within the networks, like Ann Volkes (an editor at CBS News) and Greg Pratt (a documentary video producer for a network affiliate in Minneapolis), or as independent journalists like Jon Alpert (freelance correspondent for NBC's *Today Show*)[1] and Skip Blumberg (whose portraits of Double Dutch jumpers and Eskimo athletes still appear on public television). But a younger generation eager to draw from this past to forge a new documentary video future have yet to appear on the horizon. Either they are discouraged by the lack of funding and distribution outlets for innovative and/or controversial work and a cultural milieu content with the new conservatism, or they are unaware of the past and unconcerned about the future. The goal is not to re-create that past—no one really wants to see the shaky, black-and-white, out-of-focus wild shots that suited the primitive equipment and frenzy of video's Wonder Bread years—the goal is to recapture the creativity, exploration, and daring of those formative years. Perhaps the technology and the burning need to communicate and invent forms will prevail. Independents with Beta and VHS equipment have been documenting the struggles in Central America. Lost amid the home video boom, a new generation of video guerrillas may be in training yet.

McLuhan's view that "the medium is the message" was embraced then rejected by the first video guerrillas, who asserted that content *did* matter; finding a new form and a better means of distributing diverse opinions was the dilemma. That dilemma is still with us. How a new wave of video guerrillas will resolve it and carry on that legacy, human and imperfect as it may be, should prove to be interesting and unexpected. More than guerrilla television's future may depend on it.

Note

1. But see note 5 in Chapter 7 of this volume.

Reference

Shamberg, M., & Raindance Corporation. (1971). *Guerrilla television*. New York: Holt, Rinehart & Winston.

In contrast to early video pioneers, video activists today are more diverse across gender, race, class, and sexuality, and, significantly, most recognize that they cannot afford to believe in the radical potential of technology alone. Operating within the margins of the increasingly powerful media industries, video activism and alternative television practice in the 1990s realize the futility of a "video revolution" without praxis, alternative structures, and a vision for a new social (and television) system.

9

Will the Revolution Be Televised?
Camcorders, Activism, and
Alternative Television in the 1990s

LAURIE OUELLETTE

Several years ago, in an ABC-TV news special called "Revolution in a Box," anchor Ted Koppel proclaimed that "the world is in the early stages of a revolution it is just beginning to understand. . . . Television has fallen into the hands of the people." Certainly the growing affordability of video technology does have important, if not revolutionary, implications for television: Activist video, organized alternative video collectives, and low-budget community television have, thanks to the camcorder, never been stronger. Yet, typical of what Stuart Hall (1977) has theorized as the way media "classify out the world" within the discourses of the dominant ideologies, these possibilities have generally been trivialized and ignored by media news coverage of the video phenomenon. Video activist John Walden (1990) argues:

> What the mainstream media is calling "revolutionary" (that people are now more likely to have a camera handy and running when events occur in front of them and produce footage more likely to meet the broadcast standards of the networks) is generally nothing more than the same old stuff . . . wrapped up in a brand new box.

Yet the possibility that camcorders might undermine the cultural and informational monopoly of the mainstream remains unrevealed.[1]

If news coverage of the so-called video revolution has focused on issues of professionalism (what if amateur video is mistaken for true journalism?) and privacy (Big Brother is now your camcorder-equipped neighbor), entertainment television programming has been quick to capitalize on the growing interest in camcorder media with such programs as *America's Funniest Home Videos* (ABC) and *I Witness Video* (NBC). In their early, influential critique of the cultural industries, Frankfurt School theorists Max Horkheimer and Theodor Adorno (1990) argued that forms of commodity culture such as television, which distract the oppressed classes with trivial amusements and reify radical impulses through the promise of consumption, serve as regressive societal forces and barriers to political change.[2] Situating the democratic possibilities of widespread video practice into practical jokes, amateur surveillance (capturing drug busts on video, documenting a neighbor's illegal activities), highly stylized "wraparounds," and of course advertisements, entertainment programs inevitably reproduce the conventions of commercial television by emphasizing amusement over politics, dominant values over political critique. As Dee Dee Halleck (1990) has noted of *America's Funniest Home Videos*, the actual time given to homemade tapes is at most 7 minutes of each show, while the tapes chosen to play are steeped in "the same sadism, misogyny, and contempt for the American working class that permeates the rest of TV."

At the same time, these programs serve as exemplary models of what Hall defines as the contradictory mode of media under advanced capitalism. To naturalize their ideological work of defining social knowledge and shaping hegemonic consensus, the media must also reproduce to some degree cultural countertendencies and oppositional views (Hall, 1977, p. 346).[3] Thus the idea that people can create their own media rather than relying on the monopolistic cultural industries—certainly a direct challenge to the legitimacy of those industries and the ideological function they serve—is reproduced within and around programs such as *America's Funniest . . .* and *I Witness Video,* although the oppositional potential of video is ultimately repackaged according to the logic of commercial television and dominant culture. *America's Funniest,* the most successful program in this genre, is frequently cited as an example of ordinary people creating their own media ("They will never run out of tapes . . . the video revolution assures a constant product flow," explained one typical press commentator). In its first season, *I Witness Video* even went as far as to incorporate radical rhetoric into its opening sequences. Every week the host reminded viewers of the liberatory potential of the "video revolution," including the new ability of camcorder-empowered citizens to create (as opposed to merely watch) "programming that we can all watch on television."

While Horkheimer and Adorno (1990) insisted that commercial entertainment colonized the senses of oppressed groups to the extent that they "insist on the very ideology that enslaves them" (p. 134), Hall and others have argued that such control is never total.[4] People do resist the control of stylized messages of the increasingly multinational media enterprises. Ordinary people have consistently demonstrated a desire to make their own media messages when tools such as printing presses, xerox machines, and camcorders become available. The growing interest in creating camcorder media for national television, and in watching "homemade" camcorder images on television, even programs as exploitative and co-opted as *America's Funniest,* is important in understanding how the hegemony of commercial television might be challenged. In addition to defying the passive, one-way experience of dominant television, the popularity of low-cost, camcorder video might best be seen as evidence that, as Halleck suggests, people do want something more authentic, more in touch with the everyday lives of people, than commercial television typically offers—"a flash of recognition on a box that denies it" (Halleck, 1990). Clearly this particular historical moment, when questions regarding what television can be and who can be television producers are being contested and "classified out," is too important for those who advocate a more democratic media to ignore.

Redefining Television

While the model of commercial television dominates popular conceptions of what television can and should be in the United States, relegating alternative uses to marginality, this has not always been the case. In the experimental days of television in the 1920s, when television was not dominated by giant corporate conglomerates, inventors and amateurs developed the medium, building sets and transmitting signals to each other, testing the medium while imagining uses for the emerging communication technology.[5] This often-forgotten phase in the history of television serves as a reminder that what we have since come to know as a commercial, one-way model of "television" is not inherent to the medium itself but has been constructed by specific regulatory policies and economic practices.

Despite the fact that television, patterned after radio, quickly became an advertising-sponsored, corporate-controlled enterprise, alternative visions of television have emerged. In the late 1960s video artists and guerrilla television collectives, inspired by optimistic visions of media theorists such as Walter Benjamin, Bertolt Brecht, Hans Magnus Enzensberger, and Marshal McLuhan, embraced emerging portable video technology and attempted to create liberatory alternatives to commercial television programming (Boddy, 1990). Patricia Mellancamp (1988) describes this historical moment as one in which

> portable and affordable video equipment promoted artistry, populism, and utopianism . . . with a fervent of idealism, in the face of commercial pro-gramming and cold war politics and containment, "video" would bring global salvation via access, circumventing institutions and going directly to individuals of conscience. (p. 199)

Groups like TVTV, Ant Farm, and Videofreex were founded on a belief in liberation via the democratic pluralism of television—"anyone could control the means of production, anyone could and should be an artist" (Mellencamp, 1988, p. 200). Undermining the authority of print culture and posing audiovisual culture as a positive alternative, the early days of alternative video "tipped the poles of high vs. low, or elite vs. mass culture" (Mellencamp, 1988, p. 202), and with their video Portapacks, traveling video buses, and hopes for electronic democracy, the early video artists and guerrilla television collectives promised new possibili-ties for the medium and challenged the hegemony of network television at the time (Boddy, 1990, p. 93).

In retrospect, however, the euphoria of video revolutionaries often seems based on what William Boddy (1990) describes as a "technologi-cal leap of faith" rather than on what the media theorists, who informed their work, had diagnosed as "the tension between the social formation and communications technology" (p. 101). Their belief in the utopian potential of technology put to alternative uses often overlooked the historical and political determinants of dominant media as well as the fact that "technocratic fixes" alone could not address the political inequality within the United States (Boddy, 1990, p. 93). Nowhere is this more evident than in the appropriation of "electronic democracy" by corporations only too happy to embrace the new video pluralism. As Boddy (1990) has argued:

The rhetorical similarities between the technological visions of some video guerrillas and the entrepreneurs of the booming cable industry of the 1970s seem disquieting in retrospect. The wishful thinking about the autonomy of technology and the refusal of history and politics among independent video makers may have inadvertently enlisted them as the avant garde for an (un)reconstructed communications industry only too happy to lead a "media revolution" which would leave existing power relations untouched. (p. 95)

Stephen Heath has noted the historical split between artists who counter commercial television by creating alternative uses for the medium, and those who are concerned with the broader politics of television, specifically its critique and reform. To effectively challenge the commercial monopoly on television as both an industry and a form of mass communication, it has never been more crucial that these two approaches recognize and support each other. As Heath (1990) defines the uneasy relationship between video and television:

The point in the end cannot be only to communicate "alternatives" (although this is certainly crucial) . . . but also moving beyond communication in order to grasp the reality of the television institution (and so its modes of establishment and use of communication) as a prerequisite for effective transformation, the condition finally of any alternative. (pp. 269-270)

In the remainder of this chapter, then, I will assess the way in which alternative television in the 1990s operates in the context of the dominance of commercial television, and how video activism, grassroots TV, and cable access television are, if not exactly succeeding, at least attempting to challenge and subvert the considerable power of the global commercial media industries.

Camcorders: A Tool for Activists

Patricia Williams has argued that the arrival of portable video on the consumer market confirmed the "bleak underside of visionary video politics" and its repression of consumer capitalism. Video, situated as entertainment within the private home, has become a family plot, "politics and art gone sour," the ultimate consequence of dreams of accessibility and pluralism appropriated by JVC, Panasonic, Mitsubishi, and Sony (Mellencamp, 1988, p. 219). Yet, ironically, it was the very consumerization of video that made the medium finally accessible to groups excluded from dominant television discourse as well as from the more expensive equipment used by video guerrillas in the late 1960s. One of the most contradictory (and surely unintended) results of the arrival of cheap, portable camcorders to the mass market has been the rise of video activism. An estimated 14 million Americans own personal camcorders,[6] and a growing number of them are shooting something other than family vacations and birthday parties. As consumer video became increasingly portable and inexpensive in the 1980s, amateurs, activists, and grassroots collectives began using camcorders and VCRs to document demonstrations, marches, and events; to monitor police brutality; and to create their own programs for educational and organizing purposes and for distribution on local and national cable access television.

In contrast to early video pioneers, video activists today are more diverse across gender, race, class, and sexuality, and, significantly, most recognize that they cannot afford to believe in the radical potential of technology alone. Operating within the margins of the increasingly powerful media industries, video activism and alternative television practice in the 1990s realize the futility of a "video revolution" without praxis, alternative structures, and a vision for a new social (and television) system. As video activist John Walden (1990) argues, the camcorder should not be seen as a technological liberation but must be placed within the framework of the history of resistance and opposition:

> Rather than calling this a video revolution, let's simply call it video activism. There is no arguing that the camcorder has had a dramatic impact on activist use of video in both the immediacy of its image and the new range of aggressive tactics it makes possible. But the success of video activism also relies on access to post-production facilities and access to an alternative network for the distribution of tapes. . . . Let's also remember that the camcorder—like the mimeograph machine, the bullhorn, and the photocopier before it—is just one more piece of bourgeois technology that has been pressed into the service of political activism and redefined by its use. Video activists weren't created by the camcorder. They appropriated it. They took it from the entertainment console and turned it into a weapon for change. (p. 171)

At the same time, the influence of the camcorder on oppositional organizing cannot be underestimated. For activists mobilizing around AIDS, the environment, abortion rights, racial equality, the media, and other social and political issues, low-budget video technology has become as indispensable as the ubiquitous protest sign. Ranging from abortion rights activists to environmental groups, citizens coalitions, AIDS activists, and groups organizing around the politics of race, the camcorder has become indispensable for documenting marches and events ignored by the mainstream media, for creating educational and community programming, for adding diversity to social discourse on issues, and for documenting police brutality and other oppressive encounters. *The Camcordists' Manifesto,* written by video activist Ellen Spiro (1991), articulates some of the reasons camcorders are increasingly important for activists:

> Camcorder footage contributes to a broader analysis of an event by offering an alternative to broadcast media's centrist view. It has the power to add a dimension to the chorus of voices heard, providing a platform for seasoned activists and concerned community members rather than the same old authoritative experts giving their same old scripted raps. . . . Video is a form of legitimization which ultimately is an empowering device. With insider's documentation, your group does not have to rely on mainstream media approval for legitimization. (pp. 22-23)

Shoot the Media

In the age of media conglomeration characterized by a dizzying flow of images emerging from an increasingly smaller number of corporations, many video activists are acutely aware of the powers of the mainstream media—and the need to subvert them. One way video activism challenges the mainstream media is by using video to create autonomous self-representations. Another is by creating visually interesting aesthetics that counter the expensive, slick look of network TV and questioning borders between information, entertainment, and public affairs programming. Undermining the credibility of the dominant media by exposing the constructed nature of media representations is another important tactic. Recognizing that the mass media today signify a political battlefield in their own right, many video activists, such as the Paper Tiger Television Collective, use all three strategies to focus on directly confronting the influence of the commercial media. Produced on a shoestring budget with makeshift props and low-cost special effects, PTTV has broadcast some of the most recognizable and acclaimed public access television since its formation in 1981. PTTV programs, which show regularly on Manhattan cable access, expose the biases, hidden meanings, and monopoly ownership of the mainstream media in its various forms with critical deconstructive "readings" by opinionated public interest media professionals, academics, and independent producers.

According to the *Paper Tiger Manifesto*: "Developing a critical consciousness about the communications industry is a necessary first step towards democratic control of information resources" (Marcus, 1991, p. 9). Exposing the corporate structures and ideologies of the media is only one part of this challenge. Equally important is the need to "disrupt the TV beliefs" of television viewers. PTTV member Adriene Jenik explains how this goal is achieved in the guidebook *Roar! The Paper Tiger Guide to Media Activism*:

> These beliefs, particularly those regarding the inherent objectivity and inaccessibility of the television medium, are dislodged consistently by PTTV programs. Opinionated individuals speak in their own voices at their own pace, free of the limitation of sound-bites, make-up, or the framing of an interviewer's question. Underscoring their critiques are colorful handlettered placards bearing informative graphics that pass before the camera. This handmade look, a PTTV trademark, consciously encompasses both set enhancements (colorful backdrops and on-screen characterizations) and sound cues, camera shots of the crew and other technical transgressions. These "mistakes" disrupt the insular nature of television production, proving to viewers that individuals of varying talent and economic circumstance (maybe even themselves!) can make worthwhile TV. (Marcus, 1991, p. 10)

The dual emphasis on critiquing the dominant media and promoting critical television viewing pioneered by PTTV has also been taken up by video activists taking aim at the local media in their communities. In Buffalo, New York, for instance, the 8mm News Collective uses low-end video documentation and public access television to create an alternative, interactive television medium responsive to "everyday people" and their political actions.[8] For their local cable access series *News Diaries,* the 8mm News Collective videotaped the news department of local station WGRZ to expose the construction of local news as a fiction-making, profit-oriented enterprise. This type of critique recognizes (and indeed depends upon) shared references with the viewer—in the case of *News Diaries,* the recognizable character of a local news operation. As 8mm member Barbara Lattanzi explains:

The local news operation became the prop for the 8mm News Collective qua TV viewers. The irony is that the local news self-authorizes itself to represent "the community." But if things turn around and "the community" decides to create a representation of the local news operation the result is a kind of comedic theater in which the news operators (reporters and management) are included as a cast of characters. (Hill & Lattanzi, 1992, p. 103)

At the same time, explains 8mm member Chris Hill, critical readings of the dominant mode of television news production are encouraged:

The "News Diaries" frames the news as a fiction-making enterprise. The news fictions invented by WGRZ, of course, ultimately construct their viewers as a market, asking them to buy their story. The Collective's production reveals the artifice of their own documentation process; their viewers are authorized to construct their own version/fiction of the event. While the 8mm News Collective clearly authorizes its own theater, it finally invests in a potentially media-literate audience where the performative structure of a media event—the taping of the media event and the framing of the media event—are exposed and obvious to the audience. There is no attempt to create seamless programming, to take away the artifice of the production, or to "sell" the audience. (Hill & Lattanzi, 1992, p. 103)

Damned Interfering Television

In an age when media representation and politics are inseparable, activists such as the members of Damned Interfering Video Activist Television (DIVA TV), the video arm of New York's AIDS Coalition to Unleash Power (ACT-UP), have found video an important tool for challenging the power of the mainstream media to define and represent issues central to their communities. In its mission statement, DIVA states a commitment to "making media which directly counters and interferes with dominant media assumptions about AIDS and governmental negligence in dealing with the AIDS crisis" as well as to challenge "a racist, sexist, and heterosexist dominant media which is complicit with our repressive government."[9] One way DIVA TV strips the mainstream media's totalizing power in defining the AIDS crisis is by using camcorders to document events (such as marches, teach-ins, and protests) and viewpoints relating to AIDS that the mainstream media chooses to ignore. Working from the assumption that the mainstream media will never adequately reflect the struggles, needs, and states of mind of individuals and communities living with AIDS, DIVA TV also produces videos and regular programming for Manhattan cable access documenting both AIDS activism and the experiences of people living with AIDS.

While DIVA TV has bypassed channels of commercial television by creating its own programming, the group is also interested in subverting and exploiting the dominant media in every way possible. Catherine Saalfield and Ray Navarro have described how DIVA TV often appropriates the style of music videos to create a television that is "more like newsreel and less like documentary, more like music video and less like nightly news." According to the DIVA philosophy, "This is MTV activism since it's 'More than a Virus' that is killing people with AIDS" (Saalfield & Navarro, 1991, p. 363). Despite DIVA's skepticism toward the mainstream media, creating positive self-representations of people living with AIDS and influencing cultural discourses regarding AIDS—by any means necessary—are understandably priorities over issues of media politics. As Saalfield and Navarro (1991) have explained:

> DIVA TV is propaganda on every level . . . the activists are intervening in television production and distribution, exploiting channels of public access, organizing community-based screenings, selling footage to network television produced with DIVA's point of view (and label), and operating within the politics of ACT-UP itself. What DIVA has effectively done is to image the group itself in a positive, fashionable representation, by enhancing the issues, without diluting the political urgency of the moment. Unlike television's tendency to trivialize the activist presence on the political landscape, DIVA tapes empower individual ACT-UP members. (p. 364)

Yet DIVA TV's active work to transform the ability of the mainstream media to define and control representation must not be underestimated. One particularly innovative strategy used by DIVA activists is appropriating dominant media images, subverting them, and rendering them with new meaning according to specific contexts (a history of homophobia and the politics of the AIDS crisis). In addition to engaging the audience with shared cultural references, this practice encourages active, critical television viewing. The video *How to Be a DIVA* offers a typical example. In this tape, video segments of AIDS activism, teach-ins, and encounters between activists and police are juxtaposed with mainstream news footage of AIDS-related stories appropriated from network television that have been distorted through slow-motion editing, video montage, superimposition, and manipulated sounds. The resulting contrast highlights active resistance to current AIDS policy while simultaneously critiquing and condemning the way the mainstream media have handled the crisis. Later in the tape, lyrics from Madonna's song "Like a Prayer" and more images from television news are taken from their original context and used creatively to criticize the homophobia of the Catholic church. Finally, activist footage of the Gay Pride March and candid interviews with ACT-UP members who were arrested there are juxtaposed with footage from a commercial talk show, where an insensitive host is quizzing the same protesters on the most personal (and sensational) details of being strip searched, without addressing the politics of the march. Once again, this segment distributes information and viewpoints while consciously critiquing the failure of the media to represent them.

Not Channel Zero: Afrocentric TV

Not Channel Zero, a New York-based video collective of young African American media artists, is also bridging alternative television production with an active critique of the commercial media.[10] Members, many of whom teach media production to high school students, use a sophisticated media awareness to create television that challenges "the normal viewing habits" of young African American and Latino audiences. With low-tech equipment and an extremely small budget (each video is produced for about $50), the group produces a regular news and cultural affairs program for Manhattan cable access, covering topics ranging from urban welfare to police brutality, homophobia in the black community to the antiwar movement among people of color. Despite the political and social significance of issues addressed, NCZ programs refuse to conform to the boundaries of news or public affairs.

Subtitled "The Revolution, Televised," Not Channel Zero programs begin by telling the viewers that what they're watching is "grassroots, Afrocentric television aiming at politics, culture, and re-education," thereby challenging claims of objectivity as well as the universal perspective of mainstream media. The static studio atmosphere of "serious" news and public affairs programming is replaced by a camcorder's view of the streets, where events ignored by the black press and the mainstream media are addressed by ordinary people in everyday situations. Reporters cover everything from urban welfare to police brutality to homophobia within the African American community, and frequently give their own commentary and opinions. (As one collective member put it, "We don't believe in objectivity.") NCN programs are Afrocentric not only in content, but in form. Music by popular rappers such as Ice T and Public Enemy, unconventional camera angles, slow-motion and fast-forward sequences, repeated back-and-forth video segments (a visual analogy to "scratching" in rap music), and editing tricks like superimposition translate hip-hop culture into a visual style that speaks directly to young African American and Latino viewers.

Not Channel Zero programs are not viewed within the commercial logic of "narrowcasting" but are grounded in a broader vision for the role of television within the African American and Latino communities. NCN conceives of a model of television that is community oriented, based on collective participation, that encourages critical and active viewing and is actively working toward those goals. In its mission statement, NCN announced a "Ten-Point Plan" for creating television radical both in content and in form that reflects the scope of their vision:

1. To provide a forum for the education of the African community, promoting a cultural connection among all people of the African Diaspora
2. To promote political, social and economic empowerment
3. To act as a forum to discuss issues and evaluate problems
4. To locate and provide resources that will develop problem solving techniques
5. To acknowledge the cultural contributions of Africans in the United States and abroad
6. To provide a provocative alternative to mainstream media
7. To reflect the concerns of our community and provide an outlet for their grievances
8. To celebrate and honor the memory of our African ancestors
9. To act as a creative venue for emerging artists
10. To provide a positive and respectful analysis of the African American community[11]

Similar to DIVA TV, Not Channel Zero works toward building alternative media structures while simultaneously encouraging critical readings of the commercial media industries. By appropriating, recontextualizing, and redefining images from television, films, news, and popular culture, NCN encourages viewers to develop the deconstructive skills necessary to locate and challenge the biases of television and other media. This practice, often accomplished with inexpensive and interesting stylistic techniques, yields a powerful effect. In *Sexual Politics,* an episode about the role of women in black revolutionary movements, stereotypical images of mammies are taken from advertisements and films and juxtaposed with the pause of blank television static. Countering these images are interviews with black women who present an alternative portrait of intelligence, commitment, and resistance. Other exploitative images of black women taken from films, television, and music videos are slowed down and stripped of their original sound, a tactic that decontextualizes them from their original meaning and leaves them open for reinterpretation and critique.

The Nation Erupts, created in response to the L.A. riots and ensuing rebellion within inner-city Los Angeles, is a powerful example of how alternative production and sophisticated media critique can work though video. This program, which aired nationally on the Deep Dish TV cable access satellite network, used amateur camcorder footage, appropriated commercial news images, historical footage of previous riots, commentary from black leaders, and textual analysis to address the L.A. riots from the perspective of African Americans and other groups exploited under racism and consumer capitalism. The video begins by showing the familiar amateur footage of the Rodney King beating over and over without sound. This footage leads into historical black-and-white film footage of riots that has been enlarged and distorted. The riots are unidentifiable: They could be taking place in Los Angeles or in Chicago or Harlem or Watts. As the subsequent textual history of rioting in the United States demonstrates, that is exactly the point. By historicizing the L.A. rebellion within the history of rioting and protest in the United States, the riots are provided a context largely absent from mainstream coverage.

In this important hour-long episode, capitalism and the promotion of an inaccessible commodity culture are connected to the oppression and rebellion of the African American community and other people of color. Interviews and news footage collected from activists and citizens in Los Angeles and elsewhere document the living conditions and day-to-day struggles that led up to the crisis in Los Angeles. Music by James

Brown, Prince, Ice T, and other black artists combined with speeches by Martin Luther King and Malcolm X provide another layer to the African American struggle for freedom in the United States. Mainstream news footage of the L.A. riots is repeatedly distorted and manipulated in a way that exposes its biases and encourages critical interpretation. Images taken from film and from popular culture and appropriations such as a David Letterman-style "Top Ten Reasons Why the LA Riots Happened" (number one reason: racism) situate the mainstream media's handling of race relations within a history of racist media practices and the absence of the African American experience on commercial television. Throughout the program, the King beating is periodically interspersed, as are other beatings captured on amateur videotape and footage from previous uprisings and riots. Together, these images historicize what happened in Los Angeles within centuries of economic injustice and racism against people of color, while at the same time exposing and critiquing the role of the media in condoning such practices.

Deep Dish:
Alternative TV Goes National

DIVA TV and Not Channel Zero are just two of many examples of community-based alternative television practices engaged in participatory models of production. Until the creation of the national cable access satellite network Deep Dish TV, alternative television reached its largest audience via local cable access channels. Negotiated by cities when cable operators were bidding for local franchise agreements during the 1970s, access channels provide a rare public space where free speech and alternative discourse can thrive amidst the commercial arena of television. At the low end, access facilities might be limited to a single electronic listing of community events; at the high end, they can include full production facilities and several channels. While activists and community groups use local access to create programming, until recently such programming rarely received national attention. Deep Dish helped solve a frustrating dilemma in which hundreds of hours of important programming was being produced but little of it was able to reach the sizable audience that it deserved. With its commitment to grassroots, community-based television and its capacity to beam alternative views into living rooms across the United States, Deep Dish

TV today is no doubt the closest thing to democratic, pluralistic television that has ever existed in this country.

The network was created in 1986 by Paper Tiger TV to assess whether a national audience existed for locally produced grassroots television and to discover if an alternative to the existing commercial model of television was possible technically and in terms of content. When the pilot series, aptly called *Fearless TV,* was beamed out via satellite to home dish owners and cable access channels, the response was overwhelming. Producers, access programmers, and viewers found grassroots television exciting and empowering because it provided local angles and multiple viewpoints to issues that were national in scope. Building on the success of the first series, Deep Dish TV set out to build an ongoing grassroots television network—the first of its kind. The goal was to create a national, alternative satellite network that produced and distributed multiracial, multiregional representation—"Television with a point of view."[12]

Since then, Deep Dish has evolved into the hub of alternative, grassroots video distribution, enabling video activists and access producers of every stripe to share their work with each other and with a national audience. The day-to-day operation of the Deep Dish network ensures that a diverse range of subjects, perspectives, and innovative and experimental visual styles are represented in the network's programming. This mission is also articulated in the Deep Dish catalog: "Where commercial networks present a homogeneous and one-dimensional view of society, Deep Dish thrives on diversity. Instead of television that encourages passivity, Deep Dish distributes creative programming that educates and activates." The network defines its major goals as follows:

1. Promoting local grassroots organizing;
2. Presenting a multicultural analysis of issues and events;
3. Revealing information not usually available in mainstream media;
4. Presenting perspectives of individuals and groups (such as women, working people, and people of color) that are continually excluded from mainstream discourse. (from Deep Dish promotional material)

The operations of the Deep Dish network support a commitment to participatory, inclusive television. Grassroots producers from around the country are asked to suggest ideas for compilation programs, or for a series of programs, based on a dominant theme or idea. Deep Dish staff then announce topics (AIDS, national race relations, the environment, labor, reproductive rights, U.S. military intervention, housing, and alternative TV—to mention just a few that have been covered) and mailings are sent to cable access channels and grassroots video producers all across the United States asking if they can contribute. Coordinating producers representing diverse regions and backgrounds are then selected to edit the incoming contributions—which might range from amateur camcorder footage to short video documentaries to innovative video segments featuring special effects, multiple imagery, and sophisticated editing—into 28-minute finished programs ready for transmission. This format enables amateurs and activists who can create a 5-minute segment, but lack the time, skills, and resources to produce a full program, to become active media producers for national TV.

The programs are organized into two 16-week series—one in the spring and another in the fall—and some programs are organized around particular themes, such as censorship, the L.A. riots, colonialism and native peoples, the environmental crisis, and health care, for example. Each week during the broadcast seasons, Deep Dish rents time on a national satellite to beam an hour of programming—free of charge—to more than 5,000 home satellite dish owners and 300 cable systems across the United States. Viewers who don't have a satellite dish see Deep Dish TV on their local cable access channel, which can transmit the program directly as it comes in by satellite or can tape the programs for airing on later dates. Because it operates on a shoestring budget and relies on volunteer efforts from hundreds of grassroots producers, Deep Dish programs are able to reach a potential audience of 14 million (including satellite owners and cable subscribers whose system receives the program) for about $2,000, including production costs and renting satellite time—a tiny fraction of what most network TV programs cost.

Deep Dish TV has pioneered a democratic, pluralistic alternative to the monolithic, commercial model of dominant media, a fact that is reflected in its programming. Shows are very different than the slick, professional look of commercial television, yet low-cost, innovative special effects and creative aesthetic styles influenced by the cultures of the producers make the programs visually interesting and fun to watch. Deep Dish programs are generally fast paced and full of multiple, even contradictory viewpoints. The Deep Dish philosophy and style is perhaps best witnessed in the program *Vibrant Voices: People of Color Speak Out.* In this program, an image of a black woman in dreadlocks is superimposed over the picture of the all-white, all-male board of a commercial television network. She asks: "How can these men relate to the masses?"

Season after season, programs presented on Deep Dish reflect the view that "TV should let a community speak for itself." One typical series, *Beyond the Browning of America,* documents the struggles for equality of the Puerto Rican and Chicano peoples and also explores their search for cultural identity. It begins by documenting the history of Latinos migrating to America to claim their share of a society they have been forced to dream about. Testimony from Mexican workers living in cardboard houses in the richest counties in California then give viewers an opportunity to reflect on notions of "democracy" and "freedom." Finally, Latino writers, musicians, painters, and performers seize the screen in a celebration of Latino voices. Deep Dish also envisions the possibilities of grassroots television on a global scale. One step in that direction was *Will Be Televised: Video Documents from Asia,* a series compiled from video gathered from five regions in Asia meant to reverse the one-way flow of information by bringing video from people's movements to the United States.

Interactive television that challenges the passive nature of the dominant television experience is also a part of the Deep Dish philosophy. The Deep Dish staff does extensive outreach to cable access channels and viewers to arrange local "wraparound" shows, panel discussions, and phone-in shows to run after Deep Dish every week. Live call-in shows, produced in conjunction with activist groups currently working on their local cable access systems, have addressed topics such as environmental racism, the decay of the cities, and violence in children's media. Viewers are encouraged to contribute views, comments, and questions to the program by calling a toll-free number.

In addition to its own productions, the Deep Dish TV Network also transmits grassroots and activist programming created by individuals and groups in sync with the Deep Dish philosophy, which range from the International Women's Day Video Festival to programs created by the Amalgamated Clothing and Textile Workers, DIVA TV, the Nicaragua Network, and Testing the Limits, a video collective committed to

AIDS activism. By providing inexpensive satellite time, the Deep Dish network has become a rare forum for progressive groups to get their productions on the air.

Eventually, Deep Dish TV would like to expand its schedule and provide a regular source of alternative information and perspectives not seen on other television channels. With an annual budget of less than it costs to produce 8 minutes of commercial programming, however, that goal could take years to be accomplished. Generating wide distribution of Deep Dish shows—which can mean everything from pressuring cable access channels to tape Deep Dish TV and show it on a regular basis, to ensuring that viewers are aware of air dates and times (programs are not generally listed in TV programming guides)—continues to be a major challenge. New developments in this area include negotiations with independent PBS stations, some of which broadcast *The Gulf War TV Project* and the acclaimed *Behind Censorship: The Assault on Civil Liberties* to a larger, more mainstream audience. But the vast majority of Deep Dish programming is inevitably too feisty, political, and home-grown for PBS.

The Television Revolution Will Be Appropriated

The success of camcorder activists, cable access producers, and the Deep Dish network in challenging the hegemony of commercial television can, as was previously discussed, be attested to by the appropriation of the "video revolution" by entertainment television. *America's Funniest Home Videos* and *I Witness Video* attempt to define the legitimate boundaries of home video usage by structuring visions of how the new communications might be used—or, as Hall (1977) puts it, ruling certain interpretations "in" or "out" (p. 345). Importantly, progressives are not the only groups struggling for a place within this dominant discourse. It hardly seems a coincidence that, as cable access became a viable medium for community groups and activists, reactionary extremist groups also began exploiting video technology and cable access, often with the result of effectively undermining the potential of the medium. The controversial *Race and Reason*, a Ku Klux Klan-sponsored program promoting white supremacy that has been shown on more than 50 cable access channels, is just one example. By generating national publicity and outrage, this program has further marginalized cable access and in some cases led to the silencing of other voices on the system.

Serving as a reminder that cable access, a major vehicle for alternative video, operates within the boundaries of government policy and the cable industry is recent federal legislation hostile to the freedom of expression on access stations. An amendment to the Cable Television Consumer Protection Act passed in 1992 authorizes cable companies to prohibit "obscene" programming as well as material "promoting sexually explicit conduct" or "unlawful" conduct from airing on cable access channels. For the first time ever, the cable industry is now authorized to enforce vague content standards that could pose a threat to the feisty, activist-oriented programming on cable access, a power that even the government does not have (Ouellette, 1992a). While this legislation may limit programming generated by extremist right-wing groups, it could conceivably restrict activist video that addresses issues of civil disobedience (such as not registering for the draft) and sexually explicit material dealing with AIDS, among other issues.

The highly monopolistic, profit-minded cable industry, which has long complained about the expense of providing cable access, could also thwart this vehicle for alternative expression. Cable operators lobbied for and won the right in 1984 to take back access channels not being used by their communities, inspiring the Deep Dish slogan: "Use It or Lose It." Recently, Daniels Communications, one of the most powerful cable companies, has promoted a plan to effectively incorporate cable access within the structures of the cable industry with a "National Cable Access Network." Jointly owned and operated by the cable industry, this network could, if adopted, eventually replace local and national cable access programming with programming that, perhaps not unlike *America's Funniest Home Videos,* is less controversial, more homogeneous, and more firmly structured within the boundaries of dominant commercial interests (Ouellette, 1992b).

Perhaps the most serious obstacle facing alternative video and television is the possibility that a new system of fiber optic media delivery will replace traditional cable systems. If anything demonstrates the relationship between technological opportunity and social and political tensions, it is this. Under current FCC "Video Dial Tone" policy overseeing this development, cable access television could not exist because grassroots and community groups would have to pay the same rates as

HBO and MGM for access to the system. While the barrage of media attention surrounding this technological development often promises pluralism in unlimited entertainment "choices," the reality is that the policies shaping the media system of the future are currently poised to deliver more television without true diversity—unless activists and the grassroots community intervene now to ensure otherwise.[13]

The Future of Grassroots TV

Despite the tenuous relationship between alternative television and dominant structures of media, alternative television production continues to proliferate as growing numbers of activists and communities realize the potential of self-representation made possible by the camcorder, and producers of grassroots and alternative television work toward a democratic and pluralistic model of television that was inconceivable only a decade ago. This work is important not only in offering an alternative to commercial television programming but also in challenging the television industry and promoting critical media awareness as well. Indeed, perhaps it is precisely because so many of today's video activists recognize that they are operating within the margins of a corporate-owned, monopoly media system that new directions in alternative television (and other forms of oppositional communication)[14] continue to emerge.

In the end it is this contradictory situation—the promise that television might foster a new communication among and between diverse communities, coupled with an understanding of the constant need to organize and struggle so that this potential might be realized—that is pushing today's video revolutionaries further. In assessing the new wave of media activism, Marlon Riggs has argued that "the burden of today's historical moment, when identities world-wide are radically reformulating, is for us to speak to and with each other, across the borders of identity, across our multiple positions and strategies of self-empowerment, in ways that build a truly radical multicultural coalition, perhaps even, community" (quoted in Zando, 1991, p. 44). Camcorder activism, coalitions of video collectives, and structures such as Deep Dish TV, as well as effective organizing around the policies and practices that are shaping emerging media technologies and systems will be central to accomplishing this goal.

Notes

1. Walden's (1990) "How Much Is that Revolution in the Window?" is in Faber, *A Tool, A Weapon, A Witness: The New Video News Crews*, a handbook created in conjunction with video presentations at the Randolph Street Gallery in Chicago, which provides an excellent introduction to video activism. Copies can be obtained for $4 from Randolph Street Gallery, 756 North Milwaukee Avenue, Chicago IL 60622.

2. Horkheimer and Adorno's (1990) "The Cultural Industry: Enlightenment as Mass Deception", an influential essay originally published in 1944, continues to influence leftist suspicions of mass culture as "duping" the unsuspecting masses.

3. Hall uses Antonio Gramsci's insights on hegemony, or a system of rule that depends on both force and consent, to build on his theory of the contradictory mode of media under advanced capitalism.

4. Hall, for instance, argues that audiences interpret media texts according to dominant, preferred, or oppositional meanings depending on particular conditions. See "Encoding/Decoding" (Hall, 1980).

5. For a history of the development of television, see Barnouw's (1990) *Tube of Plenty* or Head and Sterling's (1987) *Broadcasting in America*. Recently, the media arts journal *Felix*, named after one of the earliest images transmitted on television, the popular Felix the Cat cartoon character, was founded to revive the air of "magic and mysticism" that defined the early days of television. The journal is a good source for articles on media and video activism. *Felix*, The Standby Program, P.O. Box 184, Prince Street Station, New York, NY 10012 (212) 219-0951.

6. This figure comes from an article in *Newsweek* titled "Video Vigilantes" (1991), which, typical of mainstream news coverage of the camcorder phenomenon, emphasized the surveillance aspect of videotape.

7. The book *Roar! The Paper Tiger Television Guide to Media Activism* (Marcus, 1991) provides a comprehensive overview of the history of Paper Tiger TV as well as the how to's of cheap, effective alternative video production.

8. For an overview of the collective, see Chris Hill and Barbara Lattanzi (1992).

9. Taken from promotional material from DIVA TV, 12 Wooster St., New York, NY 10013 (212) 226-8147.

10. Not Channel Zero, P.O. Box 806, Wakefield Station, Bronx, NY 10466 (212) 926-4650.

11. As outlined in Not Channel Zero's manifesto, distributed by the collective.

12. The *Deep Dish TV Catalog* is available from Deep Dish TV, 339 Lafayette St., New York, NY 10012 (212) 473-8933.

13. For more on how emerging technologies could affect alternative television, see Chester and Montgomery (1993).

14. Two examples, for instance, are computer bulletin boards and amateur "zines," both mediums that have been used to bypass channels of commercial media to foster community and build alternative structures of information outside dominant structures.

References

Barnouw, E. (1990). *Tube of plenty.* New York: Oxford University Press.

Boddy, W. (1990). Alternative television in the United States. *Screen, 31*(1), 91-101.

Chester, J., & Montgomery, K. (1993). Technology in transition: From video dialtone to DBS—Where do independents fit in? *Independent Film and Video Monthly, 16*(3), 29-34.

Fuss, D. (Ed.). (1991). *Inside/out, lesbian theories gay theories.* New York: Routledge.

Hall, S. (1977). Culture, the media and the "ideological effect." In J. Curran et al. (Eds.), *Mass communication and society* (pp. 313-348). London: Edward Arnold.

Hall, S. (1980). Encoding/decoding. In S. Hall, D. Hobson, A. Loew, & P. Willis (Eds.), *Culture, media, language* (pp. 128-137). London: University of Birmingham.

Hall, S., Hobson, D., Loew, A., & Willis, P. (Eds.). (1980). *Culture, media, language.* London: University of Birmingham Press.

Halleck, D. (1990). Towards a popular electronic sphere, or options for authentic media expression beyond "America's Funniest Home Videos." In M. Faber (Ed.), *A tool, a weapon, a witness: The new video news crews* (pp. not numbered). Chicago: Randolph Street Gallery.

Head, S., & Sterling, C. (1987). *Broadcasting in America.* Boston: Houghton Mifflin.

Heath, S. (1990). Representing television. In P. Mellencamp (Ed.), *Logics of television* (pp. 267-302). Bloomington: University of Indiana Press.

Hill, C., & Lattanzi, B. (1992). Media dialects and stages of access. *Felix, 1*(2), 98-105.

Horkheimer, M., & Adorno, T. W. (1990). The cultural industry: Enlightenment as mass deception. In *Dialectic of enlightenment* (pp. 120-167). New York: Continuum.

Marcus, D. (Ed.). (1991). *Roar! The Paper Tiger Television guide to media activism.* New York: Paper Tiger Television Collective.

Mellencamp, P. (1988). Video and the counterculture. In C. Schneider & B. Wallis (Eds.), *Global television* (pp. 199-224). New York: Wedge.

Mellencamp, P. (Ed.). (1990). *Logics of television.* Bloomington: University of Indiana Press.

Ouellette, L. (1992a). Cable bill threatens cable access. *Independent Film and Video Monthly, 15*(4), 10-13.

Ouellette, L. (1992b). Publisher pitches national access network. *Independent Film and Video Monthly, 15*(10), 6-8.

Saalfield, C., & Navarro, R. (1991). Shocking pink praxis: Race and gender on the ACT UP frontlines. In D. Fuss (Ed.), *Inside/out, lesbian theories gay theories* (pp. 341-370). New York: Routledge.

Schneider, C., & Wallis, B. (Eds.). (1988). *Global television.* New York: Wedge.

Spiro, E. (1991, May). What to wear on your video activist outing (because the whole world is watching): A camcordist's manifesto. *Independent Film and Video Monthly,* pp. 22-24.

Video vigilantes. (1991, July 22). *Newsweek*, pp. 42-47.

Walden, J. (1990). How much is that revolution in the window? In M. Faber (Ed.), *A tool, a weapon, a witness: The new video news crews* (pp. not numbered). Chicago: Randolph Street Gallery.

Zando, J. (1991). Censoring to silence. *Felix, 1*(1), 44.

For the Warlpiri cameraman (and presumably his Warlpiri viewers) the camera is tracking inhabitants of the landscape, historical and mythical figures who reside there but are not apparent to normal vision. This attention to landscape is so persistent in all Aboriginal videomaking that it seems unlikely that it can be analyzed as naive or unintentional. Instead, it seems that these techniques derive from the ways that this nomadic culture looks at the landscape, . . . associating all this with stories that serve mnemonic locational and historical functions.

10

The Aboriginal Invention of
Television in Central Australia 1982-1986

ERIC MICHAELS

Television at Yuendumu

> The satellite was a threat to the Aboriginals, but now we have our own TV
> and video, we can put our things on too. We can fight fire with fire. . . . We
> could have been watching ABC News all the time and nothing of our own
> culture. . . . We like to watch our own things on the video. Now that we've
> got our own equipment we're able to do this ourself instead of Europeans
> doing it for us. Europeans only show what they want to show, not what we
> want to show.

Kurt Japanangka Granites (from *Yuendumu Sampler*,
Yuendumu Video, 1984)

This is a descriptive history of the introduction and use of video and
television at Yuendumu. It traces developments from a comparatively
passive audience of commercial videocassette viewers in 1982, to the
beginnings of video recording by a single Warlpiri interested in taping
sporting events, to the establishment of the AIAS television project and
the transition to a local, low-power TV station administered by the
Warlpiri Media Association.

The Education Department was the major innovator in video use. In
1975 DAA distributed Shibaden black-and-white video equipment to
bush schools, a legacy of the Whitlam government's Video Access
Programme. "Some local events were recorded and shown by both
European and Warlpiri operators, but the equipment was so bulky and
subject to breakdown that production was abandoned after only a year"
(Toyne, 1986, p. 2). These tapes were mainly of sporting events and

official visits. Some tapes still exist, but it is impossible to view them on the now inoperable equipment.

Yuendumu, and Warlpiri people, also served as media subjects, and considerable documentary film footage was shot by the Australian Broadcasting Corporation (ABC), government researchers, and even some commercial filmmakers. Only occasionally did the subjects ever get to see the finished product.

Home videocassette recorders appeared on the Australian market in the late 1970s, but the videotape rental outlets that made these systems appealing to bush people only began to appear in outback towns in the early 1980s. From then on, growth was phenomenal. Alice Springs by 1983 had 17 video outlets (one for every 1,250 residents) and penetration had surpassed 50% by most estimates.

The first home system was brought to Yuendumu early in 1982, by a European family. But by 1983 Aboriginal penetration was effectively total in that every extended Aboriginal family group had access to one of nine video recorders. One of the advantages was that the mass audience of film night, which brought many people into inappropriate proximity, could be broken down into more manageable and traditionally based units in the camp settings. Where necessary, programs could be replayed so that, for example, men could watch separately from women. In surveying the situation, it became clear that various other advantages were associated with personal ownership, which can be understood in terms of Warlpiri traditions.

Aboriginal VCRs were socially and geographically dispersed so that it appeared that every area of the community was serviced, and all major family groups had at least one member with a VCR the family could watch.

Because the costs of owning and maintaining a video may exceed annual per capita income at Yuendumu (Young, 1981), various strategies to share costs are employed that also distribute responsibility and ownership.

A VCR owner finds that he is sponsoring an ongoing entertainment service, which may mean he will play host to 20 or 30 people a night, incurring costs for supplying new tapes and other expenses. In a generalized way, this will obligate his audiences to him and may later be exchanged for political support, reciprocal goods and services, perhaps even ceremonial authority. But many video owners underestimate the costs, the interruption to camp life, and the extent of their own resources. As a result, in the early years of video, exchanges were quite frequent.

These exchanges seemed to occur most often between brothers, which would be fairly direct exchanges, but occurred also between brothers-in-law, mothers' brothers'/sisters' sons, fathers and sons, and others, which suggests various direct and indirect exchange routes. As might be expected, when exchanges were direct, the equivalence of vehicles and videos was quickly established; in some cases, these were swapped directly. But videos also became items of mortuary exchange, a somewhat more complicated matter.

The kinds of tapes available through this system are also limited. It is popularly believed among Europeans that Aborigines only like action/adventure films, preferably highly violent ones. The evidence for, and qualifications on, this will be discussed below but it is clear that other genres are equally popular: slapstick comedy, wildlife documentaries, and musicals, for example. But these are not as likely to be supplied through Europeans. Indeed, the most popular tapes of all, those by and about Aboriginal people, are never available from commercial Alice Springs outlets.

Because of the short life span of tapes and of machines, the initial capital outlay represented by the high commencement costs could not automatically be expected to decrease, as equipment maintenance and replacement costs might actually exceed initial capital expenditures in subsequent years. Nor would the number of VCRs grow significantly.

It was at this point that Kurt Japanangka's suggestions about extending the video project into a local community station were considered. The production and transmission hardware would cost considerably less than was privately spent on video supplies and, by making programs available for free (and without a VCR) to everybody, we would bypass the most expensive and unreliable aspect of the system.

Viewing and Interpreting

The "Effects" Fallacy

Because people concerned with the introduction of television in traditional communities want to know what the eventual effect of this introduction will be on Aborigines and their traditions, there is a tendency to jump directly from Western evaluations of television content to effects on Aboriginal audiences. Usually, they employ simple cause-effect assumptions.

This simple "cause-effect" model has mostly been abandoned in media studies simply because the evidence was contradictory and unconvincing. Current media research now rejects the notion of a passive audience who receive media messages identically everywhere and helplessly respond to what they see. Instead, audiences are now regarded as active seekers, selectors, and interpreters of media messages. The situation in cross-cultural studies is even more complex, and it may prove especially dangerous to jump to simple cause-effect conclusions here.

In cross-cultural situations where the programs are produced in one language/culture setting, but viewed in a radically different one, as is the case with rented videotapes at Yuendumu, the question, "What sense are people making of these programs?" is crucial.

Very early in the fieldwork, it became clear that European interpretation of videos was radically different than Aboriginal interpretation at Yuendumu. We laughed in different places, got upset at different scenes, and, afterward, told different stories about what we had seen. Most Europeans in Aboriginal communities notice this quickly. Some think that the Aborigines just have it wrong, but in time will learn. Others, like myself, suspect that Aboriginal interpretation is internally consistent, makes sense perhaps in terms of some traditional forms, and will have to be accounted for because it is likely to persist.

Understanding the varieties of fiction, and being able to evaluate the mix of truth and fantasy contained in fictional frames, is one of the marks of proper Western socialization, achieved well before adolescence. Are these also characteristics of Aboriginal thought, expression, and interpretation? For approaches to this question, we can consider the traditional forms of Aboriginal story.

Traditional storytelling forms. It is not clear that Aboriginal storytelling includes any *fictional* genres in the European sense of the term. Rather, the Warlpiri tell stories about the "Eternal Dreaming," historical and current events, and, according to Munn, relate personal, revelatory dreams. All these stories are "true."

Indeed, the justification given for requiring only certain people to be entitled to tell particular stories is the insistence that they be told "right" and "proper." *Kurdungurlu* witnesses (who stand in prescribed subsection kin relationships) may have to be present as well as the *Kirda* performer who owns the story to assure the correctness of the telling. The rigorously restricted transmission of the most important (e.g., secret/sacred) stories is typically accomplished in highly engineered ceremonial dramas to assure the continuity (and authority) of precise information over many generations.

Traditional story structure. In classic (ceremonial) Aboriginal song and storytelling, moments of special significance may be drawn out, repeated, or elaborated at the expense (from a European perspective) of the connections between these moments, how the plot moves from one event to the next. In fact, plots move self-evidently in Aboriginal stories— literally by the transportation of the characters over the landscape.
Munn (1973) says,

> The typical ancestral narrative is built upon a framework of site se-
> quences . . . [a] macro-temporal scaffolding . . . [which] can include the
> daily cycle of activities (for example, some of the men's narrative accounts
> describe daily hunting and gathering activities at the site along the route). . . .
> Some accounts of an ancestral track consist almost entirely of a list of site
> names connected by phrases indicating the movement of the ancestors
> between sites. (p. 132)

At least in the Warlpiri Centre, where sites (ceremonial and resource) are widely dispersed, the circumstances of the site and the associated activities are told or sung, but the tracks connecting the sites by contrast may be merely glossed.

The sources of motivation and psychological explanation in Warlpiri stories appear to be categorical rather than individualistic. A character acts (or fails to act) in a particular manner because (a) she/he is a dingo, snake, eagle hawk, and so on, and this is the manner in which such beings are known to act, and/or (b) he is Japanangka (subsection name) and Japanangkas always act that way toward Nangalas (subsection name).

The rapid adoption of video technology (at considerable personal expense) at Yuendumu suggests that television, when it is offered cheaply by AUSSAT, will rapidly become part of life in remote Aboriginal Australia. And while we need to recognize that TV can be many things (including Warlpiri videotapes), much or most of the diet will be in English language and Western-culture based. So our problem is also to predict what meanings Aboriginal people will construct from these programs, and to what effect.

In the following, we examine how Warlpiri themselves make video-tapes. From these accounts, we may extrapolate to further predictions about the interpretation of Western stories. Here, I can only note that considerable differences do exist in interpretation, and that these make predictions very difficult.

Video Production at Yuendumu

Direct observation of how Aborigines are using, viewing, and interpreting introduced video and TV tends to produce equivocal and speculative predictions about how the new media may affect their lives. In this section, an alternative kind of investigation is described, based on experiments made by providing the Aboriginal community with the resources to produce their own media and observing and analyzing the results.

This approach was pioneered in the late 1960s by Sol Worth and John Adair (1972) in an experiment with Navajo Native Americans. Worth and Adair were asking a more discrete and abstract question, not so much about Navajos but about the film medium itself. Linguistic philosophy predicts that members of different language/culture groups not only perceive the world distinctly on the basis of cultural differences but express these differences in their art and performance. This being the case, Navajos ought to make movies that look quite different than those made by Europeans. Eisenstein, Morin, and other film philosophers claim to identify a basic "language" of film based on "shots" and "scenes." Would people of a non-Western culture develop a different filmic language?

Worth and Adair provided six Navajo with the resources to make a brief, silent 8mm film, providing little or no guidance in what a film should look like, what was a "good" or "bad" shot, what was a "correct" editing sequence, and so forth. Training was limited to basic instruction in the technology: how to operate a camera and how to do editing. The rest of the choices were left for the Navajo, most of whom had never seen a film at all, to discover for themselves. Worth and Adair carefully documented the entire process. The result was films that they claim differ in fundamental ways from European films, and these differences in framing, editing, topic, narrative, and so on are said to have their basis in unique properties of Navajo culture and thought.

This approach was chosen for the Warlpiri study, but with somewhat different objectives. After a generation of studies that followed the work of Worth and Adair with diverse cultures, it is generally agreed that differing cultures can produce differing audiovisual media. But even though it is clear that different cultures make different media in experimental settings, in real life they usually don't, except for these occasional brief interventions by anthropologists and researchers. Third World people quickly succumb to Western media and end up producing imitative forms when provided with the resources.

The Economics of Home Video

Growing concern about the loss of Aboriginal culture and language was motivating the first Aboriginal media groups—broadcasters such as CAAMA, TAIMA, and Radio Redfern. It became possible therefore to take the basic premise of the Worth and Adair studies and apply them to indigenous media development. We might demonstrate that Aboriginal people would produce unique media suited to their needs, and determine as well what the conditions would be to turn this discovery into the basis of local development schemes for traditional communities.

Warlpiri Video: Early Days

Difficulty at the Beginning

One kind of mistake was to rush in with preconceptions and find these too quickly confirmed. For example, the Navajo films revealed that the pointing of the camera was consistent with the etiquette for making eye contact in a culture. Among the Navajo, where direct eye contact is far more limited than among, for example, most Europeans, few close-ups were observed. It was inappropriate for the cameraperson to intrude this closely, as it would be embarrassing for an audience viewing the film. Cavadini and Strachan used a similar observation in filming *Two Laws* among the Boroloola Aboriginal community to justify exclusive use of wide-angle lenses to shoot medium or long distances.

On reviewing the first Warlpiri-made videos, this long-distancing technique reappeared. Surely this confirmed the hypothesis. But on the first day's outing to join in location shooting, it became clear that Japanangka's preference was not so much for a type of lens but to remain wired to the cigarette jack of the Toyota. The instructions that came with the battery pack were inadequate and so batteries were not used and the cameraman could not get close to the action. As soon as the batteries were properly inserted, Japanangka moved in close to the action and close-ups became commonplace. But, as became apparent later, not everyone could be shot close-up; this depended on the kin relationship between the cameraman and his subject. A simplistic hypothesis then had to be replaced with a far more subtle and less obvious one.

A second kind of mistake concerned the assumption that anyone could be trained in video and that, for the project to become community-based, we should simply equip a broad spectrum of people.

The fact that Japanangka was the first videomaker gave him particular rights over the medium at Yuendumu, so that he quickly became "boss" for both shooting and showing. But there were many occasions where he could not perform this role and people wanted something recorded and shown. For some time, Japanangka was unwilling to share this responsibility or train others in the technology.

During the first 6 months, therefore, the project seemed especially vulnerable, in that all video expression was tied to one individual's skills, interests, kinship relationships, and personality. It was only after this initial period, when Japanangka developed sufficient expertise and authority, that he began to identify other participants and finally to transfer some of his authority and skills through his brother-in-law.

Attempts by myself or the adult educator to involve women in production were even less successful during these early stages, as we were unable to identify appropriately related women and instead effectively stalled women's video by inappropriate choices.

For the Warlpiri, it is social context and structural circumstances, more than personality characteristics, that determine who may introduce novelty. The choice or accident of the innovator will determine the route through the community that the innovation will take, and this will vary depending on the social position of that individual. Likewise, all such innovations ought to be spatially located, so that there needs to be some agonizing over where to locate facilities.

Case Histories: Video Subjects

Sports videos. The first videos made at Yuendumu were almost exclusively of sporting events. This reflected the interests and involvements of both Japanangka and his audience. Indeed, throughout the project, sports would remain a priority subject.

Traditional dancing. It was not long before some of the older people, not directly involved or especially interested in European sports, began to make suggestions for taping events. These mainly involved public traditional dancing. The Women's Museum at this time was becoming a highly active dancing group, with the assistance of anthropologist Francoise Dussart. They sought to have the dancing taped for three purposes: (a) archiving of traditional dances, (b) training and review functions to improve dancing, and (c) possible communication and exchange with women in other communities.

Because Japanangka was the son of the senior Nampijinpa who served as coordinator for the Women's Museum, it was especially appropriate that he be enlisted for assisting the women's dancing. But this also raised problems. As a man, Japanangka was less desirable than a female videomaker for these purposes; there would be Napaljarri mothers-in-law who needed to be filmed but might pose a problem for a Japanangka cameraman.

Traditional subjects remained Japanangka's responsibility and he soon added dances of both women and then men to his repertoire. This brought about a lively and more widespread interest in the project. Review of tape by the participants became hilarious events in which a good deal of joking and correction took place in the audience, as tapes were reviewed as many as a dozen times by the same groups.

It soon became obligatory to have the camera at any important dance and participants would wait for the arrival of the video to begin. At one time when both Japanangka and I were unwilling to come with the camera (we were having a disagreement), senior men visited each of us at our camps and engineered a rapprochement, assuring us that an important dance event would be recorded, arguing that it couldn't take place until we arrived.

Message sticks. I brought video equipment along on my early visits to central Australia, but I was mostly unwilling to use it. I did not want to be mistaken for a videomaker, as I was less interested in the footage I would shoot than what Aborigines chose to make. The exception was my willingness to tape "messages" in one locale to be delivered at another. These included quite mundane information, for example, from the Central Land Council to remote community councils regarding plans for meetings, messages from CAAV regarding distribution of audiocassettes, and tapes of families to be shown to their relatives elsewhere. In making these tapes, I wanted to underscore the functional, informational value of video and deemphasize the entertainment, high-production type that people were becoming familiar with.

During the first year, many people thought the video message stick idea a good one, but there was not much development in this direction. The most elaborate tape was made by the Women's Museum and filmed by Japanangka. We were planning a trip to Lajamanu, and the women requested that we make a tape to take to the Women's Museum there.

We arrived at the museum to find the women all dressed up and prepared to deliver a series of quite formal speeches. The substance of these was that Lajamanu women ought to emulate the Yuendumu women by constructing a museum to house ceremonial objects, seeds, ochres, and other ritual paraphernalia. In this way, when Yuendumu women came to Lajamanu to dance, they would be assured of the proper materials.

Following the speeches, the women displayed some of these materials, although Japanangka and I were not allowed into the museum and could not see any of the restricted objects or designs housed there.

This tape was edited, reviewed by the women, and sent up to Lajamanu, where the senior women there gathered and reviewed it twice. At Lajamanu, we met with the community council and made a tape of our discussions that was then aired at Yuendumu. The subject was the combining of forces between the two communities for videotape production and distribution to begin a "Warlpiri Network."

This tape was then viewed by the video workers and others at Yuendumu, but this network never quite developed. I believe this has much to do with the personalities and social identities of the video workers in the different communities as well as a certain competition that is evident between them. Following these directed experiments, the message stick idea lapsed. At least tapes were not shot for this purpose explicitly.

Editing

The women's message stick was the first tape to be edited completely on the half-inch to half-inch editing deck.

(Note: Much of the uniqueness claimed for Navajo film was associated with the editing process in which Navajos produced sequences that, while unacceptable or unreadable to European viewers—such as jump-edits, sudden appearances and disappearances of people and objects—were sensible to Navajo viewers. For these to emerge, Worth felt it was essential that the Navajo discover the editing process themselves, and no instruction was provided until the filmmakers inquired about whether the film could be glued together. It is possible to make this discovery with film because the film strip itself corresponds indexically to the image perceived with the naked eye; you can hold the film up to the light and see the chemically engraved pictures. But video encodes images electromagnetically and casual examination of a videotape reveals nothing to the naked eye. Film editing involves an obvious operation: physically reassembling the transparent pictures. Video editing, by contrast, is a complex electronic feat; the details of how the editing machine accomplishes an edit are difficult to understand and are never fully apparent without extensive technical explanation. It was impossible for the Warlpiri to be expected to "discover" video editing for themselves. Furthermore, Worth and Adair assembled cinematically naive Navajos for their project. If by 1983 it was possible to find a community of Aborigines who had never seen a movie, they would have been so atypical as to make any study impossible to generalize to media development models. This resulted in a deemphasis on the editing process, both for research and among the Warlpiri themselves in the early stages.)

Japanangka considered the time and effort involved in editing unwarranted for most purposes. For sports videos, editing had severe disadvantages. On at least one occasion, teams who were reviewing basketball tapes nearly came to blows because the official score and the number of baskets recorded differed. At a hostile meeting, Japanangka had to give a formal accounting of the theory and practice of camera work and editing. Even then, many thought the discrepancy a failure of Japanangka's skill. "It should be true!" one referee complained.

For Japanangka, the utility of editing at this stage was essentially the ability to delete material that proved unacceptable for general audiences or that contained images of people who had died since the taping, both of which could be achieved without elaborate equipment. The limitation of half-inch editing equipment in 1983 was that the deterioration of image quality in each generation was so severe that edited masters (second generation) could rarely be copied so as to produce an acceptable distribution tape (third generation).

Soon, the editing deck was being used mostly for playback, and it was decided to disassemble the facility (rather than risk its deterioration) until such time as it might be required. When this point arrived a year later, the deck was no longer capable of producing acceptable edits, and Yuendumu video workers mostly traveled to Alice Springs to use CAAMA's equipment for this purpose.

Discussion: Warlpiri "Direct Cinema"

As a result of the genres preferred by Japanangka and the lack of interest in editing, Warlpiri were in 1983 producing mostly in a documentary style approximating what in the West is called "direct cinema." All the events filmed (except the "message sticks") were happening irrespective of the camera's presence, although interactions between the camera and the event, such as waiting for the camera before beginning to dance, or dancing "at" the camera, were noted.

The conditions for inventing stories partly explain why Japanangka, and the few other Warlpiri who were beginning to work with the camera, were reluctant to "make up" things for the tape. But this posed certain problems for description and analysis.

Obviously, where events are fictional or constructed especially for the camera, these distinctions become more clear to the observer. I discussed these issues with the video group (who, through a funding coup by the adult educator in late 1984, now included six people whose job descriptions included video production). I inquired whether anybody might like to make something happen just for the video.

The following day, a Jupurrula who had not before worked with a video camera announced that he would like to make a tape of old Japangardi's story about Coniston. On Sunday, he would come by my camp in the morning and we would travel east to Coniston station.

Coniston: Description of a Production Event

The Coniston Massacre serves the Warlpiri as the single most telling history of their encounter with Europeans. It concerns events following the murder by two Japanangka brothers of the prospector and dingo trapper, Frederick Brooks, at Crown Creek near Coniston station in 1928.

In general, it is conceded that the murder was related to Brooks's appropriation of an Aboriginal woman, and that in the raids that followed over the following year, between one dozen (official estimates) and 100 (Warlpiri estimates) people were killed. For the Warlpiri, the story is important for a number of reasons.

First, many if not most people at Yuendumu have relatives who were killed in these raids. Indeed, from their accounts it appears that these included many assembled for ceremony, so it is possible that an entire land-holding patrilodge was lost and, with it, the expertise for certain tracks in the area. This implies even greater social disruption than just the murder of many people; a disruption that still seeks resolution.

Second, this event clearly spelled out to the Warlpiri their tactical disadvantage in the European invasion and the futility and costs of resistance.

Third, the presence at Yuendumu of families descended both from the victims of Coniston and from the police tracker suggests a contemporary social tension within the community. Because different families were all affected by these events, each can claim rights to tell its version of the story, and because the story has become of interest to Europeans (especially since it resurfaced in land claim hearings), versions have been recorded in books and on film, and shown on TV. Whose version finally emerges as "true" may be of some consequence to the community.

As one hears these versions told repeatedly, one begins also to detect elements of dreaming construction entering the accounts, suggesting that these tales might become, in future generations, dreaming stories for the land around Coniston where they took place and where, perhaps, older stories were lost in the massacres.

Taping. The storyteller that Jupurrula was to videotape was the son of one of the two Japanangka protagonists, the senior member of his lineage. But when Jupurrula arrived Sunday morning, he also brought two carloads of people, and it became apparent that this was to be a major production; 27 people came along.

As it developed, only old Japangardi and his two Japanangka sons would be on the tape. But even though almost all the other people would attend mostly to hunt, picnic, or otherwise simply enjoy the bush trip, on closer examination, what was assembled was an entire kinship group, all related in various ways to the Coniston story and the land on which it would be filmed. These people, although never on camera, effectively authorized the filming of the story and assured its credibility to Warlpiri audiences (see Michaels & Kelly, 1985, for kinship details).

Analyzing the video product. The resulting video (edited only to exclude intrusive setup shots) is not immediately remarkable as a uniquely Warlpiri expression. The most striking characteristic is exceptionally long landscape pans; indeed, there is more attention to landscape than to actors or action. This could easily be dismissed as the result of naive filmmaking in which static landscapes, which prove easier to record than moving people, receive more attention. These extremely long, uninterrupted takes are also associated with unsophisticated filmmaking.

Conventions that are employed, such as Japangardi telling the story to the children or walking into the picture, are commonplace in European cinema. But as Jupurrula discussed the tape with me, and as evidence accumulated from other indigenous productions, it became clear that it would be a mistake to attribute European readings and sources to these conventions.

Reviewing this tape, the long landscape pans were discovered to include considerable camera movements; the panning motion is interrupted by zooms, refocus, and still shots. In interview, Jupurrula provided a purposive explanation for every motion of his camera. "This is where those policemen came over that hill," or "that is where dreamtime figures are in that tree," or "this is the track old Japanangka came round."

Explained in this fashion, it became clear that for the Warlpiri cameraman (and presumably his Warlpiri viewers) the camera is tracking inhabitants of the landscape, historical and mythical figures who reside there but are not apparent to normal vision. This attention to landscape is so persistent in all Aboriginal videomaking that it seems unlikely that it can be analyzed as naive or unintentional. Instead, it seems that these techniques derive from the ways that this nomadic culture looks at the landscape, recalling details of topography, outline, vegetation, associating all this with stories that serve mnemonic locational and historical functions.

Likewise, the movement of the storyteller into the picture before speaking seems to be a variant of "bringing in the dreaming," which begins ceremonial dances. Here, performers will dance into the ceremonial ground along a track from which direction the story being danced comes. This appears again and again in other videos where important or traditional content is conveyed. Both these conventions arise from the elaborate attention to location that characterizes Aboriginal expressive culture, translated here by Jupurrula into video.

The technique of telling the stories to children is also a convention that appears in European cinema as a rhetorical device providing an empathic alternative to taking head shots and that underscores the historical continuity of the content and invites younger viewers to become involved as well. Even if this is not the intention here, it would not be inaccurate to see a similar process occurring. But the dominant reading for Aboriginal audiences has to do with patrilineal rights to stories and restrictions on speaking about the dead. Japangardi is in the alternating generation with his father, about whom he is mostly speaking, and has a different skin name. His sons, however, are in the same subsection, maintain identical rights to their grandfather, and in a symbolic sense are equals. Indeed, the prohibition on recalling the names of the dead are only relaxed for close family with the emergence of the second descendant generation, at which time names of the dead may be recycled and *kumunjayi* restrictions lifted. Therefore the presence of the protagonist's grandsons, who may have more "right" to the story than the son, authorizes its retelling as well as underscoring the continuity of tradition.

The appearance of these conventions on the tape that suggest unique Warlpiri concerns cannot be regarded as definitive. Rather, they are experiments made by Jupurrula in carrying rules for expression from oral tradition into electronic media. They intend to make the video product not only readable to Warlpiri audiences but credible as well. Remember that there are competing versions of the Coniston story extant at Yuendumu, and it may matter very much which of these in the future becomes dominant.

The social organization of production. Worth and Adair argued that at least as important as the content of the Navajo films themselves was the way in which the Navajo made these films. The unique conventions of indigenous media arise through the particular social organization of production. This observation, derived from Marxist scholarship, is now commonplace in accounting for why Hollywood media look the way they do. This is equally true for indigenous media.

The startling aspect of the Coniston production was the assemblage of 27 people to make a film that featured only 3 and required only 2 operators. What is the function of the other people? Often Aborigines engaged in activities defined as "work" by Europeans are criticized for involving many more people than would seem to be required, typically for reasons and advantages seen to have little to do with the expressed objective of the activity. This has been described as "kinship riding," and, indeed, it first appeared to me that the excess 22 people were along mostly to enjoy an unrelated hunting trip occasioned by the availability of resources (cars) and my sponsorship. Only when the kinship relationship between these people was charted did it become clear that these were all close relatives of the protagonists of the Coniston story and their presence was somehow necessary for the event to take place.

On the one hand, most of these people are identified as having ownership interests in the land on which we filmed. Aboriginal (if not

European) law required their consent to conduct an activity on this land. But they also maintain interests in the stories associated with the land, and this interest was expressed by their presence.

The situation recalled the relationship described earlier between Kirda (owner) class and Kurdungurlu (manager) class. In particular, Kirda for this story were in the Japangardi/Japanangka semipatrimoiety. It is not incidental that Jupurrula the cameraman is in a Kurdungurlu relationship to Japangardi and other people represented here. When I asked why others who attended and had direct knowledge of these events did not appear on camera, Jupurrula said: "They're Kurdungurlu. They want to stay on the side for this story."

In ceremonial activities, Kirda will paint up, dance, and express the story, which they are said to own. Kurdungurlu usually remain unadorned, to the side of the dance, and are said to manage it, like stage managers in this sense. Without Kurdungurlu, a dance cannot proceed, and it seems likely that they, rather than the owner/dancers, have final responsibility for correct performance. But they do not dance themselves.

In all reports from Warlpiri country, the camera is perceived to be Kurdungurlu for events. Women dancers at Yuendumu have directed a "cameraperson to physically replace the Kurdungurlu on *the* dancing ground" (Francoise Dussart, personal communication), and in the taping of ceremonies, senior people insisted that only Kurdungurlu, not Kirda, could operate the camera.

Warlpiri Media Association

The Coniston production signaled the next stage of development in media production at Yuendumu. The establishment of the video room at the Adult Education Centre, the availability of additional salaries, and the arrival of a new school principal supportive of the project all contributed to increased community participation. At this time, Japanangka moved to Lajamanu in response to family obligations and transferred his authority (and his Institute research assistant salary) to his brother-in-law, Jupurrula—a sensitive negotiation.

This transference of the video from an isolated research project to a community-based institution was an essential move in the direction of media development objectives, but it posed some organizational problems with respect to funding, accountability, authority, and ownership of tapes and equipment. The solution was to officially incorporate, which was done under the Northern Territory Companies Act, as a nonprofit community institution.

For convenience and speed, and to solve several problems at once, the Warlpiri Literature Production Centre Inc. was expanded and its constitution rewritten to cover video production as well as literature. The constitution also was revised to require an Aboriginal director and a majority Aboriginal board to assure Warlpiri control and to conform with suggestions made by CAAMA and the Central Australian Aboriginal Legal Aid Service (CAALAS).

It must be admitted that the primary function of this reorganization was to satisfy the requirements of the State, not of the Warlpiri, and, as is typically the case in such reorganizations, the corporation becomes European, not Aboriginal in structure. But the move also benefited Warlpiri interests. It removed the Literature Production Centre, as well as the video, from a vulnerable and ambiguous relationship with the school as a facility of the Northern Territory Education Department as well as the Institute, both of which were ultimately outside interests. It established a mechanism for holding copyright to videos and protecting the interests of the videomakers. It provided a conduit for funding, staffing, and control of equipment.

The revised constitution was drafted late in 1984 and submitted. A Japangardi involved with video in his role as assistant adult educator was elected chairman, and Jupurrula's role as director of video was formalized.

This use of video to "open up country" is of special significance to Aboriginal people and has been developing for some time in association with land rights efforts. Videotape has been used occasionally as evidence in hearings, where it demonstrates how much more comfortable Aboriginal people are in accounting for their land in situ than in a courtroom. Land councils are now expanding their video activities on field trips for the purpose of collecting evidence.

Community meetings. One of the most politically important genres to develop has been the recording and reviewing of meetings. Here, not only the production but the viewing and distribution of tapes becomes important, as this example demonstrates.

In September 1984 the principal of the Yuendumu School announced his resignation after only 6 months as headmaster. The resignation precipitated a series of actions in which the community attempted to achieve far greater control over education for their children. On September 10, the Yuendumu School Council, an Aboriginal parents' organization, left Yuendumu at 5:00 a.m. and drove for 4 hours into Alice Springs to the regional office of the Education Department. They announced their intention to sit in the lobby until the district supervisor would see them. When this was arranged, they presented a list of demands for certain controls over local education. They did not wish to negotiate but simply to be heard.

The first demand was for the session to be videotaped. Dave Japanangka, reading from the demands list, said, "We want this to be videotaped so that we can prove we really did come here, and so the Education Department can't lie about what was said." A member of the Yuendumu Video Unit taped the entire session, as did representatives of the Central Australian Aboriginal Media Association (CAAMA) and the Australian Broadcasting Corporation (ABC).

The next day, as requested, the superintendent came to Yuendumu and attempted to answer the council's demands. This meeting was videotaped. There followed several days of meetings with concerned parties, culminating with the visit of the chief minister for the Northern Territory. All these meetings were videotaped. During this process, the community used the videotapes in several ways:

1. They reviewed their own performances and analyzed their effectiveness as well as the negotiating strategies of the department.
2. They showed the tapes to people unable to attend the meetings, especially those who could not go into Alice Springs.
3. They showed the tapes to bureaucrats, politicians, and others who came late into the dispute.

School holidays meant a 10-day break in activities a few days after the crucial chief minister's meeting. It was feared that the momentum would be lost. But, instead, people realized that various community members would be traveling throughout the Territory during the holidays, and a list of all destinations was assembled. The 12 hours of taped meetings were edited onto a single 3-hour cassette; 18 copies were made and provided to people traveling to various communities and to meetings and conferences.

Within 2 weeks, approximately 4,500 people had seen some or all of the tape, including the local members, federal politicians, education administrators, Aboriginal organizations, as well as the teachers, staff, and parents of at least nine other remote Aboriginal schools. Additional requests for copies exhausted the supply of tape at the Video Unit, and only communities sending blank tapes could be provided for. The tape was still being requested and duplicated several months later.

Some of the demands were met, and considerable progress made on others. Although the long-term results were not convincing, there emerged a general optimism in the community based on the perception that they had taken a stand and exerted some real control over their lives.

A number of things about these events deserves attention. First, the videotape wasn't the only medium used to communicate the situation. The story was well covered (and responsibly handled) by regional newspapers. The ABC tapes were aired by the station in Darwin, and transmitted to Alice Springs. But even though almost half of the major remote communities were by then receiving television from satellite (Intelsat), they received a feed from Brisbane or Perth, and so did not get Territory news. Remote communities remained largely uninformed. However, the Territory minister for education and departmental officials did contact, by telephone and other means, various remote schools to publicize these events from their own perspectives. Thus, when we arrived at certain communities, they were already aware of the situation, although the tape offered a very different, and sometimes opposite, impression of what officialdom had reported.

Second, the tape is of terrible quality. Recording conditions were sometimes impossible, as in crowded meeting rooms; lighting was erratic, sound was worse. And as the camerapeople were also participants in the events, their attention was often divided. Twelve hours of raw tape was edited in a marathon all-night session as people waited at the door for copies so they could depart on holiday or to meetings. Editing was half inch to half inch. The Portapack source recorders were off-the-shelf home VHS systems. Anyone with a technical background realizes these are below minimal standards for video production. Yet the tapes galvanized audiences, who sat riveted for 3 hours in almost every community I observed.

Third, the tapes were unquestionably authentic because of the images and because it was known that they were taken by Aboriginal camerapeople. They also clarified complex issues. As documentaries, without narratives or voice-over explanation, they allowed people to come to their own conclusions and to appreciate the complexity of the issues. No single person, or written document, was able to do this. It also matters that we are dealing with communities whose literacy rates tend to fall below 25% and further in the older age groups. Written documentation could never have involved this range of people.

These tapes were also part of the first community television broadcasts in a number of remote communities where satellite dishes were disconnected and the tapes played over the transmitters.

Discussion

When the remote television project began at Yuendumu, I suppose we expected that Aboriginal people would want to record certain aspects of their lives that interest Europeans, such as ceremonies and other traditional activities, and perhaps some form of home movies. Interest in using local media as a means of cultural preservation and a teaching tool for the children did develop early in the project. Perhaps this was partly due to familiarity with European interests in ethnographic film subjects.

Some of the older people, upon seeing filmmakers enter the community, quickly gathered traditional implements and dressed up in ceremonial garb, to offer themselves as media subjects. In a curious reversal of traditional roles, the younger video workers began to intervene in these situations and attempted to negotiate with the filmmakers. They explained to me that the old men don't really understand what a camera is for (as opposed, perhaps, to what it is). They do not consider that they may be giving away their own image, their stories and designs, in a manner that is outside their control, and that this might jeopardize tradition.

The problem with using video as a tool of cultural preservation resides especially in the implications of mortuary restrictions. If you record the senior authorities for Warlpiri traditions telling stories, making implements, dancing, and so forth, it will not be long before these tapes cannot be shown, when these people die. This is a limitation that people at Yuendumu will now resolve themselves.

There have been a number of occasions where images of the dead have inadvertently been shown (and, more recently, even broadcast), and the consequences have been severe, including the shutting down of the facility for a period of time and the dramatic destruction of offending tapes. But in these cases, where Warlpiri themselves controlled production and transmission, there was no external agent to blame for the violation, and it had to be resolved within the community. Video-making can be a dangerous business.

We did not anticipate the passion of people to use the medium so directly as an agent of political communication as is described in the school tape example. But increasingly, the percentage of tapes that recorded meetings in and away from the community has grown.

This is partly because the great distances between communities in Aboriginal Australia means that people are often having decisions made for them in distant places by others; their lives are affected constantly by endless rounds of meetings that only a few representatives can attend. The taping of meetings enables the whole community to become involved in the decision-making process and makes their representatives accountable.

The taping of travels and bush trips may prove to have emotional and political consequences. It encourages people to "think about their country" and may well become significant in the land rights struggle.

Other tape genres have economic as well as political value. The Warlukarlangu Artists Association mounted three major gallery shows in its first year of operation, 1985. Each of these openings was attended by a few artists, but videos were taken at the openings so everyone could see what had happened, as with other "meeting tapes." But video also was displayed in the more recent shows and provided valuable documentary background about the making and meanings of the paintings. Video is now also used in place of photography for cataloguing and identifying paintings (old people seem to have less difficulty with scale in video), and an art marketing publicity tape including current works for sale has been edited.

Transmission

The distribution as well as the production of tapes also informs us of the kinds of distribution systems that Aboriginal producers will require in remote areas. The system builds from the ground up. Communications to outstations are the first requirement. For example, we can imagine solutions to outstation education that video and its transmission from the central community school could provide, based on examples in Canada, Alaska, and elsewhere.

People at Yuendumu will want to communicate to other remote people, to network the "bush people" throughout the region, and perhaps the continent, as was attempted in the example discussed above. Then will come the more traditional, and cost-effective, links to major supply and information trunk lines.

As early as 1983, Japanangka expressed interest not only in making videos but in transmitting them as well. For him, this meant, first, transmission in the community and also throughout Warlpiri country, extending to outstations, then to Lajamanu, Willowra, and everywhere else where Warlpiri people lived. During the second year, one of the videomakers designed and painted a logo in traditional sandpainting style to express this concept.

Of the difficulties and expenses that have been described for video and television in this report, the provision and distribution of programs stands out. Locally, the acquisition and maintenance of tapes has been shown to be expensive and unsatisfactory. The short life span of expensive VHS machines in Aboriginal camps in a desert climate involves major capital outlays and recurrent expenses. The borrowing of locally produced master tapes took a continual toll on the WMA video archive. The provision of viewing facilities within the unit did not solve this problem. Where possible, people prefer to view at home. Exchange of tapes with other communities proved expensive and unreliable. In the case of the important school meeting tapes, the cassettes were personally transported and shown by community members across great distances. People at Yuendumu and in other communities were unwilling to trust master tapes to the erratic mail services, and no community had adequate facilities or funding to make duplicates for distribution.

The economics of satellite transmission do not readily invite a solution to the distribution problem. The costs of uplink and transponder rental are not justified by the erratic output and limited audience for community tapes in local language. Other solutions are required. But local transmission can easily and economically solve the problem of getting programs around the community. This was the solution explored and eventually developed by the Media Association.

I was enthusiastic about this proposal because producing videos seemed to fulfill only half the project objectives. Video production without adequate distribution was unlikely to evolve into a community media facility. Analytically attempting to generalize from videotape production into television effects ignored the immediate reality of television as a unique household appliance. Only when Yuendumu began broadcasting could many of the questions facing the community be worked out, both by the community and by the researcher.

On paper, this solution is quite simple. A low-power community television transmitter is fairly modest technology and should cost only a few thousand dollars, the cost of a single VHS system. If a reliable local station could be established, people could watch video without the expense of a VCR. A simple color receiver costing less than $500 would be the only necessary equipment, and these had proved to require considerably less maintenance than did the VCR component.

The problems that faced the community involved the law and licensing. It is illegal in Australia to transmit radio waves (which also carry television signals) without a license. And no licensing category was available appropriate to an operation of the sort Yuendumu was proposing. Television licenses were designed for large, essentially urban operations, based on economic and social assumptions of mass electronic distribution from the 1950s.

The only licenses being applied to remote communities are "Self Help" licenses, a fairly ad hoc scheme designed to allow for community retransmission of in-coming ABC Intelsat signals. Not only did this license not provide for any local origination, but it was only available as part of a dish/retransmitter scheme, typically provided by subsidiaries of Hills Industries. Worse yet, from the community point of view, the licensee was sometimes (as in Lajamanu) the hardware supplier rather than the community itself.

License Applications

In November 1983, Japanangka, Nampijinpa, and myself edited a sample of tapes produced at Yuendumu and included a speech by Japanangka explaining clearly his objectives for media development there. He proposed on this tape the establishment of a local TV station, airing community-produced, Warlpiri language/culture tapes. This way, when the satellite "came in," Yuendumu could mix the imported signal with local programs to produce what they would determine was an appropriate TV schedule for the community. He explained the community's fears about television intruding on Warlpiri culture but admitted an attraction to the medium. He described the proposal as "fighting fire with fire."

Over the next several months, the issue was discussed at Yuendumu. By now it was known that Ernabella and other communities were also producing and planned to broadcast, so that it was agreed there should be broader consultation. This was achieved at the Australian Broadcasting Tribunal's public inquiry into Satellite Program Services at Kintore Aboriginal Homeland, a Pintubi community near the West Australian border, in March 1984.

This important meeting (the only direct consultation by a government agency with remote Aborigines on the question of satellite television) also provided the opportunity for the video-producing communities of central Australia to confer on issues and strategy. Following the meeting, both Yuendumu and Ernabella wrote to the secretary of the Department of Communications explaining their needs and requesting a license.

Six months later, despite my own and other follow-up inquiries, there was no official response from the department. Then, an "expression of interest" form was provided to fill out, which the community did. At this point, however, the Task Force on Aboriginal and Islanders Broadcasting and Communications was sitting, and the department expressed an unwillingness to proceed on these and related issues until the Task Force reported and the government responded (which finally occurred in December 1985, after both satellites were launched and AUSSAT was operational). The urgency that the community had expressed to have their facilities in place in advance of the onslaught of imported signals was ignored.

Meanwhile, the community had made inquiries regarding the purchase of a transmitter. Hills Industries, the supplier of Self-Help equipment, seemed unenthusiastic about providing a transmitter without a dish, and, it is believed, made inquiries to the department regarding the situation (although the supplier is not implicated in any license violations that might arise from use of their equipment if it meets technical standards). Moreover, the price quoted for the transmitter seemed extraordinarily high (approximately $10,000) for what was being requested.

Yuendumu was able to locate a ham enthusiast willing to supply privately a transmitter for $1,200 if his anonymity was preserved. Members of the Media Association, following some dramatic politicking, managed to arrange with the council the reallocation of the old community laundry, which the football club had intended to restore, for use as a television station. Money ($8,000) for the transmitter and the renovation of the building was voted from Social Club profits, and CEP trainees were enlisted to do the work. Thus by 1985 Yuendumu was poised to undertake local transmission.

Test transmissions from the studio in the Adult Education Centre were begun on April 1, 1985. In a meeting with the council, it was decided to embark immediately on a 4-hour schedule from 12:00 to 2:00 p.m. (lunch time) and 5:00 to 7:00 p.m. (following work) on weekdays. The schedule went into operation on April 2.

By the end of the month, the community decided to make its activities public in an attempt to pressure the DOC to resolve their licensing ambiguities and also to communicate their achievements to other remote Aborigines. This was done by having the ABC videotape reedited to include an announcement from the Community Council and WHA and including sections taped off-air of the first broadcasts. This was played at a media development conference in Sydney. CAAMA was authorized to issue press releases and the media attended the conference. Japangardi, the WMA chairman, and Jupurrula, video director, came in to Alice Springs to meet the press at CAAMA. There followed a dramatic weekend during which it developed that Canberra had failed to brief the State Broadcasting Engineer, who publicly issued threats of inquiries, closing, confiscation, and penalties. Ernabella community was enlisted and announced that they too were broadcasting and offered their support to Yuendumu.

The DOC in Canberra responded by promising the issuance of special licenses to both Ernabella and Yuendumu. In fact, the community never received direct confirmation from the DOC regarding this license, and my own inquiries suggest that it is essentially an "in principle" decision not to interfere rather than a license that can be identified as a policy commitment or a document that can be cited for attracting funding, resources, or support. It did produce a $25,000 equipment grant from DAA, from an end of the fiscal year surplus, outside any policy or planning context. Even so, Yuendumu television by May 1985 was well and truly launched.

Operations

Daily transmission created an entirely new set of challenges and problems for the video workers and the community. Unlike video, which could be produced and viewed whenever people were motivated, a TV schedule demands that operators be on the job at specified times and that they have preselected and reviewed tapes for airing. Neither of these requirements was entirely convincing to the video workers.

In the studio, a camera was trained on a compere, or host, seated behind a desk with the WMA logo behind him or her. This camera went through a Portapack and was then wired to a home video deck, which was jacked into the transmitter and went to the aerial. This unwieldy setup was necessitated by the incompatibility of the components but had the advantage of allowing for the live segments to be recorded if the compere got up from behind the desk and switched the Portapack on. Occasionally a cameraman would assist, but usually one person operated the entire system.

The format that evolved was originally very much like a radio program. The compere would greet the audience, tell any news or make whatever remarks he or she chose, and then announce the program, rising from the desk to switch on the tape and turn off the camera. Following (or in between the tapes) there might be additional live segments or remarks.

Soon this format was expanded. Jupurrula, for example, began to play music as an introduction on a tape recorder set on the desk. Sometimes he would train the camera on an appropriate graphic—this might be a Bob Marley t-shirt draped over a chair when he was playing his favorite reggae music. Sometimes people were invited in for interviews, and different people, including senior men, took turns at being comperes. Children were invited to the studio to show pictures and read stories they had made at school that day.

Because of frustrating but familiar delays in wiring the new station, all this was taking place in the old Adult Education room of approximately 6 × 4 meters. Far too many people tended to crowd in during broadcasts, and equipment was being damaged; it was also difficult to control the camera.

Comperes developed a habit of disappearing occasionally while tapes were playing, and cameras would come on and broadcast people unaware, including young men telling risqué jokes. It was decided to abandon the live segment as a regular feature until the new studio opened and simply to play tapes.

This led to a general slackness in the transmission schedule so that, during some periods in mid-1985, it was difficult to predict when the station would be operating. However, when an important tape was to be aired, say of the Ayers Rock handover, which was shot the previous day, the station might run the tape continuously until the entire community had viewed it.

Evaluation

These early months of transmission were very exciting for the community but also quite frustrating for the video workers. The long delays in opening the studio were mostly due to problems with outside electricians and a several months' delay waiting for the electrical inspector to come from Alice Springs. But development work in remote communities always has these delays, and the ability to tolerate these are crucial to eventual success.

A major worry was predictability. I saw no way that the station could survive without a reliable schedule. How could viewers know when to tune in? There were certainly periods when the video workers seemed to treat the procedure more as a chore than anything else, and this was disturbing because they seemed unaware whether anyone was watching or not. They sometimes appeared just to turn the transmitter on, unconcerned whether it was being viewed.

The objective of freeing people from their video recorders did not materialize either. Video was every bit as active during this period. Moreover, no one bought TV sets just to watch the station. The store manager was unsupportive and unwilling to stock either color sets or inexpensive black and white ones. Because the audio signal could also be received on the FM radio band, some Warlpiri only listened to the TV. It was a curious sight to see an Aboriginal household sitting down watching a radio.

There was also a reception problem. Aerials were advised but were initially unavailable. And video viewers who had spent untold hours fiddling with the channel knobs on their sets (to tune in radio-frequency VCR connections) had great difficulty tuning to the local station. While we all assisted in tuning sets and setting up aerials, this could only be on request and wasn't always successful. As a result, I often thought that I might be the only person watching TV at Yuendumu. But as soon as anything very good or very bad happened, it quickly became apparent that penetration was far more extensive than it seemed.

This was demonstrated most clearly when a tape was inadvertently shown containing sections with a child who had very recently died. The community was quick to anger, and elaborate measures were taken by the video workers to correct the offense, as their failure to preview tapes was the cause. Now during mourning ceremonies, the station usually shuts down, because people don't want to operate it and because people don't want to watch.

The utility of the station is demonstrated more positively when important tapes arrive in the community and the transmitter runs all day. This variable scheduling seems somehow more appropriate to the routines in Aboriginal communities, but it is difficult to imagine how to make this work with television and maintain viewership.

Related problems have been noted in the contexts of Aboriginal employment, school attendance, and many other activities that demand regular scheduling. The notion of regular schedules is alien and intrusive to traditional community rhythms, responsibilities, and seasonal routines. Mediation between clock time and Aboriginal time is not always easy, and how the local television broadcasting schedule might intervene remains unclear.

When imported signals become available, and if the community chooses to insert its signals into the imported schedule rather than maintaining their own channel, it may be possible to develop a variable transmission. More recent suggestions have been to train the camera on a still image (or even out the studio window to Yuendumu's main intersection) while retransmitting the new ABC/CAAMA HF shower signal. This would mean all-day TV transmission as well as fortuitous FM radio retransmission for people without short-wave capable of receiving the new CAAMA service.

These are matters whose solution lies in the future as media introduction proceeds. The problem at this point is to ensure that sufficient flexibility is built into the system to allow for these developments rather than closing off options in a manner that alienates both the community and the video workers. It should be emphasized here that Yuendumu Video is very much an experiment in process, and should remain so; it is premature to devise prescriptive solutions to all problems.

But it should also be noted that both Yuendumu Aborigines and media development advisers conceptualize local television not as an isolated facility but as a node on a larger network of many stations. Evaluation of Yuendumu television, in isolation from such a network, can be only speculative. For the local system to work, it will need to be linked to other stations, identified as a class for training, funding, licensing, program exchange, and other essential support and services. In short, it will need to be part of a regional or national Aboriginal communication scheme, not merely an interesting, but exceptional experiment.

References

Michaels, E., & Kelly, F. (1985). The social organization of an Aboriginal video workplace. *Australian Aboriginal Studies, 1984*(3).

Munn, N. D. (1973). *Warlpiri iconography: Graphic representation and cultural symbolism in a central Australian society.* Ithaca, NY: Cornell University Press.

Toyne, P. (1986). The development of local television broadcasting units. In B. Foran & B. Walker (Eds.), *The application of science and technology to Aboriginal development in Central Australia.* Melbourne: CSIRO; Alice Springs, N.T.: Centre for Appropriate Technology.

Worth, S., & Adair, J. (1972). *Through Navajo eyes: An exploration in film communication and anthropology.* Bloomington: University of Indiana Press.

Young, E. (1981). *Tribal communities in rural areas.* Canberra: ANU, Development Studies Centre.

Interactive television is not a single technology or service but a family of diverse systems and applications that trace their history to the very beginning of television.

11

Interactive Television

JOHN CAREY
PAT O'HARA

In the mid-1970s, there was a flurry of excitement in the commercial telecommunication world as well as in education and government about the potential of interactive television. A "wired nation" appeared to be just around the corner and with it came a promise of a technological promised land in which every home would have a two-way link to virtually unlimited information and entertainment. One of the projects begun during this period was based in Reading, Pennsylvania: interactive cable television for senior citizens. Created with funding from the National Science Foundation and implemented by a consortium of New York University and Reading groups, the project was field tested in 1975 and formally launched in 1976. Berks Community Television (BCTV), as it was later to be called, is now approaching 10 years of operation. Curiously, it is one of the few interactive cable television projects launched in the 1970s that still operates. Indeed, the two-way cable service has expanded over the years to include many other user groups and origination sites within Pennsylvania's Berks County. Why has the Reading interactive cable service succeeded while many others have not? Further, why has this apparently successful community channel not been imitated by others? To tackle these questions, it is useful to trace the history of interactive television, describe how the Reading system was created, and review its current status nearly a decade later. Emerging from this assessment is a picture of a social communication innovation in which technology played an important but secondary role.

EDITORS' NOTE: This essay represented the state of the art of interactive television when it was first published in 1985.

Interactive Television

Interactive television is not a single technology or service but a family of diverse systems and applications that trace their history to the very beginning of television. Among the earliest experimental television projects in the 1920s was two-way video communication. In the 1950s a few rather primitive interactive formats were introduced to commercial television. A children's program in New York, *Winky Dink and You,* created simple interaction through the use of a plastic screen that viewers attached to the regular TV screen. In the programs, a cartoon character Winky Dink would encounter a series of problems. For example, chased by a tiger, Winky Dink would run to the edge of a chasm. Children watching in their homes were then exhorted to help Winky Dink escape by drawing a bridge with crayons, on their plastic screen, over the chasm. One problem with this format was the participation of kids who failed to purchase the special plastic screen and simply drew with crayons on the glass TV screen. Another well-known interactive format was employed by Edward R. Murrow in his interview program *Person to Person,* in which a guest in his or her home was interviewed by Murrow, who remained in the studio. Often, there was a considerable distance between the two locations. While the program enjoyed commercial success, the interactive format was very crude. In fact, the guests could not see Murrow though they often pretended to see him.

Interactive television received a major promotional boost at the 1964 New York World's Fair with the display of AT&T's picture telephone. "Picturephone," as it came to be called, was presented as a forerunner of a new telephone service that would be in every home within a decade. While the picturephone drew enthusiastic response from many in the 1960s, it was soon apparent that the cost of interactive video telephones in every household would be prohibitive for the foreseeable future. However, many began to explore commercial or institutional applications for interactive video. Thus, in the late 1960s and early 1970s, a series of pilot projects were begun using interactive video for business meetings, medical training, education, and police work. These pilot projects employed a range of transmission technologies, for example, microwave, cable television, and special telephone lines. Also, they employed a range of communication configurations, for example, two-way audio and video, one-way video and two-way audio, and data transmission accompanying audio-video communication. Many of these early projects experienced severe technical problems, as they were testing new types of equipment. Others experienced resistance from user groups who felt that the technology might replace their jobs. Still other applications addressed needs that did not really exist or were too costly for the institutions using them.

While the early projects experienced many problems, enthusiasm for the *possibilities* of interactive television continued to grow. One manifestation of this enthusiasm was a multimillion-dollar pilot program undertaken by the National Science Foundation in the mid-1970s. The National Science Foundation fixed upon interactive cable television as a resource for the delivery of social services and education. Their interests were tied to questions about the costs and effectiveness of delivering social services via interactive television. It was felt that, if interactive television could be demonstrated to be cost-effective, it would be adopted by many communities and used to extend services to those who did not have access to them and improve services to those who received information and education in limited face-to-face settings or through traditional one-way media.

The National Science Foundation funded three projects, in Reading, Pennsylvania; Spartanburg, South Carolina; and Rockford, Illinois. Collectively, the three projects were intended to provide training for firemen and teachers, education for high school students, training for day-care workers, and social service information delivery to senior citizens. In addition to these stated intentions, the three projects provided a range of further services. And, in each case, extensive research was conducted about the applications.

Just as the National Science Foundation projects were concluding, a commercial interactive cable project was begun with great fanfare: the Warner Amex QUBE system in Columbus, Ohio. QUBE used one-way audio and video into homes and simple data transmission from each home back to the cable headend studio. The principal format in QUBE programming was multiple choice responses to opinion questions posed in programs, for example, how viewers felt about a planned shopping center in town.

While the National Science Foundation projects in Rockford and Spartanburg yielded a wealth of valuable research (Baldwin, Greenberg, Block, & Stoyanoff, 1978; Lucas, 1978), the systems did not flourish after the research ended. Similarly, QUBE provided extraordinary publicity value for Warner Amex and helped them to win many franchises. However, use of the system (still in place in Columbus, Ohio, and a few other cities) has been low and interest has generally declined (Kahan, 1983). The system in Reading, Pennsylvania, stands as a curious oddity. Research about the system suggested that it provided only moderate cost benefits for social service information delivery (Moss, 1978). Yet, it took root in the community and flourished. The reasons for this, along with some general findings about how the system has been used, are discussed in the brief case study that follows.

Interactive Cable Television in Reading, Pennsylvania: Setting Up the Organization

The Reading interactive cable television project was first and foremost a community-based social innovation. Before any equipment was purchased and before any programming was planned, the project team undertook extensive organizational work within the community. This began with the formation of the consortium that received funding from the National Science Foundation. It included the local cable company, the senior citizen council in Berks County, the local housing authority, and the City of Reading itself as well as the Alternate Media Center and Graduate School of Public Administration from New York University. Second, some of the NYU staff took up permanent residence in Reading during the entire course of the project; they joined the community. Then, several important organizational decisions were made to help implant the innovation within the community. A staff of technicians and camera operators who could run the equipment were hired locally. A community board was established to provide counsel and support initially and, eventually, to take over the system. Also, a programming committee of senior citizens was set up to advise on programming decisions. Finally, a nonprofit local entity was created. These organizational elements provided early credibility within the community and anticipated the eventual need for local fund-raising to continue the system and a local management group to run it. In this sense, the transition process from federally funded experiment to ongoing local system was begun on the first day of the project.

System Design

Early technical design decisions contributed much to the style and conventions that evolved over time. There was a conscious effort made by the NYU project team to build a simple and modest technical configuration that would lend itself to operation by individuals with little or no technical background. It was hoped that this would place more emphasis on the quality of human interaction patterns and less on the technical demands of the system. Thus, instead of studio environments, community spaces were selected for program origination. Also, these were called "Neighborhood Communication Centers" rather than "studios." There were three Neighborhood Communication Centers in the original design. The interactions among participants at the three interconnected centers formed the basis for most programming. In addition, a few remote sites could be linked into the system when needed, for example, city hall and the local social security office.

One of the early technology choices, selection of off-the-shelf black-and-white cameras and fast zoom lenses, was directed by a concern for reducing technical problems and providing more comfort to participants. For example, the fast zoom lenses necessitated minimal adjustments to existing room lights, thus reducing heat and glare. The fabled hot lights of stage and screen are simply not suitable for ordinary people's comfort. Further, the zoom lenses allowed informal and staggered seating arrangements with no loss of image size. This became a very important issue several months into the project when a split screen convention emerged. That is, a split screen was used to show two people from different centers interacting with each other. The simple camera arrangements and zoom lenses allowed the camera operators to quickly align the image size and position on the screen of the two interactants.

In keeping with the simplicity of design, only one camera was used at each location to capture participant behavior (a separate graphics camera and videotape feed were also available for use). This camera was placed next to the television monitor that displayed the downstream video feed, that is, the image being sent out by the cable system to home viewers as well as to each neighborhood communication center. Because the monitor conveyed the video communication from other centers as well as what was "going out" to homes, participants directed their gaze toward it most of the time. And, when interacting with someone at another center, a participant spoke to the monitor, not the camera. However, because the camera was located right next to the monitor, a person speaking to the monitor gave the appearance of eye contact to a participant viewing at another center.

The design decision of one camera per location to capture participant behavior also helped everyone to understand shifts in action from one location to another. That is, any time a viewer saw a cut from one camera perspective to another, it meant that the action had switched to another center. Since three or four sites were commonly participating in a given program, the issue of "location" for a given person at a given moment was very important and potentially problematic. The one camera per location decision helped viewers identify where a shot was originating, along with occasional comments by a program host, the distinct appearance of each center, and the regularity of participants at each site (that is, viewers learned that certain regular participants always went to the same center).

The video signals from each center were transmitted to the cable headend where a technician selected the shot or combination of shots (split screen) that became the downstream feed to home television sets and the video monitor at each center. The technician was called a "switcher," not a "director" (there were no directors). He was instructed to follow the action and show the person or persons who were speaking. For this reason, there were very few reaction shots or other techniques used by directors in commercial television to comment about the action. For example, in commercial television, a director might instruct a camera operator to zoom in for a close-up shot of a person's shaking hands to show that the person is tense. This type of shot was not used in Reading's interactive programming. Further, the technician-switcher in Reading, unlike the invisible director in commercial TV, was often brought into the programming by a comment from a participant at one location. For example, a speaker commonly said, "Bruce, punch up Horizon Center," instructing Bruce, the switcher, to show a particular neighborhood communication on the video monitor.

In many ways, the configuration of the audio system was more problematic. Everyone involved felt that the ability to interrupt easily and speak informally would be crucial to successful programming. However, the presence of more than a dozen microphones spread over three or more locations, each one "open" all the time to pick up spontaneous comments, can create noise, feedback, and confusion. After much trial and error, the project team selected directional, hand-held microphones for use by most participants supplemented by a few lavaliere microphones for use under some conditions by a program host or guest. This microphone mix helped to reduce ambient noise while allowing wide pickup in each center. The directional microphones were placed strategically throughout the seating area at each center. Participants learned quickly that they had to grab one of these microphones and speak into it in order to be heard at the other centers. The audio output at each center was enhanced by appropriately placing high-fidelity speakers in each center, based on the size of the room and seating arrangements. The difficulty of finding the right balance so that participants could speak and hear without disruption to the interaction needs to be stressed. Indeed, the overall process of getting the audio to function effectively required more work than setting up the video.

Programming

Most of the programming on Berks Community Television, Reading's interactive channel, may be categorized as a talk format, with interaction taking place among participants at two to four origination sites during a given program. In the early years of operation, all programming took place during the day, from 10 a.m. to noon. Programming was in black and white, and 90% of it was live. Individuals who wanted to participate fully in programs (be seen and heard) went to one of the neighborhood communication centers near where they lived. Those who watched the interactive programs from their home could call in and participate in an audio-only mode. Calls from home viewers were solicited frequently during many of the programs.

Some of the early programs included *Scrapbook,* a discussion of local history and folklore; *Inside City Hall,* an interview/discussion program between seniors and the mayor or a city council member; *Singalong,* a very popular program in which participants at all the centers sang favorite songs together; *Yoga for Health,* a 5-minute exercise program; *Sense and Nonsense,* a quiz program; and *The Eban and Herb Show,* a polling-discussion show on a broad range of topics. Most programs were 30 minutes long, though a few ran a full hour and a few were 5 minutes in length.

A major goal of the National Science Foundation, in funding the Reading project, was to determine if interactive programming could effectively deliver social service information. This was explicitly reflected in some programs such as a question-and-answer session with the local director of the Social Security Administration. Other programs mixed social service information with entertainment. For example, *Sense and Nonsense,* a quiz program, mixed trivia questions, questions about Hollywood movies, and social service or nutrition questions designed to educate those who might not have known the answer. Still other programming, for example, *Singalong,* involved pure entertainment. A major finding of the research conducted about the Reading project was that, while interactive TV was a reasonable way to convey social service information to senior citizens, an equal or greater benefit was the socialization that followed from an individual's participation in the programming. Participants made new friends, became more active, communicated more, and in some instances gained renewed self-esteem.

In most of the programs a strong emphasis was placed on center-to-center communication. Thus, in a discussion show with local politicians, the host of the program and the guest politician were commonly situated in separate origination sites. The seating arrangements also fostered center-to-center interaction. Everyone at a given center—host, guest, and participants—faced in the same direction: toward the monitor, where they would see participants from the other centers. Indeed, if two individuals who were seated side by side in the same center began a dialogue, they commonly maintained an orientation toward the monitor rather than facing each other directly. The center-to-center communication flow quickened the pace of the programming, because the visual action moved from location to location in any dialogue between participants at separate origination sites.

During the first few months of system operation, programs did not keep to a rigid schedule. A 30-minute program might run from 28 to 32 minutes. Along with this relaxed sense of time, programs often began and ended with a few minutes of chitchat totally unrelated to the topic or purpose of the program. Within a few months, scheduling requirements of the cable system (the interactive programming was bracketed by commercial programs that began and ended within precise time constraints) and a general concern about managing the interactive programs led the project staff to adopt more precise time schedules. However, the informal chitchat feature (which almost everyone liked) was maintained in a more controlled way. Indeed, it evolved into a convention of "sweeping" the centers. At the beginning and end of the program day as well as at the beginning of many individual programs, the host asked the technician-switcher at the cable headend to show each center one by one. During this sweep of the centers, participants frequently smiled or waved, greeted a person at another center, asked about someone's health, and so on.

The issue of appropriate structure for the interactive programs was from the earliest days a major issue for all. A number of competing models existed. The programs could attempt to imitate commercial TV, treat the participants' interactions like other community social gatherings such as church or town meetings, or explore totally new formats that built upon the unique characteristics of the interactive technology. By and large, the NYU team wanted to explore new interactive formats; most seniors recognized that they were involved with a new technology but also naturally fell back on formats and behavior borrowed from their social experiences with town meetings, church, and so on; and a few seniors envisioned themselves to be a Johnny Carson or Phil Donahue.

These competing models were readily apparent in early programming, where there was much variation in format and style. Within a short time, however, many program conventions emerged based upon the characteristics of the technology and system configuration, for example, the center-to-center communication flow. Competing formats based upon the seniors' social experiences, for example, town meetings, were somewhat less influential as the new interactive conventions emerged. It may also be argued that the new technology and existing social formats merged, as in the interview/discussion program between seniors at three neighborhood communication centers and the mayor at city hall. The influence of commercial TV is more complex. Those who tried to imitate commercial TV formats by reading from a script fared poorly and the practice was soon discouraged. Other commercial TV practices such as opening a program with a standard video sequence led to parallel practices: displaying a designed graphics card and playing a short musical theme at the opening of some programs. And the aspirations of a few to imitate the style of Johnny Carson or Phil Donahue remained. Indeed, while Berks Community Television has evolved into a clear and distinct form of television, with its own set of formats and conventions, the subtle influence of commercial TV models in the minds of producers and participants will likely always remain.

Communicating on Interactive Television

How do ordinary people, in this case senior citizens, adapt to a new communication technology like interactive cable television? Berks Community TV provided a fertile ground in which to examine this question. In Reading, people came to the new situation with existing communication patterns based upon their experiences in everyday face-to-face situations and with other technologies such as the telephone. Early usage of interactive television in Reading demonstrated that people initially borrow behaviors from other, more familiar situations and treat the new communication form as if it were the more familiar form. Thus some individuals, after completing a speaking turn, would conclude with "over," a pattern borrowed from amateur radio operators. One participant, after speaking into a microphone, placed the mike next to his ear to hear the response. He treated the microphone as if it were a telephone receiver. This pattern is not new or unique to Reading. Alexander Graham Bell is reported to have begun his telephone conversations by saying "Ahoy."

Because individuals in Reading borrowed from different areas of experience, there was much variation in the early communication patterns on Berks Community TV. Over time, as people learned about the system and as shared codes of behavior evolved, communication patterns became more consistent and efficient. They were more consistent in that most participants said or did similar things to communicate a given meaning. They were more efficient in that they could communicate a given meaning in less time and did not require the same degree of redundancy to make sure others understood the message.

Interactive programming in Reading also demonstrated how many of the fundamental prerequisites for a communication exchange can become disrupted when people exchanging messages are separated physically. For example, in a face-to-face situation, it is relatively easy to establish that someone else is in your presence and therefore able to communicate with you, whether they are talking to you or someone else, who they are, and what you are talking about. With these prerequisites in place, communication can flow relatively efficiently between individuals. On interactive TV, individuals have to do more work to establish these prerequisites. Moreover, the prerequisites once established are subject to disruption, for example, a technical problem at one of the neighborhood communication centers can eliminate someone from your "presence." Similarly, a comment seemingly addressed to everyone at all the centers might be a response to a side comment spoken off-mike and heard only by those at one center. These communication issues are not unlike those we experience when using a telephone. However, an elaborate and shared set of conventions has evolved for managing telephone interactions. Many of these conventions are unexamined because they seem natural to us at this point. For example, the occasional "uhuh" of a listener in a telephone conversation not only signals "I agree" or "I'm following what you're saying" but also "I'm still on the line and in your presence." If a listener in a telephone conversation does not provide these minimal signals of continued presence on the line, a speaker is likely to inquire after 2 or 3 minutes, "Are you still there?"

On Berks Community TV, much of the work to establish and maintain the prerequisites for communication has evolved over time as a job for the program host and a secondary host at each center. They help to establish who is speaking, what the topic is, when someone leaves the room, and so on. In addition, the television monitor in each center serves to establish and maintain the communication channel between interactants. It conveys who a person is interacting with, where the other person is, and what information is being transmitted throughout the system. For all these reasons, the monitor has served as a powerful regulator of interaction.

The communication behavior of participants on Berks Community TV was also affected by the regularity of the interaction, the narrow geographic locale of participants and viewers, and the synchronous relationship between programming and day-to-day life. That is, the programming was live and took place each weekday. In addition, each program had many regular participants; participants and viewers all lived within a few miles of each other; and nearly everyone shared knowledge about local streets, stores, schools, and people. Thus, if a regular participant had a cold *yesterday* during a program, another person could ask during a program on the following day if he were feeling better. No such assumptions can be made about programming that is prerecorded and broadcast or cablecast over a variable time period.

Communication patterns in Berks Community TV were also characterized by the use of specifics rather than generics ("You can get it at Boscov's" rather than "You can get it at your local drug store"). Participants assumed that the audience shared their knowledge about Reading. This contrasts markedly with most programming on commercial television in which accepted communication conventions eliminate most temporal references (news is an exception), frequently employ generic references rather than specific ones, and assume little shared knowledge by the audience (major public items of knowledge such as the name of the U.S. president or a football star are exceptions). This also means that much of the programming on Berks Community TV would be difficult to follow for a cable audience in Houston or Boston.

Evolution of the System

To an observer familiar with the early Berks Community Television programming, there has been relatively little apparent change. In 1977 evening programs were added to the schedule. They emphasized communitywide issues and included many participants in addition to senior citizens. In 1981 Berks Community TV changed to color and added a new "studio" space in downtown Reading. Over the years the number of originating sites has expanded to more than a dozen. Additional high schools have linked into the system as well as local colleges, hospitals, and more government agencies.

In 1977 national funding for the Reading "experiment" ended and local funding as well as local management took over the system. Since then, 8 years of community support have strengthened the position of Berks Community TV within the City of Reading and surrounding areas. The current annual budget of $250,000 comes from a healthy mix of sources, including the City of Reading, the County Office of Aging, local corporate and foundation grants, the local cable company, and viewer donations. Most of the budget goes for seven full-time and two part-time staff. The paid staff is supplemented by an army of local volunteers, both technical and programming.

The programming conventions appear to be well embedded. While an interview style borrowed from commercial television is somewhat more evident, the continued use of split screens and a center-to-center information flow maintain an overall style that is quite similar to programming in the early system. Many of the original programs and program producers persist. Their expertise and participation in the now expanded system has helped to provide a continuity of style for the new programs and user groups. For example, Oda Miller, a retired social service worker who joined the project at its earliest stages, has continued to contribute programming concepts and interviewing and hosting responsibilities. So too has Gene Shirk, ex-mayor of Reading, chairman of the Berks Community TV board, and host of *Generation Gap* from its beginning. It was Gene Shirk who developed the idea of opening the system to young people and, in this way, began the transition to a broadly based community channel. Many other early participants have continued as program producers, hosts, and regular participants. Mae Fieck, who hosted the original interview program with city hall politicians; Ed Yost, who hosted *Scrapbook;* and Marie Pelter, who hosted the quiz show *Sense and Nonsense*, have all since died. When Marie Pelter died, her obituary in the local newspaper ran under the headline, "TV Personality Dies." This was one of many indicators that those who created and maintained Berks Community TV have achieved both respect and notoriety within the community.

Conclusion

Having outlined a brief case history of interactive television in Reading, Pennsylvania, it is appropriate to return to the questions we posed earlier: Why has the Reading system flourished while many other interactive systems did not and why has Reading not been replicated elsewhere? The two questions may be interlinked.

The apparent success of Berks Community TV has relatively little to do with interactive technology as such. Berks Community TV flourished, first, because the timing and location for the service were propitious. The conditions of time and place that fostered growth and acceptance for the service were a heavy cable penetration, no local broadcast television, and a cohesive community of viewers. Reading, Pennsylvania, is one of the "gritty" cities in the Northeast whose population has dwindled but that holds deep traditions of railroading, textile mills, and Pennsylvania Dutch ancestry. Served by television in Philadelphia and Harrisburg, the community naturally yearned for "local" programming. Also, local government agencies with a mandate to provide information services to the public and funding to pay for them found Berks Community TV a good way to do the job. It did not hurt, as well, when a local city councilperson who appeared regularly on early programs and won popularity through that participation was then elected mayor of Reading at the next general election.

Second, while the lure of advanced technology helped to secure early funding from the National Science Foundation, the implementation of the system was not technology driven. The needs and wants of people participating in the programs, watching as part of the home audience, and serving on the many committees associated with the system, were emphasized above all technical considerations. This helped to create a loyalty and tenacity that was crucial to the ultimate survival of the system.

Third, the continuation of the system has been tied to the skills of those who have run it for the past several years, a manageable budget, and sources of local funding. Further, there is no guarantee that Berks Community TV will continue for another decade. Like other community services, it is subject to changes in the local environment as well as the resources and desires of people who provide, consume, and pay for the service.

Berks Community TV has not been replicated elsewhere, nor should it, because its system design, program style, user groups, and content have been specifically tailored to conditions in Reading. If there is a lesson in Berks Community TV for other communities, it is to begin with a clear understanding of local conditions, needs, and resources, then to build communication services based upon that understanding.

Finally, Berks Community TV may be used to discuss some fundamental questions about interactive television. Specifically, is interactive television thrown into the mix, just a new format for normal one-way television, or a new medium entirely? This is not simply an academic issue. If we treat interactive television as a form of face-to-face interaction, users are likely to place demands on the system to do what people can do in face-to-face situations. No telecommunication system can duplicate an exchange that is mediated only by the human sensory apparatus. Interactive television will, under these circumstances, fall short of the standard we match it against. Conversely, if we adopt one-way television as a general model for interactive TV, users will likely imitate program formats and styles of behavior present in commercial television. This presents at least two obstacles. First, few interactive TV systems could match the production budgets of commercial television. Programs that attempt to copy commercial TV formats may therefore look like cheap imitations. Second, the likely users of interactive television are not actors and will not be able to match the performance of commercial TV actors.

An alternative approach is to carefully examine the characteristics of interactive television systems and to explore the kinds of communication for which they are best suited. Berks Community TV provides some examples of suitable applications but it by no means exhausts the possibilities. There are many examples of successful interactive television applications other than those in Reading. Collectively, the work of those who create interactive programming and the behavior of audiences that participate in it will forge a set of shared conventions. In this sense, it may be argued that interactive television is a distinct communication medium that is in the process of being formed.

References

Baldwin, T., Greenberg, B., Block, M., & Stoyanoff, N. (1978). Rockford Ill.: Cognitive and affective outcomes. *Journal of Communication, 28*(2), 180-194.

Kahan, H. (1983). *The cable subscriber speaks: Channels, choice or chaos?* New York: Advertising Research Foundation.

Lucas, W. (1978). Spartanburg, S.C.: Testing the effectiveness of video, voice and data feedback. *Journal of Communication, 28*(2), 168-179.

Moss, M. (Ed.). (1978). *Two-way cable television: An evaluation of community uses in Reading, Pennsylvania.* New York: The NYU-Reading Consortium.

Not a surprise, the so-called exploratory or experimental arts environment permits the most evolutionary and least restrictive use of interactive video. Relatively less affected by the marketing demands and formulas of commercial media, the fine arts most frequently provide an environment for "bottom-up" processing. In a "bottom-up" environment, unexpected events perpetually trigger greater direct-response behavior on the part of the viewer than in a "top-down" regulated video game context.

12

Boundaries and Frontiers: Interactivity and Participant Experience— Building New Models and Formats

DAVID TAFLER

On the horizon, as the human population expands, sprawls, and threads its way around the globe, electronic networks connect the most remote communities with their inner-city counterparts. At the intersections where broadcast image and sound, telephone, fax, and electronic data fill the satellite, microwave, fiber optic, twisted coil corridors, raw junctions and clusters shape the exchange of information. This matrix operates on many levels, forging and maintaining commercial enterprises while at the same time linking individuals and sustaining social contracts.

Much of the writing devoted to these information highways has spoken of the systemic corridors channeling the traffic. This chapter speaks to the activity at the terminals where the human operator interfaces with the electronic screen, with the mechanical keyboard, with the buttons, joysticks, levers, touch-, heat-, motion-generated apparatuses. As much control as the individual exercises over the conception of a message generated by his or her fingertips, other operations condition his or her cognition. Their source lies in the environment, where everyday subsistence becomes increasingly contingent on rapid responses to a plethora of light, sound, and kinesthetic activity.

The din filters down on every telecommunication level from retail catalogues to shopping channels, from cellular phones to automatic teller machines (ATMs). New instruments present new portals for accessing information. Electronic governors intercede and regulate production. Advanced digital systems monitor output and mediate inventory.

Multiple arcade devices and entertainment channels siphon off excess fascination and free time.

What does it mean to reach out and touch someone on the Internet? What significance lies in witnessing the television set becoming an active part of the traditional school, museum, or even public entertainment environment? Does an encounter with a screen experience stitch the group together in a public place, or does the ubiquitous television set perpetuate the congenital isolation bred from the home relationship with cable, broadcast, or computer characters?

Besieged by multiple solicitations, multiple seductions played across a confluence of mass marketing outlets and entertainment options, the individual struggling for some vague consciousness in a society constantly driven by new technotools and toys actively tries to pursue a rational course, or at the very least monitor his or her own evolving role and relationship to the media environment. The struggle not only means exercising some control over the delivery of information but understanding the way that control itself generates information or meaning.

Different models emerge along the way. Perhaps most prevalent, video arcades become trysting grounds for the new machines. New consoles drive the participant through star wars and race tracks. Bystanders watch as drivers manipulate joysticks and jettison themselves through imaginary space.

Quickly, these phenomena spread to the home. Video drivers handle remotes that annoyingly disrupt continuity patterns for other family viewers. Siblings battle for the controls directing the adventures of their surrogate electronic combatants. A two-tier hierarchical and unstable relationship evolves between the active button pushers and passive onlookers. The interactive dance becomes a running dialogue, a series of exchanges among the individuals in front of the screen.

An implied dialogue also evolves within the system itself, at the interface between the programmer and the user. Who controls the other? When an individual encounters an interactive system and makes a commitment to cognitively map its cybernetic corridors, the early trials signal the extent to which the program will allow the viewer-participant the latitude to determine the conditions shaping his or her exploration.[1] At some critical moment, the programmed parameters reveal whether or not the viewer-participant exercises control or remains positioned by the controlling program. At that junction, each player anticipates the other in the sequence of options, forks, branches, routes, and procedures written into the structure of the experience. To the extent that the piece remains fixed, this interaction either falls within or beyond a fabricated set of anticipated parameters. Motivated interest wanes and waxes accordingly.

Increasingly complex technology fortifies a growing user-friendly environment. The environment's routines and subroutines cloak the differences between control and being controlled, between production and reception. These differences lie along the boundaries of those technological functions mediating control.

New control systems predicated on talking to technology breed a new form of orality quite different than earlier communication models. An antiseptic machine logic prevails at the surface of the screen. The relentless deductive corridors sever emotional contact. Preconfigured pathways breed alienation. Cloaked in a void, the individual gestures toward an illegitimate mirror, which, in turn, conveys an array of programmed paradigms.

A seductive nomenclature camouflaging alienation in a fragmented environment, so-called interactive systems increasingly misrepresent and idealize the status of the alleged viewer-participant. Interactive tools and applications often do little more than realign old practical, pedagogical, economically driven, social methodologies. Prevailing systems restrict most pseudointeractive applications to fixed switching operations. Most participatory target games, information-testing devices, and computer-assisted training, design, and manufacturing (CAD-CAM) operations still remain linear and lack the multiple branching options essential for legitimate interactivity. The interactive challenge lies beyond the level of simple, reflex activity required to complete an electronic circuit and to move a targeted raster onward.

For most individuals, video interactivity remains wedded to the common practices of switching channels, selecting commands, moving pointers, choosing tools, generating text, and drawing images on a computer screen. With the facade of a GUI (graphic user interface) cloaking thousands of lines of coded instruction, the alleged viewer-participant responds enthusiastically to the immediacy of this new technological contact while his or her cognitive awareness regresses to the level of the child and remains confined to the parameters set by the task-related situation.

Admittedly, commercial applications such as choosing channels, products, or services do guarantee viewers some direct, discriminating involvement as long as the system of choosing, and the sequence of choices, remains profitable. Most commercial applications confine the viewer's freedom to a thoroughly regulated field of profitable branches or channels. Open-ended decision-making environments, symptomatic of moving within a multichannel television experience, provide the viewer with predictable passages that, at best, open up on expected programming patterns.

Certain alleged interactive communication corridors serve as unmarked lairs for electronic data gathering. Early on, as a lure to sell cable systems, a media company promoted what became the short-lived QUBE experiment in Columbus, Ohio, by publicizing the deployment of response buttons in the viewers' homes. The viewer could participate by expressing his or her preference and interest in products, programs, or argued positions. On a practical level, the viewer could automatically solicit, with the touch of a button, mail-distributed follow-up literature sent to the home. Only the more esoteric programs capitalized on the interactive controls. Interest waned. The company focused on its true mission, expanding its cable distribution, and not on pioneering interaction.

The flip side of QUBE's wired exchange bore a more sinister interactive layer with much greater rewards for programmers and their advertisers. QUBE constantly monitored and compiled viewing preferences and patterns. The system tracked and measured viewing behavior and calculated its television programming accordingly.

Though experiments such as QUBE have not endured, other, similar interactive mediators, for example, a new generation of television metering devices, more effectively track and register viewer involvement and identity. By directly monitoring the precise duration of time spent viewing each selected channel, the meters assemble and organize viewership data that accurately reflect the fragmentation and frequent fluctuations of contemporary viewing. These concise, concrete, and reliable measuring devices mean more manipulation, a worrisome byproduct of so-called interactive systems.

As a capitalist manifestation of George Orwell's horrific vision of 1984, a multitude of new measuring devices record, calculate, and report individual behavior. The Arbitron Ratings Company introduced a "people meter" that not only measures television audiences but also measures what products the viewers are buying. Individuals operate handheld, interactive devices in sample audiences ("Arbitron 'People Meter,' " 1988). In a commercial environment, the tracking of specific consumption patterns becomes an obvious asset to the stations or networks marketing their advertising services. Other feedback systems record ATM use, utility consumption, purchases, telephoning patterns, and innumerable spending and earning activities. Every utility bill paid, every credit card purchase, every purchase from a store that maintains running tabulations of each consumer's activity (usually through telephone number referencing) feeds this gluttonous compilation of information. The compiled data form as much a part of the post-television experience as do the images that dance on the screen.

The desire for concrete marketing data does not negate the individual's capacity for elusive behavior. Nor are those latent forces that promote the viewer-participant's speculative probing and questioning easily discernible in these extended marketing ventures. Statistical readings do not preclude or sufficiently encompass the infinite number of variables that work against a tight-knit theory of human interaction. The data merely serve as one among many efforts or tracks for articulating a particular response pattern. The conclusions cannot exclusively describe the reception of a particular text, nor can they adequately address the social-cultural milieu surrounding any production and reception. The data simply illustrate one aspect of the existing interface between the respective constituencies. Though the residual statistical data may lend insight to certain manifestations of interactive behavior, the conclusions remain speculative.

Another mediating data device, the public opinion poll, similarly highlights what the media describe as a new interactive democratic corridor stretching the boundaries of the participatory body politic. On numerous occasions, major American newspaper, television, and radio outlets have described and/or provided "interactive" operations whereby members of the electorate express their positions, though always in response to the media's structured options. Contrary to direct and open encounters, polls restrict their participants' response activity within a fixed and confined range. The predetermined options frequently offer dubious choices. Deceptively, the black-and-white alternatives mask the subtlety of content, structure, or thought that underlies the process of selection. Though interactive channels on some level acknowledge the individual's existence, that individual identity remains submerged beneath a stifling and often meaningless, though exceedingly manipulative, statistical blanket. Statistical generalizations fortify the anonymity of the individual while building the myth of consensus in an increasingly homogenized audience.

Some advocates of interactive video forgive their objective-oriented constraints and their participant's relative confinement. In 1988 David Clark, director of the University of London Audio-Visual Centre, argued that "a good interactive video program must deal directly with the user's concerns and requirements in ways that do not eat up scarce thinking capacity for tasks unconnected with the job in hand" (p. 41). Clark harbored no reservations with an explicit, direct system presenting an implicit series of fixed procedures and closed branches that limit the format, regulate events, and control the viewer.

Correlating individual response activity to influence or control group behavior works against a more open-ended and flexible interactive system contingent on the frequent fluctuations of individual behavior. A system predicated on selling ideas and expanding the size of an indulgent audience programs to the largest common denominator. It produces programming that takes few risks and requires little expended energy by the viewer. The potential response range remains a foregone conclusion.

In essence, the overall design of the system overrides any particular content that the system conveys. A tenuous equilibrium among conflicting forces characterizes the terrain. Herbert Marcuse wrote in *Eros and Civilization* (1955):

> The individual is not to be left alone. For left to itself, and supported by a free intelligence aware of the potentialities of liberation from the reality of repression, the libidinal energy generated by the id would thrust against its ever more extraneous limitations and strive to engulf an ever larger field of existential relations, thereby exploding the reality ego and its repressive performances. (p. 48)

A series of junctions mark the territory where new electronic systems interface with their constituents. At each location, the locus of repressive boundaries and libidinal frontiers positions the individual's relationship to nature, to culture, to the outside.

The question of closure goes beyond the individual viewer-participant's cognition and outward efforts. At some level of activity, the viewer-participant's private process of personal discovery must overlap his or her relationship to other individuals, including the producer, as part of the larger interactive consortium contributing to the experience. By necessity, the viewer-participant's active efforts to fabricate coherence operate on the flip side of the (artist)producer's intent when the (artist)producer constructs a premeditated and deliberately structured cycle of events for the viewer-participant(s).

In the mid-1980s a number of video pioneers opened up this turf and enhanced the qualitative value of the interactive experience. New territory, however, does not remain neutral. A human struggle situated comfortably within easily comprehensible contours changes repeatedly with each new wave of transition. New options trigger a sometimes gradual, other times more rapid onslaught of new events. Some stretch the fence while others explode open the gates, promising a limitless array of renewed physical, emotional contact and experience.

Unfortunately, when it comes to stimulating heightened awareness, novel patterns atrophy rapidly. Most continue to prescribe and circumscribe traditional roles and predictable behaviors. In an essay on the operation of language, Jacques Lacan (1977a) sketched the parameters. He appropriated the cybernetic interface as a model describing the patient-doctor relationship in a psychotherapeutic dialogue. His description of the presumptions and exchanges applies equally to the interactive encounter itself.

> If I now place myself in front of the other to question him, there is no cybernetic computer imaginable that can make a reaction out of what the response will be. The definition of response as the second term in the "stimulus response" circuit is simply a metaphor sustained by the subjectivity imputed to the animal, a subjectivity that is then ignored in the physical schema to which the metaphor reduces it. This is what I have called putting the rabbit into the hat so as to be able to pull it out again later. But a reaction is not a reply.
>
> If I press an electric button and a light goes on, there is no response except for my desire. If in order to obtain the same result I must try a whole system of relays whose correct position is unknown to me, there is no question except as concerns my anticipation, and there will not be one any longer, once I have learned enough about the system to operate it without mistakes. (p. 86)

Expectations played against unanticipated responses trigger new levels, new planes, new desires, and new awareness. In a human exchange, the process evolves indefinitely, contingent on the involved parties, their individual response activity, and their respective commitments to an ongoing communication. A machine, even an interactive apparatus, threatens to supplant that communication with a reductive, causal, operational exchange.

The interactive debate lies at this threshold. New touch-and-feel, point-and-activate technospheres promise to reach beyond the senses. Suddenly, the standard devices by which one distills and comfortably encounters external events disappear. The establishment of a subject position distinguishable from the obligatory behavior assigned by an external program becomes a major challenge. An individual must find a position whereby he or she may confront and sustain the range of emerging and soon ending possibilities. Toward this goal, conceptual entrepreneurs prospect and plow the imagination.

In 1951 legendary radio news correspondent Edward R. Murrow demonstrated his and coproducer Fred W. Friendly's willingness to adapt to television by adapting television to a new way of thinking about telecommunication. Murrow broke symbolic ground by presenting the Atlantic and the Pacific, the two oceans that bracket the continent, side by side in an over-the-air edition of his program *See It Now*.

> From the start Murrow and Friendly seem to have been clearly aware of what TV could do. The first *See It Now* program presented a startling innovation, one that highlighted the potential of the medium. Making use of the just-developed coast-to-coast broadcasting facilities (a combination of coaxial cable and microwave relay), Murrow sat on a swivel chair before two TV monitors that could be viewed by his live audience and called on Camera One to "bring in the Atlantic Ocean." Then he called for a picture of the Pacific Ocean on the other monitor, and these live pictures of the oceans were followed by simultaneous live views of the Brooklyn and Golden Gate bridges and the New York and San Francisco skylines. A gimmick? Yes. But an extraordinarily effective gimmick, for, as Murrow told his audience, the telecast allowed "a man sitting in his living room . . . for *the first time* to look at two oceans at once." (Leab, 1983, p. 8)

Following on the fascination of Edward R. Murrow's Atlantic and Pacific oceans simulcast, contemporary installations reach beyond the projection screen. Exploring emerging media systems, Kit Galloway and Sherrie Rabinowitz's interactive television project *Hole in Space* excavated the technoturf of satellite communication. Their uplink project established, temporarily, a bicoastal toll-free bridge across North America. With one portal in New York's Lincoln Center and another in Beverly Hills, California, live interactive television grabbed and dramatized differences in time and climate to unsuspecting individuals on the street. The sounds made by these people triggered conversations that led to time-space revelations. The magic moment transpired every time another individual discovered the corridor. The phenomenon expired when the mainstream media publicized the monitors' existence, thereby contextualizing their presence. At that point, this electronic corridor became nothing more or less than an electronic watering hole, an extension of the telephone, a link between communities unifying families and friends.

A computer-directed experience through a constructed, mediated, and regulated image environment such as a high-resolution interactive video laser disc allows but does not necessarily guarantee an exploratory interactive platform. Through the marriage of the pathways that are programmed in the software with those that are edited on the disc, the viewer confronts a much more complicated system of collaborative design that promises a reward that is substantially richer or, on the other hand, potentially more frightening than the random ironies of continuity generated through broadcast channel "switching" or programmed video game encounters.

Not a surprise, the so-called exploratory or experimental arts environment permits the most evolutionary and least restrictive use of interactive video. Relatively less affected by the marketing demands and formulas of commercial media, the fine arts most frequently provide an environment for "bottom-up" processing. In a "bottom-up" environment, unexpected events perpetually trigger greater direct-response behavior on the part of the viewer than in a "top-down" regulated video game context.

The first generation of interactive laserdisc art installations during the 1980s exemplify a bottom-up environment.[2] The interactive laser disc environment transcended the simple platform of selection. It transcended the linear field of the gallery, the theater, and the cinema. Rather than simply allowing the spectator to work his or her way through a particular and, no doubt, challenging exposition, a condition exemplified by most electronic video games, or to expand quantitatively their possible viewing options, through cable, direct satellite, and videocassette programming, interactive laserdisc art permitted a real open-ended experience.

For computer-driven laserdisc programs to reach legitimate interactivity, they had to stretch beyond older formats. Allowing high-quality moving images to simulate "real-life" situations meant wedding the enactment with the decision-making framework structured within a particular viewer-participant's mind. Not all interactive engagements can achieve such a committed response. For that reason, those that do succeed must operate on many open levels.

An open-ended experience emerges from the patterns defined by the branches and pathways through the disc, the viewer-participant's movement through that virtual space, the duration of the interaction, the pattern of the interactivity, and the social context of the viewer-participant's activity with other attendant or participating viewers. Because interactivity integrates the spectator's behavior with the text, that genesis complicates old relationships including those among the participant viewers. New models are required.

The earliest project in this field, the work of the Massachusetts Institute of Technology's Architecture Machine Lab in the late 1970s, set the stage. Their most famous application, *The Aspen Movie Map* project, a "drive through" of Aspen, Colorado, allowed the viewer-participant to make a logical sequence of alternative choices at each of a number of motivated junctures when proceeding through the program.[3]

> " 'Aspen' wasn't a travelogue, . . ." "It was the whole town. It let you drive through the place yourself, having a conversation with the chauffeur." There was a season knob—any street you were driving down, any building you were examining could be seen Winter-Spring-Summer-Fall. Many buildings you could go into. Some, like restaurants, you could go in and read the menu. Some had "micro-documentaries"—brief interviews—inside. Some had a time knob—you could see historical pictures of the building. And much more. (Brand, 1987, p. 141)

The system simulated the viewer-participant's passage through the streets of Aspen with each intersection and with key buildings serving as those decision-making junctures. Exploration drove the interaction. Each viewer-participant had the freedom to find his or her own way through the information maze.

Other dimensions augmented the viewer-participant's movement through the maze. The viewer not only explored physical layout but had the option of viewing certain key civic figures. When passing the respective departmental headquarters, the viewer-participant could choose to enter and be greeted by the appropriate departmental chief, for example, the city's chief of police.

On its own terms, *The Aspen Movie Map* did what it did well. Stewart Brand (1987) summarizes that early fascination in *The Media Lab*:

> "Aspen" shook people. Scales fell from eyes at conferences where it was demoed about what computers could do, about what videodisk could be, about how *un-authored* a creative work could become. For the first time

the viewer could be thought of as an animal instead of a vegetable, active and curious instead of passive and critical. (p. 141)

By simulating a drive-through experience, however, *The Aspen Movie Map* cushioned experience in the same way that automotive travel in general shields the driver and passenger from the more direct subtleties of an on-foot encounter. As close as it came, the Aspen project did not truly approach a virtual reality, the asymptotic realization of Bazin's myth of total cinema, what Bazin (1967) described as an "integral realism, a recreation of the world in its own image, an image unburdened by the freedom of interpretation of the artist or the irreversibility of time" (p. 21).

Nor did *The Aspen Movie Map* attain an open-ended level of interactivity. No matter how many streets, buildings, and events the individual encountered in this dramatic leap toward total cinema, the viewer's actions were always restrained not only by the frame limiting and controlling his or her vision but by the prerecorded grid of the city. Unlike the experience of walking through an actual environment where the body registers a plethora of sensations, the viewer's attention remained responsive to the events recorded and framed through the window of the car. These streets lacked the potential for the unexpected, a vital component of everyday experience.

The predetermined and prioritized sequence through the prerecorded streets of Aspen, and the controlled and measured velocity of the viewer-participant's passage, inhibited legitimate exploration. The installation's branching restraints continued to burden the viewer-participant with the preconstructed experiential artifice. Historically, the Aspen project presented an alternative to the traditional linear program. Without an open-ended break from formulaic procedures, however, this pioneer interactive experience offered only an abbreviated alternative to a more programmatic display or production.

When simulations become representations, the reader acquires new responsibilities. Those responsibilities compensate for the automatic operant conditioning procedures of interactive toys. In Jeffrey Shaw's interactive project *The Legible City,* the viewer-participant bicycles through a projected maze that replicates the grid of a section of midtown Manhattan. Instead of buildings, words and sentences conform to the scale and layout of the city. This "architecture of text" follows color-coded story lines vested in the respective authors' relationships to Manhattan. According to Shaw (1990),

Travelling through this city of words is consequently a journey of reading. Choosing direction, choosing where to turn, is a choice of the storylines and their juxtaposition. In this way, this city of words is a kind of three dimensional book which can be read in any direction, and where the spectators construct their own conjunction of texts and meanings as they bicycle their chosen path there. (pp. 185-186)

Pedaling through a written text represents a novel approach to reading but it does not expand upon the challenges and pleasures of bicycling through a city. A video graphic display responsive to handlebar and pedal output does not convey the dynamic of bicycling, nor does it substitute an interactive dimension for the multiple perils and thoughts, encounters and reactions, that stimulate the most placid of urban cyclists on an everyday basis. While *The Legible City* embraces another interactive genre, the underlying questions remain.

Certain early interactive laser disc artwork in the 1980s began to examine the conception and force underlying their own innovative programs (Tafler, 1990). *Lorna,* by Lynn Hershman, was a level one interactive installation without a computer program controlling the branching operations on the disc.[4] There was no touchscreen component allowing an immediate field of contact between the viewer-participant and the screen. By choosing the chapter or branch on a handheld remote, the viewer-participant made direct contact with the laser disc player, which allowed for an indirect communication with the screen.

DOUBLE YOU (and X,Y,Z.) by Peter d'Agostino, and Grahame Weinbren and Roberta Friedman's *The Erl King*, did not require the viewer-participant to use a separate control to access branches during his or her inquiry. The touchscreen computer-driven interface changed the parameters of interactive experience, and will be discussed later in this text.

Lorna challenges the viewer-participant to build an analytical relationship with an agoraphobic character. As the viewer-participant grows increasingly familiar with the protagonist Lorna, he or she enters into a compact. The challenge that he or she faces is to recognize the interactive pattern as being somewhat distinct from the subject's obsessions and fantasy. The demands of accommodating new discoveries to the protagonist's symptoms and behavior leave a narrow window of exploratory opportunity for the viewer-participant. Though the clues and traces to Lorna's behavior remain limited by the elements and events woven onto the disc, the inferences and associations that can be sparked by these clues stretch to the depth and limits of potential awareness of the viewer-participant.

When viewer-participants interact with the disc, the "players get to know (the character) Lorna through the objects in her room. Each object represents a chapter of the disc that, once accessed, lead[s] to a series of short vignettes that reveal aspects of the protagonist's life" (Hershman, *Lorna* pamphlet, p. 5).

> THIS IS LORNA'S LIVING ROOM.
>   CAN YOU IMAGINE SPENDING THE LAST 16,325 DAYS HERE?
>   JUST LOOK AT ALL THAT JUNK SHE KEEPS AROUND.
>   GO AHEAD, LOOK.
>   EACH OBJECT WILL GIVE YOU A CLUE ABOUT LORNA.
> (*Lorna*, Frame # 3436)

Each object designates a "chapter" or branch; they become avenues of investigation. They include Lorna's watch, mirror, television, telephone, fish, and wallet.

The branching pattern is straightforward. Moving through the disc, the viewer-participant has a relatively easy time reconstructing branches that form a logical chain of events. For example,

> Each object is given a corresponding chapter number. Players can select either a Mirror, Wallet, Fishbowl, Watch, TV or Telephone.
>
> If the player selects mirror: there is an aging sequence of Lorna. This leads to Lorna taking a bath playing with her remote switch which leads to the T.V.
>
> If the player selects the wallet: We are led to a series of still frames of photos in the wallet. This leads to her checkbook, which can be seen page by page, which leads either to the Paradise Motel sequence or her handwriting analysis. This leads to her psychologist which leads back to the Paradise Motel which leads to family photos which can lead into either MTV or a doorway.
>
> If the player selects the phone: They are led into the audio track 1 scene which routes them back to the beginning. (from "KEY TO BRANCHING," Hershman, *Lorna* pamphlet, p. 9)

Different activation values drive the viewer-participant to isolate and select different branches as part of his or her experience.

Throughout the process, the viewer-participant had to confront the terms of his or her own engagement. Complicating the exchange in

Lorna, psychoanalytic content motivates the branches that structure the viewer's experience. Deciphering the text requires examining and tagging virtual objects and treating them as clues, symbolic traces, entranceways for unraveling the protagonist's condition. The viewer-participant's deliberate or inadvertent decisions expand those junctures into narrative scenes and documentary/informative statements.

The interactive pattern lies outside of the text. As the viewer-participant probes the subject's obsessions and fantasy, the symptoms narrow the exploratory window. Eventually, the viewer-participant's involvement must go beyond Lorna, whose character remains insufficiently developed. That obsession becomes the subject.

As technology's accelerating transition spawns these new interactive arenas, established systems of address continue to perpetuate the same old contradictions. In particular, television, despite its enhanced interactive capabilities, remains a virtual presence in the home while assertively structuring the lives of the inhabitants. Constant, "live" television creates the illusion of no mediation. Its most noticeable blatant mask, the on-screen/on-air presence, positions a viewer/listener within an implied relationship that hides the deceptive distance and unidirectional flow of conventional broadcast structure. That structure not only denies the spectator the ability to respond to screen content in a meaningful way but decreases the likelihood of the spectator becoming aware of that constraint. Because self-awareness forms the axis along which all interactive models evolve, that denial impedes the essential reflexive understanding required for legitimate interactivity. Without transcending its effect, it becomes impossible to build new models that reveal and process the natural tension and stress erupting from all dramatic relationships.

Most television practice also continues to sustain the identification with characters and situations that foster those direct illusions that seemingly bind the viewer with the viewed program. Beyond the self-contained diegetic space of that great majority of narrative programs, talk shows offer a facade of the audience talking back. Carefully positioned studio audiences and professionally screened and constrained telephone participants operate as an intermediate layer shielding the preformulated programs from a legitimate interactive process. Newer formats play on other interactive facades. Today's shopping channels promote the illusion of choice and connectedness. Ironically, they program desire and capitalize on its effects. Other channels perpetuate other forms of prepackaged control.

Home television, meanwhile, sets up the contextual and technical conditions supporting interactive systems. (a) Contextually, multichannel television programming increasingly relies on experiences comprising competing fragmented moments. Though they may be contiguous, these moments or events are self-sufficient capsules of information and stimulation. (b) Technically, the spectator now has access to the controls. The home viewer decides when to begin and end an experience, adjusts the sound-to-image proportion or dimension, and alters the continuity by switching between channels. With the acquisition of a VCR, the spectator's leverage becomes that much greater. The viewer has the option to repeat segments, routines, and sequences. The interactive spectators/participants actively construct the logic justifying their involvement.

The possibility exists that there is, in fact, no logic. An "interactive" involvement does not necessarily mean that the spectator is always consciously engaged. The spectator's participation simply may be driven by a mood or condition, a sensuous pleasure, generated by the system. With a natural childlike fascination with kinetic imagery, the spectator's initial encounter with this "expanded" cinema may be a moment of jubilation, a child's play before the mirror (see Lacan, 1977b). Otherwise, aside from being seduced by the spectacle of a moving image (the electronic fireplace), the spectator may cultivate pleasure from structuring events. This pleasure, however, differs from the emotion and attention elicited by narrative expectations. It is mediated by accompanying friends and/or family, and all of the remaining heterogeneous elements that shape and embody the individual in that specific environment at that particular moment.

Meanwhile, the spectator is on a journey constantly adjusting his or her ties and relations with the images on the screen. If the viewer is not manipulating the dials near the tube, he or she is pushing the buttons on the remote. In either case, there is the pleasure of manipulation when exercising control. Regardless of the level of engagement, the objective is to sustain higher order processes of orientation and discrimination throughout the sequence of events.

While the individual certainly does have decision-making leverage, it can be argued that conscious experience is inadequate for the overall control of the spectator's interactivity. A cinema experience normally projects an enormous amount of sensory information that is processed in a very short length of time.[5] Because the presentation is uneven, in essence some moments are saturated while others are thin, some proportion of the spectator's experience must fall out of sync with the ongoing presentation of the work. This implicit and subtle unconscious interactivity, "a breaking edge nowhere present" (a phrase borrowed from Heath, 1981, p. 79), may, in fact, be the flip side of the synaptic firings that account for the conscious decisions guiding the interactive exchange. In other words, at each decision juncture, the interactive spectator both consciously and instinctively evaluates, calculates, and reconstructs the overall orientation.

This reorientation is crucial. At each interactive juncture or event, a spectator filters new incoming information through revised expectations. This reorientation is a governor buffering the spectator's reception. It inhibits and prioritizes events in their transfer to longer term memory, which subsequently affects their recollection after presentation. The impact of that filtration increases proportionately with the passage of time.

Despite legitimate efforts to transcend established norms and enhance some sort of reciprocal contact, most early interactive formats locked the viewer-participant within fixed and controlled surrogate encounters. More recent interactive video disc and virtual reality installations raise the same questions while highlighting the metaphoric problems of labeling vicarious events "interactive." Driving a mock vehicle in a video arcade may simulate the viewer-participant's active engagement at each intersection, but the experience remains antiseptic. Even highly realistic flight simulators lack the critical edge. These experiences omit the risk of issuing instructions that place an individual and others in imminent danger. Despite the libidinal fantasy, the alien television environment offers no extraordinary situations, no challenging encounters. All obstacles and demarcations merely threaten programmed penalties with limited consequences. The imagination yields to conditioned reflexes in the vicarious play of everyday reality. Driving or flying a virtual vehicle, walking in metaspace, racing a cybercar, or even riding a hypothetical bicycle hardly qualifies as a compelling stretch over the actual equivalent event.

In his keynote address to the Fifth Conference on Computers and Human Interaction on May 17, 1988, Frederick P. Brooks Jr. of the University of North Carolina at Chapel Hill articulated certain challenges confronting the designers of interactive applications. "Is all this technology for entertainment only? Or worse, for enthralling the mind while a sales message insinuates itself?" (p. 1). Beyond the text, do interactive tools provide new entry points for scientifically motivated and controlled simulations? Brooks argues that interactive tools facilitate navigation through "mental models of virtual worlds" (p. 5). Simulating "real-world" behavior, interactive tools permit the subject to steer through complex, challenging situations and environments.

In a more recent paper, Brooks's colleagues continue to explore these questions. Holloway, Fuchs, and Robinett (1991, p. 2) ask: Does "a system that gives the user a sense of being in an environment other than the one he or she is in, or of simulated objects being in this environment: a system where the user suspends disbelief and has a feeling of presence in the simulated environment," remedy the fail-safe limitations of "interactive" simulations? Ceiling trackers linked to head-mounted displays in their lab permit individuals to move and interact with a computer-generated real-time image environment that resembles its not yet constructed counterpart. As sophisticated feedback loops, "walk-through" systems offer wonderful opportunities for architects and others to refine their designs. Obviously, computer-enhanced simulation provides extraordinary advantages in a wide range of applied fields for training and exploration. The debate does not materialize at that level. The more subtle challenge lies in considering the far-reaching implications of simulative activity as interactive behavior.

A legitimate interactive procedure must become an active risk-taking venture. True interactive procedures must stretch the relationship of the spectator to the projected content and to the apparatus. Each exploratory effort must venture into the unknown—the unknown dimensions of human behavior. When hovering on the threshold separating perception and action, the individual must abandon a strictly causal track before taking the plunge. Playing resuscitates all of the uninhibited traits of childhood exploration and curiosity. Exploration evolves from the forks in the passage. Each junction demands a sorting out, recognizing different features and making appropriate associations with other events experienced along the way. Anthropologist Gregory Bateson (1972) described the nature of this transitory passage as a sorting out.

> In the hard sciences, effects are, in general, caused by rather concrete conditions or events—impacts, forces, and so forth. But when you enter the world of communications . . . , you leave behind that whole world. . . . You enter a world in which "effects" . . . are brought about by *differences*. (p. 452)

Each move kindles more complicated mental systems. From a willingness to make naive choices, the viewer-participant abandons the more deliberate evaluation of a clearly motivated structure and takes a bold step into an uncharted experience.

Similar to the child, the viewer-participant approaches this experience with little knowledge of the many pathways possible through the code and subroutines on the computer, through the many chapters and thousands of frames on the "disc." The viewer can choose to navigate these paths either at random, much like wandering through a gallery, or with an increased understanding of a new interactive vocabulary.

All interactive laserdisc systems have branches or pathways providing innumerable alternatives for the spectator. Differences form at the organizing junctures. Loops mapping the terrain's meaningful and significant content connect at these sites. Bottom-up texts set up a system predicated on the viewer making discoveries. First discovering the loops and later traveling along their routes constitutes the interactive experience. Bateson's (1972) working blueprint outlines the operating system:

1. The system shall operate with and upon differences.
2. The system shall consist of closed loops or networks of pathways along which differences and transforms of differences shall be transmitted. (What is transmitted on a neuron is not an impulse, it is news of a difference.) (p. 482)

The interactive impulse begins with the viewer-participant's own operating system.

3. Many events within the system shall be energized by the respondent part rather than by impact from the triggering part.
4. The system shall show self-correctedness in the direction of homeostasis and/or in the direction of runaway. Self-correctedness implies trial and error. (p. 482)

The viewer-participant's willingness to tread unknown paths serves as a precondition for processing new information. The individual's mental landscape extends to the loops established for the interactive experience. "Now, these minimal characteristics of mind are generated whenever and wherever the appropriate circuit structure of causal loops exists. Mind is a necessary, an inevitable function of the appropriate complexity, wherever that complexity occurs" (p. 482). Each loop weaves a complex relationship for the individual amidst a limitless array of subroutines. Each juncture permits that many more collusions among the viewer-participants themselves.

A fluid array of factors add moments of causal arrest, revised cycles of repetition, intermediate moments of closure, and loss of causal momentum. The obsessive magnetism of the traditional text diminishes. In a modular environment predicated on the glance, the continuity unites a sum of spectacles. Each spectacle, one small part of a highly repetitive, overlapping weave, permits a break in the committed spectator's obligatory gaze. The omission of any one single element or event remains inconsequential. For the channel-switching spectator, the continuous array of noncontextual spectacle flashes on the screen outside of any diachronic context. When any event may evaporate without irrevocably destroying the concept or force of reception, attention no longer means captivation. With the enhanced freedom of distraction, the risk of losing the text disappears.

Not motivated by plausible or rational conditions, segmented events do have a different emotional impact. With less causal significance, less anticipation, increasingly less surprise, constant change by itself becomes redundant. Constant change, however, sets up its own attracting conditions and threatens to dismember traditional hermeneutic systems.

The future absence of these guidance systems does not produce a structural vacuum. Filling the void left by the decline of the compelling diegesis, a multiplicity of new footholds or entry points into the text give the fractured experience some greater potential. Here, the viewer-participant climbs on board the carousel and begins a cyclical ride. The obligatory conditions of ambiguity guarantee indeterminacies that the viewer-participant either disavows or accommodates.

An open arena that both challenges and defies the viewer-participant's cognitive efforts is short-lived. Inevitably, the long-term lack of exclusivity surrounding any one production guarantees that other projects will emulate or build upon the ideas nested in that particular installation. Unfortunately, this replication omits some vital aspect of the original encounter. Because the fascination and patience with the challenging structure and content of such an original encounter depend upon its historical specificity, prescient marginal encounters suffer the consequences of the inevitable capitalization of the original's style and substance. As a consequence, in the late twentieth century—an age of accelerated communication and transition; a postmodern age of repetition, replication, and saturation—marginal events are infrequent, rhetorically obsolete, grossly oversimplified, or hopelessly handicapped by a rapid, universal communication that leads to overexposure.

Marginal events, however, do surface from time to time when the conditions are ripe. A small window of legitimate open-ended possibility surrounds the interactive art experience. The interactive text's shift in emphasis from the author to the viewer-participant marks the threshold of a post-television environment. Crossing this boundary becomes the crucial component that allows the opportunity to both destabilize and reconstruct viewer expectations. With the introduction of a multilayered, integrative textual experience, marginality no longer simply functions as part of the author's intentions, contingent on the play of recognizable and disparate codes that mark a particular film, tape, program, or text.

Marginality, not an exclusively quantitative measure, fluctuates with the qualitative degree of insight exhibited by the viewer's participation. His or her position along an active-passive scale would appear to represent a generic measure of marginality. In essence, the dynamics of an interactive experience cannot be limited to predictable or calculable conditions between the viewer and the text. True, the viewer-participant's actions match, in some alternating pattern, the events on the screen. This circular pattern or play, however, becomes more than a dialogue, it becomes a "metalogue" invested with much of the stress and many of the challenges of a conversational or even combative encounter. Most important, the total structure of the experience evolves from this interplay. As in any real encounter, the viewer-participant has the potential to come away changed. As in everyday encounters, the variables cloud the formulation of a concise schema for locking in the experience. Because interactive behavior resists simple categorization, many aspects of the process remain speculative.

The capacity to mediate an experience builds on a lifetime of learning. Interactive systems intensify and enlarge upon that experience. The linkages that an individual makes with varying elements in his or her history, understanding, and knowledge will determine the vividness of his or her encounter. The relative weight of certain events and actions are subject to a wide range of historical referents and their peculiar characteristics. Placing boundaries around an individual's cognitive construct masks the forces driving his or her ongoing perceptions and behaviors. Gregory Bateson (1972) writes:

We commonly think of the external "physical world" as somehow separate from an internal "mental world." I believe that this division is based on the contrast in coding and transmission inside and outside the body.

The mental world—the mind—the world of information processing—is not limited by the skin. (p. 454)

When the quantitative dimensions and the qualitative features of the interactive text have been transformed into a recognizable grid of self-directed branches, the evolving megatext sets up very different experiences governed by widely varying constraints.

And in addition to what I have said to define the individual mind, I think it necessary to include the relevant parts of memory and data "banks." After all, the simplest cybernetic circuit can be said to have memory of a dynamic kind—not based upon static storage but upon the travel of information around the circuit. (p. 458)

No behavior forms an inviolable closed circuit. Objective-based programs do not limit the participant's movement. Their event parameters extend beyond the screen. They embrace a wide range of activities that promote a strong sense of viewer involvement, shaped and reinforced in conversations with friends and neighbors.

Peter d'Agostino's *DOUBLE YOU (and X,Y,Z.)* challenged the hierarchical system of the artist/viewer relationship by making the duration, density, and subsequent meaning of the experience dependent on the actions of the viewer.[6] *DOUBLE YOU (and X,Y,Z.)* was designed to be encountered as a bit map through an odyssey of images and sounds focusing on a young child/infant's emergence and acquisition of language.

While the subject of *DOUBLE YOU (and X,Y,Z.)* is the acquisition of language, the underlying structure is derived from another source—physics.

"It is now believed that there are four forces that cause all physical interactions in the universe: light, gravity, strong, and weak forces." (from the prologue of the videodisc, 1986)

Through analogy and metaphor, logic and absurdity, these concepts are used to parallel four stages of early language development. They make up the four-part structure of the work:

1 Light/birth
2 Gravity/words

3 Strong force/sentences

4 Weak force/songs

Sound is the primary motivation for this progression—from cries at birth to first words, sentences, and finally to songs sung at age two. This last part also reveals that the source of the title, *DOUBLE YOU (and X,Y,Z.)* is from a children's song that concludes with "now I know my ABC's next time won't you sing with me." (d'Agostino, 1986, pp. 322-323)

Responding and exploring on a personal and metaphorical level, the viewer-participant matches sounds with images, words with places, organizes image icons representing words into sentences, and plays a "video music box" where image/music sequences can be selected from the moving images of a carousel.

DOUBLE YOU (and X,Y,Z.)'s context resides on the threshold of an individual's recognition of his or her personal history within some unfathomable phenomenological existence. On a maiden voyage, the viewer moves through real and metaphorical moments of pregnancy, birth, perceptual recognition, and cognitive map making.

As the spectator progresses, the memories of these sensory experiences are compiled. . . . At one point, the spectator travels an outdoor train or wanders through a revolving carousel on the ground. At another stage, the world appears through the window of a helicopter flying over the San Francisco Bay. At yet another interval, a series of tests examines a continuity of images that prefigures a different sort of (grammatical) landscape. (Tafler, n.d.)

Self-referential aspects abound in the text. Countless references to language and culture, for example: A child's cry "da da" = Dada; the image of a Campbell soup can = Andy Warhol; a split screen represents cubism, helps to induce an attenuated level of awareness. No specific, imposed, or conscious goals or implications govern the viewer's actions.

That cognitive development also appropriates aspects of video game playing. An image-word sentence order puzzle offering six different continuity choices takes the form of an instructional computer program for acquiring and learning basic language skills. Finally, by cruising on a carousel and moving through a music video jukebox maze, the viewer celebrates the flourishing of childhood.

When moving through an extended text, a sense of self emerges from the vortex of events and convictions that shape an individual's thinking.

In *Toward an Aesthetic of Reception,* Hans Robert Jauss (1982) sketches this extension.

> The relationship of literature and reader has aesthetic as well as historical implications. The aesthetic implication lies in the fact that the first reception of a work by the reader includes a test of its aesthetic value in comparison with works already read. The obvious historical implication of this is that the understanding of the first reader will be sustained and enriched in a chain of receptions from generation to generation. (p. 20)

The boundaries "between passive reception and active understanding, [an] experience formative of norms, and new production" fall within the viewer-participant's horizon of expectations (Jauss, 1982, p. 19). When moving through the circular encounter, the viewer-participant confronts a simulated environment that re-creates his or her coming-of-age.

On a structural level, the Philadelphia Museum of Art's installation of *DOUBLE YOU (and X,Y,Z.)* in spring 1987 destroyed the unipositional, privileged vantage point of classical production and contemporary experience. The configuration of four monitors, separated into two channels arranged on a "W"-shaped wall, created an array of differing sight lines and vanishing points in the room. At the touchscreen controls, located at the far right of the gallery, lower than the monitors, recessed in the wall, and tilted on a slight angle, the viewer-participant loses the sight line advantage. He or she must interact with others so as to contemplate the two-channel consequences of the interactive decisions made.

The architectural layout and sculptural design of the installation removed the hierarchical divide between the pilot and the observer by separating the pilot at the controls from the observer who occupied the key focal point in the articulated space. The observer became the director relaying the highlights of his or her visual experience as a series of action-triggering cues to his or her touchscreen counterpart, situated at the side of the room.

From an alternative self-directed participatory process, viewer-participants can stretch to rewrite the program of their given encounter. During this reconstruction, dream logic prevails. Fixed rules cease to govern the structure of reconstructed relationships. A legitimate interactive experience bridges the inchoate world of the unconscious with the rational demands made in a conscious encounter.

One such encounter, Grahame Weinbren and Roberta Friedman's "avant-garde musical"[7] *The Erl King,* fluidly moves through a web of dream reenactments and oral recitations, recollections from Freud's writings, academic interpretations by a Lacanian psychologist, multiple appearances by a Chinese cook and joke and storytellers; dyed chickens that are slaughtered, cleaned, and finally cooked by the Chinese chef; images of automobiles on highways and in stock car crashes; musical recitations by soul, percussion, and bagpipe artists and a soprano accompanied by a pianist who is occasionally depicted wearing a chicken's head; and the narrative enactment of Goethe's poem "Erlkönig" as a tale, dance, and a dream. Few if any prompts guide the viewer-participant's interaction with the screen. The effects of touching the screen are nearly instantaneous. The action on the screen shifts with a startling immediacy.

Through a multiple-channel, three-disc system, different tracks and combinations of tracks can accompany the same visual sequence. Recognizing and accessing patterns on the basis of sound cues therefore becomes that much more difficult. Not only does the sound not help, it may hinder branching. A floating, multiple-track system potentially adds an infinite number of variations and combinations to the branching array.

Even if this severely deficient description were to be expanded, it would fail to capture the complexity of the work's construction for it overlooks one of the generic features of this laserdisc installation: the cyclical journey through the experience that is at least partially shaped by the participant's external and internal orientation. The multiple facets of that orientation defy the linear transcription of a written text, not to mention a conventional film or video exposition.

The structure of *The Erl King* compounds the exchange with the viewer. Subscribing to the cycles of a dream, the piece leaps from section to section in a number of multiple varying unpredictable sequences. A single initial touch activates a sequence that lasts from 7 to 10 minutes, depending on the particular narrated joke that comes up in that particular cycle. After the appearance of an opening title situated on a dark screen: "WHO RIDES SO LATE THROUGH THE NIGHT AND THE WIND," the sequence shifts into a simple four-part arrangement. The first part presents the soprano Elizabeth Arnold singing Schubert's opus number one, "Der Erlkönig." Shortly after the section begins, a prompt appears on the touchscreen. To expedite the viewer's awareness of the interactive nature of the installation, a blue rectangular outline materializes toward the lower right corner of the touchscreen.

After a brief duration, if there's been no intervention by touching the screen, the blue rectangle disappears.

"Der Erlkönig" ends abruptly and one of three older actors appears reciting one of seven cycling jokes from Freud's "Jokes and Their Relation to the Unconscious." Another graphic prompt materializes that asks: "Another joke from Freud's Jokes and their relationship to the unconscious." Barring no response, the sequence returns to "Der Erlkönig." The sequence ends with the producer and director credits. After the sequence completes its uninterrupted 7- to 10-minute play, the monitors return to the image of the still life and the touchscreen freezes on the opening prompt.

Once the viewer-participant takes advantage of the limitless number of controls available to manipulate the sequence, duration, repetition, and velocity of selected images, a multiplicity of potential cinematic moments surface. They are not only nonhierarchical, they are susceptible to accidents in the viewer's perception. Intensifying the disorientation, certain sequences may reappear in two or three different contexts. Many hours interacting with *The Erl King* will continue to reveal unanticipated pathways and branches.

Reconfiguring the proscenium, the screen serves as the well, the window that beckons Alice through the gateway, a gateway that expands the experiential boundaries of the text. Outside the constraints of passive reception and inside an unfamiliar terrain, the viewer-participant searches for the tiller amidst the modular mappings. In *Gödel, Escher, Bach* (1979), Douglas R. Hofstadter describes this mental architecture.

> For each concept there is a fairly well-defined module which can be triggered—a module that consists of a small group of neurons. . . . There may be many copies of each module spread around, or modules may overlap physically. . . . Perhaps the complexes are like very thin pancakes packed in layers which occasionally pass through each other; perhaps they are like long snakes which curl around each other, here and there flattening out, like cobras' heads; perhaps they are like spiderwebs; or perhaps they are circuits in which signals travel round and round in shapes stranger than the dash of a gnat-hungry swallow. There is no telling. It is even possible that these modules are software, rather than hardware. (p. 348)

The mounting number of modules across the reception spectrum increases the number and shortens the span of each loop. As the text mutates into shorter, more rapidly consumable fragments, the single event deteriorates. Its comprehensibility diminishes within an abbreviated time frame. As the cycle shortens, the volume and frequency of short events proportionately increase. Eventually, a veritable onslaught of image elements floods the participant.

In the aftermath of this fragmentation, interactive relationships hinge increasingly on those synecdochic moments where each representation encodes some essence of the total catharsis.[8] In tracking the destiny of the text, viewer-participants must prioritize and select a certain number of these smaller events around which to hinge their experience. Hofstadter (1979) writes:

> Our thought makes use of an ingenious principle, which might be called the prototype principle: The most specific event can serve as a general example of a class of events. Everyone knows that specific events have a vividness which imprints them so strongly on the memory that they can later be used as models for other events which are like them in some way. Thus in each specific event, there is the germ of a whole class of similar events. This idea that there is generality in the specific is of far-reaching importance. (p. 352)

Separating useful from superfluous sense data, selecting the most significant modules, the respective parties order events within coherent branches. Inevitably, the loops formed amidst those branches and their respective linkages become a supporting structure that both eclipses and shapes the overall experience.

Unlike simple response patterns, more complex encounters do not allow for easily discriminable response measurements. Moving from quantifiable tasks to nonquantifiable challenges broadens the whole range of textual operations. Avoiding well-lit corridors tempers external demands and directions. Lacan defines this operation as a kind of message massage. Language loses its telegraphic economy and becomes a medium for carrying implicit signals.

> By an inverse antimony, it can be observed that the more the function of language becomes neutralized as it moves closer to information, the more language is imputed to be laden with redundancies. This notion of redundancy in language originated in research that was all the more precise because a vested interest was involved, having been prompted by the economic problem of long-distance communication, and in particular that of the possibility of carrying several conversations at once on a single telephone line. It can be asserted that a substantial portion of the phonetic

material is superfluous to the realization of the communication actually sought. (Lacan, 1977a, p. 86)

The viewer-participant's access to multiple areas of selectivity guarantees that other reactions and interactions can take precedence over the designs of the (artists)producers. This uninhibited ability to rearrange the continuity does not confine itself to any one specific choice cluster.

Other factors weigh heavily in assessing the possibilities and limitations of new interactive formats. Interactive touchscreen environments encourage the viewer to touch the screen so as to regulate the movement of the "event." While the process of discovery may parallel an initial encounter, and the process of learning the language for directing and therefore controlling an environment, the qualitative and quantitative dimensions differ. The primitive process of touching does not truly augment the more sophisticated interactivity of sight and mind. Furthermore, this immediacy forces at least one spectator to locate him- or herself within arm's reach of the screen, a notable controlling factor in the gallery limiting what might otherwise be a more open experience. On the other hand, the use of a remote opens up that distance again.

Freezing, replaying, graphically altering any networked segment of a complex, interwoven arrangement remakes the experience. When reduced to their essential characteristics, the procedures exercised emulate the mental events triggered. Hofstadter's (1979) focus on neurological states appears to describe the logic behind these processing mechanisms.

> Memories are coded locally, but over and over again in different areas of the cortex. . . . Another explanation would be that memories can be reconstructed from dynamic processes spread over the whole brain, but can be triggered from local spots. This theory is based on the notion of modern telephone networks, where the routing of a long-distance call is not predictable in advance, for it is selected at the time the call is placed, and depends on the situation all over the whole country. (p. 343)

Interactive devices naturalize this fragmented network. Abstract reality becomes an everyday phenomenon for all, even the most disengaged spectator.

Networks based on modular models represent the very premise of interactive organization. They raise the critical issues. According to Hofstadter (1979):

Philosophically, the most important question of all is this: What would the existence of modules—for instance, a grandmother module—tell us? Would this give us any insight into the phenomenon of our own consciousness? Or would it still leave us as much in the dark about what consciousness is? (p. 349)[9]

When fluctuating branches within a destabilized environment make demands on an adaptable spectator, what does it mean? The limitless cognitive realm opens an array of possibilities. Beyond some sleepy hollow, the flood of reorientation catapults the contemporary Rip Van Winkle toward an interior struggle within his or her own virtual universe.

Transcending technical performance, hypothetical conditions generate other emotions that the system might explore. Against that backdrop, the individual's own performance frames the experience within a meditative realm that mirrors the relationship of the viewer-participant to his or her own operation as pilot. Eventually, the plane crashes, not the physical entity of some virtual vehicle that flies on autopilot but the automatic relationship of the pilot to the plane crashes. It remains severed by the simulation.

Whereas directed activity conditions the viewer to participate in limited, formulaic, recognizable ways, more distinct encounters demand an adjustment to the encounter. Within this range of adjustment, the possibility exists for building an alternative, bottom-up installation or experience.

Resisting the parochial or dystopian ramifications of a constrained application, the viewer-participant's open, even naive input helps shape the programmed experience. When challenged, the viewer-participant must transcend his or her standard patterns of behavior. An emotional element jars and affects other processing abilities. Can the multiple branches reconcile all of the unknown and unanticipated patterns? No. As viewer-participant categories shift, class, race, gender, age, relationship variables shape the gaps and indeterminacies in the continuity and quality of individual behavior. Moreover, even within the same group, from one encounter to the next, an interactive process never remains the same.

Interactive experience must perpetually test prescribed conventions and laws. At the same time, those procedures and formats change in response to the new environment. With growing exposure to interactive instruments and tools, the viewer-participant's experience accommodates to that growing familiarity. Older systems motivating predictable response patterns lose their interactive condition. For an interactive condition to reemerge, newer systems must restore the challenge of the unknown.

Later, preexisting systems will integrate these radical procedures and force the interactive dimension to shrink. Before the adventure becomes automatic, however, the individual can still explore a novel universe of new territories.

Human behavior transcends the more superficial programmatic aspects of decision making. Sequestering viewer-participants within a controlled, nondistracting, and private setting means violating the basic premise of interactive experience. Because interactivity implies a communal dimension, the tailoring of experience to reconcile individual need violates the overall reality of the media experience.

Outside the home, other community dynamics exist. Interactive video sites become public. When the viewer-participants interact with the screen/installation in concert with other viewers or viewer-participants, their collective actions become an integrated part of the text. The effects of this synthesis can be labeled the "extended text," which represents the viewer-participant's self-initiated exploration, an exploration that transpires with other members of the community. Any effort to examine interactive experiences must reach out, attempt to locate, understand, and articulate what constitutes the extended text.

When the active viewer-participant interacts with the text in concert with another individual, the complexity of the interaction grows proportionately. In those situations where a single participant's input has a notable and often dramatic effect on the group, his or her operation will indeed play a pivotal role in shaping that experience.

A public interactive installation becomes living theater. Individuals interact with other individuals. The instrument of that interaction guides and mediates the interrogation, the quest, the passage, and whatever insight might emerge. Meaning erupts from the effect of any causal action. As a catalyst, the screen through its structural grid, a pseudolinguistic system, triggers that action-reaction from among the viewer-participants. Lacan emphasizes the role of the instigator-provocateur. The significance of screen activity within the structural system becomes clear.

For the function of language is not to inform but to evoke.

What I seek in speech is the response of the other. What constitutes me as subject is my question. In order to be recognized by the other, I utter what was only in view of what will be. In order to find him, I call him by

a name that he must assume or refuse in order to reply to me.
(Lacan, 1977a, p. 86)

Beyond the screen, within the theatrical/social situation, a new hierarchy of categories and relations emerges. The fundamental division between active viewer-participants and passive spectators disappears. Some individuals' interactivity becomes an inadvertent and major part of the spectacle for other individuals' observation. Viewer-participants no longer distinguish passive-spectators from other viewer-participants. One's position at or away from the controls becomes irrelevant. Widely differing parameters of involvement fuse within any single interactive situation. Operators become intermediaries open to directions and comments coming from other individuals oscillating back and forth throughout the surrounding space. The cyclical variation of events exacerbates this ensemble effect.

Events are contextualized by the environment. The theater, museum, or gallery, with its conventional narrative or nonnarrative formats, will shape the spectator's expectations. For example, in a gallery presenting a wide range of abstract work, incoherence and fragmentation become a part of the context. In turn, the spectator's tolerance for linear abstraction expands.

The museum or gallery setting serves as the natural and profound site for this play. The gallery restores all of the possibilities of random access and self-determined duration and repetition previously denied by the cinema. The installation permits the temporal and spatial freedom of moving at will from image to image, experience to experience, and thus conforms to the historical conditions mediating the act of looking at art. That mediation becomes a crucial part of the meditation. Nevertheless, the same constraints present themselves—the restraint of the walls or branches that reveals the curatorial or production design motivating the way in which images and objects are organized.

Systemically, the community splits and subdivides into modular constituencies. Mercurial and forever in process, those constituencies perpetually dissolve and reassemble again as part of a circular play transpiring in front of the screen. Nothing forces the viewer to participate in the structuring of his or her experience. Maintaining some form of legitimate selectivity rests on developing a community of distinctly different participants who remain acutely aware of their tenuous relationship to the interactive installation.

Beyond the screen, institutional architecture and interior design play a prominent role in shaping the interface. The viewer-participant's movement through the structure sets up rhythms and patterns that become a key part of the interactive design. The infinite possibilities of repetition and juxtaposition in the gallery allow for varied and marvelous accidents of experience.

Unfortunately, mainstream media experience remains a harbinger for future trends. Most interactive systems will continue to distribute information with little possibility for activating the experience. Despite these limitations, the viewer-participant/spectator can prepare to fixate, select, restrict, and manage those features of an encounter that will result in a personal and unique experience. Never fully compliant or resistant to linear and recognizable causal-temporal relationships or themes, the evolution of the viewer-participant(s) will oscillate between this accommodation and resistance. In the interactive arena, the challenge remains to position the imagination beyond the manipulative contours of an immaculate cyberspace.

More advanced interactive models will oblige the system to keep track of deviant response patterns; they will possess the algorithmic capacity to form their own branches. A flexible type of multiple branching procedure requires a very different approach than a fixed response pattern. An open-ended application requires a much larger program that covers a broader cycle of events. Only on a much larger scale will the field allow for the multifaceted approach to a specific problem, that moment of discovery when the limitless depth of the experience itself takes over.

Notes

1. From early childhood, through crying, pointing, and eventually speaking, the individual stretches the boundaries of contact, learns the limits of his or her influence, and realizes the inevitable constraints.

2. While this novel televisual experience is unprecedented, there are historical traces to be found in the arts and the cinema, particularly in certain "avant-garde" or European films. The interactive "megatext" can trace its history to those abstract film experiences where the absence of a dramatic narrative or documentary theme has forced the viewer to discover his or her own justification for the sequence of images. This new televisual experience draws upon a richly endowed foundation developed by exploratory work in both language and film, coupled with the formats and devices inherited from the older arts.

3. Funded by the military after the Entebbe hostage-freeing raid of 1973, the Aspen project was originally conceived as part of a project to determine if computers could simulate real environments for commando preparations. Aspen was chosen for its size, grid, and visual characteristics.

4. "The first level is direct address . . . that speaks directly to the viewer" (Gayeski & Williams, 1985, p. 121).

5. An individual's short-term memory can only allegedly "hold up to seven items in full consciousness for about twenty seconds after immediate sensory registration." In cinema, this would ordinarily represent the length of two shots. "Information retained for longer than this period is transferred to 'long-term memory.' " In other words, by the third shot in a sequence, information would have to be transferred to longer term memory for an experience of continuity to be realized (Palombo, 1978, p. 27).

6. In describing *DOUBLE YOU (and X,Y,Z.)*, reference was made to the following articles: Tafler (1986) and d'Agostino (1987).

7. Reference was made to notes by the artist Grahame Weinbren.

8. Sergei Eisenstein (1949, pp. 130-133) rides a similar route when he talks about the synecdochic syntax of inner speech.

9. Hofstadter (1979) goes on to assert: "The crucial step that needs to be taken is from a low-level—neuron-by-neuron—description of the state of a brain, to a high-level—module-by-module—description of the same state of the same brain" (p. 349).

References

Arbitron "people meter" to measure purchases. (1988, June 22). *New York Times*, p. D24.

Bateson, G. (1972). *Steps to an ecology of mind.* New York: Ballantine.

Bazin, A. (1967). The myth of total cinema. In *What is cinema?* (H. Gray, Trans.; pp. 17-22). Berkeley: University of California Press.

Brand, S. (1987). *The media lab: Inventing the future at MIT.* New York: Viking Penguin.

Brooks, F. P., Jr. (1988). Grasping reality through illusion: Interactive graphics serving science. In E. Soloway, D. Frye, & S. Sheppard (Eds.), *CHI'88 Proceedings* (pp. 1-11). Reading, MA: Addison-Wesley.

Clark, D. (1988, March). Hard lessons for interactive video. *Educational Computing*, pp. 41-45.

d'Agostino, P. (1986). Interventions of the present: Three interactive videodiscs, 1981-90. In D. Hall & S. Fifer (Eds.), *Illuminating video.* San Francisco: Aperture/BAVC.

d'Agostino, P. (1987). DOUBLE YOU (and X,Y,Z.): Concepts and sources for an interactive videodisk project. *TELOS, Journal of Communication, Technology and Society, 9,* 153-158.

Eisenstein, S. M. (1949). Film form: New problems. In *Film form* (J. Leyda, Trans.; pp. 122-149). New York: Harcourt Brace Jovanovich.

Gayeski, D., & Williams, D. (1985). *Interactive media.* Englewood Cliffs, NJ: Prentice-Hall.

Heath, S. (1981). On suture. In *Questions of cinema* (pp. 76-112). Bloomington: Indiana University Press.

Hofstadter, D. R. (1979). *Gödel, Escher, Bach: An eternal golden braid.* New York: Vintage.

Holloway, R., Fuchs, H., & Robinett, W. (1991, October). *Virtual-worlds research at the University of North Carolina at Chapel Hill.* Unpublished paper.

Jauss, H. R. (1982). *Toward an aesthetic of reception* (T. Bahti, Trans.). Minneapolis: University of Minnesota Press.

Lacan, J. (1977a). *Écrits: A selection* (A. Sheridan, Trans.). New York: Norton.

Lacan, J. (1977b). The mirror stage as formative of the function of the "I" as revealed in psychoanalytic experience. Chapter 1 in *Écrits: A selection* (pp. 1-7) (A. Sheridan, Trans.). New York: Norton.

Leab, D. J. (1983). See it now: A legend reassessed. In J. E. O'Connor (Ed.), *American history/American television: Interpreting the video past* (pp. 1-32). New York: Ungar.

Marcuse, H. (1955). *Eros and civilization.* Boston: Beacon.

Palombo, S. R. (1978). *Dreaming and memory: A new information-processing model.* New York: Basic Books.

Shaw, J. (1990). Interaktive Kunst. In *Der Prix Ars Electronica* (pp. 185-186). Linz: Veritas.

Tafler, D. (1986, Summer). DOUBLE YOU (and X,Y,Z.): Video's new interactive frontier. *SPOT, the Journal of the Houston Center for Photography,* pp. 6-7.

Tafler, D. (1990). *The electronic megatext: A theory of telereception and reformation.* Unpublished doctoral dissertation, Columbia University.

Tafler, D. (n.d.). *Video's new interactive frontier.* [Notes printed on the videodisc jacket for *DOUBLE YOU (and X,Y,Z.)* by Peter d'Agostino, distributed by Electronics Arts Intermix]

It seems that video games may be just the beginning of a new post-television scenario where unique hybrids of TV and computers are creating hypertheaters of the absurd, high-tech forums that seem analogous to the function and practicality of the "self-contained comforts" of an RV.

13

Virtual Realities: Recreational Vehicles for a Post-Television Culture?

PETER D'AGOSTINO

With prognostications for the demise of television and mass media within the next decade, various forms of virtual reality (VR) seem positioned to become the important new technology for the twenty-first century.[1] With little informed commentary on this matter, the promoters and polemicists have lined up on the utopian and dystopian sides of the issue. Often they represent VR as a cutting edge technology. They depict VR with the image of a head-mounted display with data gloves, and describe it as an interactive immersion experience existing within a controlled computer-generated environment.

On the utopian side of this post-television culture, we cruise unimpeded along electronic superhighways. Under a technologically determined blue sky, everyone has access to databases of information and democratically interacts in a continual town meeting. Here networks comprising people and institutions will equally participate in shared governance on local and global issues.

On the dystopian side, those views of cyberspace popularized by writers William Gibson and Bruce Sterling also envision the wide use of high-tech computer networks. Here, huge surveillance systems monitor the populace at every turn and are under the control of centralized big brothers from multinational corporations and governmental agencies. Interface cowboys operate "on an almost adrenaline high . . . jacked into a custom cyberspace deck . . . projecting a . . . disembodied consciousness into that consensual hallucination that was the matrix" (Gibson, 1984, p. 6).

Somewhere between the perils and pleasures of the utopian/dystopian future, the virtual reality experience begins to seem more like the experience provided by the recreational vehicles (RVs) of the twentieth century.[2] VR's immersed experience resembles that of taking to the road in an RV. As if to emphasize that, a recent RV owner's manual states:

> Your recreational vehicle has been designed and engineered to provide you with many self-contained comforts of home without having to be connected to outside sources. . . . [I]f operated within recommended procedures, [it] should provide you with many miles of virtually trouble free travel (*RV Owner's Operation & Maintenance Manual*, 1985, p. 8).

It may seem for the few who can afford RVs like a way to escape it all, at least for a while. But this kind of escape is, of course, illusory, originating with those industries that stand to profit.

Of course, this idea of autonomy and RV travel is a myth. Many RVs, in fact, are fully equipped with TVs and phones. Cellular telephones, microwave towers, and satellite dishes transmit signals that reach out everywhere. Regardless of whether one roams through the wilderness of a national park or travels to a fantasy theme park, there is no escaping television and radio news broadcasts. The on-line capabilities of computer networks to link users globally brings the RV substation even closer to that aspect of virtuality that encompasses the broader implications of what is popularly known as cyberspace.

As evasive tools, RVs, TV as well as VR have a lot in common. To a certain degree they insulate and disembody human experiences, but their differences are also especially significant. The RV drives on an actual road even if it ends up in simulated places. Television simulates the sights and sounds of reality at a distance. VR technology is promoted as an interactive experience that parallels actual experiences including the ability to see, hear, and touch within an immersed 3-D surround environment. Claims are being made that real interactions become indistinguishable from those that are simulated in a computer. Although images on a computer screen can mimic the movements of a VR user's hand in a data glove, the actual sensation of handling objects through this kind of device was overstated by an October 1987 *Scientific American* cover story and still remains an elusive goal of virtual reality proponents.

Questions of verisimilitude have arisen before with the advent of new media. Reportedly, some of the first moviegoers attending the Lumière brothers' film *Train Coming Into the Station* actually ran out of the movie theater when the train appeared to approach the audience. Newspaper reports documented accounts of radio listeners who believed that

Martians had landed in New Jersey when Orson Welles's Mercury Theater broadcast its version of H. G. Wells's *War of the Worlds*. There is sufficient evidence that audiences can believe or at least react to the illusions that they see and hear through the media.

In my own experience, I ducked when those first 3-D arrows and spears appeared to be shooting out of movie screens in the 1950s. With VR, however, I have yet to feel any sensation similar to that of handling actual objects. In a VR kitchen or any other lab demonstration, there is no mistaking actuality from virtual reality unless the user's sensation of handling objects is more than minimally impeded. But this is the beginning of VR development. Its computer graphics do accurately mimic movement. The levels of real-time interactivity far exceed any simulation that has been experienced before.

From the promotional literature, the novels, and films, to the growing military, medical, and entertainment industry applications, some of the concepts generated about virtual reality may seem quite visionary. Many of these ideas, however, have been "in the air" for some time. The following progression of ideas (poetics, technics, and politics) works toward a conceptual framework for defining an emerging post-television culture and gauging the potential consequences of the virtual future at the close of this century, on the threshold of the coming millennium.

TV: No Sense of Place

Though it presents a form of hyperreality that can reverse classic territorial relationships, television is still an analog medium wedded to the possibilities and constraints of the late twentieth century. When the transmission lines were unplugged during the 1989 democracy movement uprising in Beijing's Tiananmen Square, the resulting television snow became a lasting example of the one-way flow of information. Although two-way interactive television has been technically feasible from the beginning of television's invention, it has only been employed on a limited basis. New models for transmission and reception are needed.

Today's television programming seems increasingly reality based, through talk shows, tabloid newsmagazine formats, and the docudrama-styled movies of the week. Cyberspace, a subject of science fiction and military research for some time, has also recently become a hot topic in the mass media, primarily through the vivid display of "smart" bomb technology during the televised coverage of the Gulf War. Much of it is myth.

During operation Desert Storm, how much did we really learn about the war in the Persian Gulf through watching TV, getting our information from what amounted to infomercials promoting the purported success of the U.S. high-tech industries? The war put on display some of the applications of VR in warfare, highlighted by point-of-view video images carried by smart bombs during the now infamous "surgical strikes." With much of the most important information from the front lines censored, the live press conferences presented by the military brass merely perpetuated the fallacy that the new "smart" weapon systems were a highly efficient means for destroying targets while preventing civilian casualties, referred to as "collateral damage." On the other side of the virtual battlefield, some of the firsthand reports from the field indicated that the Iraqi SCUD missiles were being intercepted by American Patriots in the skies above Israel and Saudi Arabia. Much of this proved to be myth when these cultivated assumptions reported in the press were later proven to be either misleading or completely inaccurate (Freedman & Karsh, 1993).

Watching satellite transmissions from global networks, television's broadcast and cable viewers, captive or otherwise, are apparently more connected to others in distant parts of the world who are watching at the time than to their own neighbors. The concept of physical proximity loses meaning in a virtual world. A sense of place disappears when an individual can travel around the world in 30 hours, when a message can circle the globe in 30 seconds, when an image can be transmitted instantaneously. On the Internet, a global trip takes a fraction of a second. Only the location of the body makes a difference between electronic transmission and physical transportation. Joshua Meyrowitz (1985) writes in *No Sense of Place:*

> The phrase [no sense of place] is an intricate—though very serious—pun. It is intricate because the word "sense" and the word "place" have two meanings each: "sense" referring to both perception and logic; "place" meaning both social position and physical location. (p. 308)

The separation of the physical body from its perception and logic, this stretching of the senses through electronic technology, as we shall see, has some important ramifications.

A prime example of a "sense of place," vis-à-vis social position and physical location, was demonstrated in Los Angeles. In the infamous Rodney King beating, the home video camcorder footage of his body, beaten and bloodied by the police, had been repeatedly televised in slow motion and analyzed with authoritative "voice of God narration" by newscasters. TV producers everywhere literally made this footage into a broadcast TV logo shown over and over and over again during their local and national news programs. After the mass uprisings, rioting, and civil unrest following the first police verdict, Rodney King finally spoke, asking simply and eloquently, "Can't we all get along?" At a TV press conference, he spoke directly to an international audience who had, prior to this time, hardly caught a glimpse of or heard a word from the man himself.

Having addressed the international press, King, himself now out of the shadows and into the glare of the spotlights, became a personification of the "Other." He became a spokesperson to quell the anger and violence of society's "Others," the minorities and marginalized who continually face bias, discrimination, and violence as a consequence of color, gender, or some other identifiable characteristic. Paradoxical and double edged, TV programs and formats at once create stereotypes and can serve to challenge them. According to Meyrowitz (1985), television has fostered "the rise of hundreds of 'minorities'—people, who in perceiving a wider world, begin to see themselves as unfairly isolated in some pocket of it" (p. 309).

Beyond the Gulf War and the L.A. riots/uprisings, isolation becomes a misnomer in a world being processed, conveyed, and disseminated through satellite telecommunication systems that transmit at the speed of light. The movement of the body through cyberspace becomes tied to economic determinants that foster identity and allocate relative privilege and access. Despite the interactive facade, these delivery systems are still predicated on the one-way and nonresponsive framework of broadcasting. Examples of two-way technology, such as the QUBE system in Columbus, Ohio, and the present/future of HSC (the Home Shopping Network) and QVC (Quality, Value and Convenience), do not move forward. On the contrary, they lead the way back to TV's primary modus operandi: developing more efficient ways of delivering consumers to commercial products and services.

Utopian projections of high-tech digital telephone and television combinations, "on-line" and "on the air" information systems, have already absorbed the dystopian visions of the William Gibson novels and of films such as *Bladerunner* and *The Lawnmower Man.* Cyberpunks may now "jack in" to the simultaneously limiting and limitless realm of cyberspace. "The sky above the port was the color of television, tuned to a dead channel" (Gibson, 1984, p. 3). The parallels to 1960s psychedelic culture are unmistakable. Former LSD guru Timothy Leary now promotes high tech for the VR generation, but with a distinct difference from what motivated him in the 1960s. Instead of a focus on self-discovery, this new high-tech movement has all the baggage of the materialist 1980s. Ironically, high-tech transmission contributed to the stock market "crash" of 1987. The crash was fueled in part by automated computerized trading.

Despite the daily attention being paid to cyberspace and VR, the telecommunication paradigm has not yet begun to shift. In the face of many of the prognostications that new technologies such as virtual reality will eliminate television, it seems that, on the contrary, TV is still a predominant model being perpetuated and appropriated by the computer industry. With the merging of video and computer on-line activities along the proposed electronic information superhighways, some of the lowest common denominators formularized by television are still being employed.

Video games, meanwhile, may be the beginning of a new post-television scenario where unique hybrids of TV and computer technology create hypertheaters of the absurd, new recreational vehicles for a post-television culture. Contrary to the promise that new electronic superhighways will provide unlimited access to information, these forms of surrogate travel begin to resemble the analogy of escapism provided by recreational vehicles, presented earlier. Lingering efforts to develop a technologically advanced interactive participatory democracy may indeed reveal that the gulf between information rich and information poor is growing at an exponential rate as opposed to being narrowed.

Here and There

While television and some of the on-line activities mentioned seem to dissolve a sense of place, simulated "virtual realities" are beginning to develop new ersatz places. Jerzy Kosinski's description of Chance Gardiner, in *Being There* (1970), presents an ultimate dystopian view of an enveloping virtual future.

Chance went inside and turned on the TV. The set created its own light, its own color, its own time. It did not follow the law of gravity that forever bent all plants downward. Everything on TV was tangled and mixed and yet smoothed out: night and day, big and small, tough and brittle, soft and rough, hot and cold, far and near. In this colored world of television, gardening was the white cane of a blind man. (p. 5)

For the general public, VR is merely the next stage of "shoot-'em-ups" found in the video arcades of shopping malls and in the video games at home. VR laboratory simulations, meanwhile, have become quite sophisticated. In fields as varied as architecture and medicine, they range from flight simulators to interactive 3-D modeling systems for examining molecular structures.

For the present, the VR industry relies upon a combination of input-output devices attached to the individual's attire: a computerized head-mounted display (HMD) incorporating 3-D video goggles, data gloves, and an exoskeleton body suit.[3] Although still primitive when compared with the promise of VR, this apparatus has become an icon for computer-generated immersion technology. Mass media use this image to represent a wide variety of past, present, and future applications from war to virtual sex (teledildonics).

The quest for totalizing immersion experiences has precedents in other cultures. The merging of space and time in the Japanese use of "Ma," a concept exemplified by the sixteenth-century Karesansui-style rock gardens, was described in E. T. Hall's *The Hidden Dimension* (1969):

The Ma, or interval, is a basic building block in all Japanese spatial experience. Part of the Japanese skill in creating gardens stems from the fact that in the perception of space the Japanese employ vision and all other senses as well. Olfaction, shifts in temperature, humidity, light, shade, and color are worked together in such a way as to enhance the use of the whole body as a sensing organ. (p. 153)

New techno/cultural interfacing can begin to explore and integrate other realities from around the shrinking world, a shrinking world within an expanding universe that began with a big bang and is supposed to ultimately end in a big crunch. Here on Earth, the fundamental problems of the human condition need to be addressed, especially in the context of what has been referred to as a post-cold war new world order.

No There, There

Gertrude Stein reportedly said of her hometown Oakland, California: "There isn't any there there." She was comparing life there with the cosmopolitan provincialism of Paris during the early 1920s. It is well known that Stein had a central role in the Parisian cafe society comprising artists, writers, and musicians in the final phase of that seminal historical period that has been referred to as "The Banquet Years" (Shattuck, 1968). There was a strong fin de siècle spirit to all this:

> Artists sensed that their generation promised both an end and a beginning. No other equally brief period of history has seen the rise and fall of so many schools of cliches and "isms." Amid this turmoil, the fashionable salon declined after a last abortive flourishing. The cafe came into its own, political unrest encouraged innovation in the arts, and society squandered its last vestiges of aristocracy. The twentieth century could not wait fifteen years for a round number; it was born, yelling in 1885. (Shattuck, 1968, p. 4)

In our own era, with a new millennium at hand, issues of survival primarily focusing on the body, from the immune system to the ecosystem, have become controversial and contested matters. For the species to survive, values and meanings must change as we plunge more rapidly toward the twenty-first century.

The phrase *there isn't any there there* has a familiar ring to it when incorporated into *Mona Lisa Overdrive,* the last of the trilogy of William Gibson's novels that introduced the concept of cyberspace.

> "There's no there, there." They taught that to children explaining cyberspace . . . images shifting on a screen: pilots in enormous helmets and clumsy looking gloves, the neuroelectronically primitive "virtual world" technologically linking them more effectively with their planes, pairs of miniature video terminals pumping them a computer generated flood of combat data. (Gibson, 1989, p. 48)

This is a scenario right out of CNN's Gulf War coverage playing video images from the "smart" bombs exploding on impact with their targets.

Perhaps, in some ways, the twenty-first century has arrived. A vivid portrayal of a virtual future can be found in Donna Haraway's 1985 essay "A Manifesto for Cyborgs," a chilling projection of our entry into the next millennium. She writes that "by the late twentieth century, our time, a mythic time, we are all chimeras, theorized and fabricated hybrids of machine and organism; in short, we are all cyborgs" (p. 66). This manifesto speaks eloquently to many current issues of the body, especially those of displacement and disembodiment. Haraway (1991) states that she is "trying to explore bodies, technologies, and fictions as they are constructed through the mediation of late twentieth century communications sciences, in the simultaneously organic and artifactual domains of biology and medicine, industry and the military" (p. 24). No boundaries exist between the body and technology, between the virtual future and our concrete present. Once more the body must be transformed in order to be made ready for its assimilation within a brave new world.

As an updated myth of the monster, the cyborg is emblematic of a postsimulated world in which a return to the Garden has become an unlikely metaphor given the global ecological crises that now engulf us. However bizarre this utopia, at least it provides the prospect of starting over. According to Haraway (1985), "the cyborg is a creature in a post-gender world" (p. 67). Simians, women, and cyborgs all can begin again on equal terms. A virtual environment sheds the constraints of a world burdened by overpopulation and its concomitant pollution and pestilence, by history and its attendant anger and fear.

Beyond the kind of existential alienation that influenced previous generations, the loss of a Western notion of paradise is seen here, ironically, as a positive step. Within the context of a postindustrial age, the outmoded dichotomies of "nature versus culture" or "human versus machine" may have all but withered away, at least in theory, though obviously not from what we see on television.

The phenomenon of the electronic church may have also peaked during this same period of the mid-1980s, when it became a clearinghouse for what appeared to be a mass search for salvation. The "second coming" may have seemed imminent to those broadcast TV watchers and cable subscribers who were seekers of the faith until the various scandals slowed, if not deterred, some of the momentum of the television evangelists. Here, the "New Right" alliances applied the political theory of a trickle down economy to the practices of TV call-in shows, where toll-free numbers were used to solicit the direct funding necessary to broaden these mass-mediated empires of religion and politics.

Much of the central focus remains on the body. Some key social issues such as AIDS, gays, abortion, pornography, and censorship remain and are still prominently portrayed in the media as right-wing/left-wing political controversies. Always relevant as a concern and fascination, the body takes on an urgency that isn't limited to a Cartesian mind/body split or to questions as to whether computers, such as HAL from Arthur C. Clarke's *2001,* can become more intelligent than humans. Our latest fears relate to those biological monsters of the *Alien* films, those creatures that occupy our bodies and consume us from within (see Kuhn, 1990, p. 73).

Enormous social stress triggers these fantasies. This stress originates not only from within our own biological systems but from the impact of our species on the natural environment. The depletion of the ozone, global warming, and the shifting post-cold war sociopolitical landscape have become major topics, especially with regard to the future.

The Invention of the Future

The future does not merely arrive in its prescribed chronological time. It is an ideological construct, an invention that is sold in the marketplace of ideas and mythologized through the mass media. Long before the development of contemporary electronic technologies, the power to create life and the capacity for replication and reproduction were powerful subjects.

Descartes presents a historical point of departure for tracing the classic dichotomy of body and mind. His work led to the invention of algebra and calculus, a mathematically based artificial language that in many ways reduces human experience to a logical mathematical system. J. David Bolter writes in *Turing's Man: Western Culture in the Computer Age* (1984): "Descartes and his followers helped to make the clock a defining technology in Western Europe. With that, even animals were perceived as 'clockwork mechanisms' " (p. 11). When Descartes separated the spirit symbolically from the material world and its physical limitations, Europeans had a model for separating the mind from the body. "I recognized that I was a substance whose whole essence or nature is to think and whose being requires no place and depends on no material thing" (Descartes, *Discourse on Method*, 1637). By the eighteenth century, the notion "I think, therefore I am" had become a dominant philosophy.

Mary Shelley's *Frankenstein or, The Modern Prometheus* (1965) reignites the fascination with the power to create life, the capacity for rebirth and replication:

> The stages of the discovery were distinct and probable. I became capable of bestowing animation upon lifeless matter. (p. 51)

I saw the hideous phantasm of a man stretched out, and then, on the working of some powerful engine, show signs of life and stir with an uneasy, half vital-motion. Frightful it must be; for supremely frightful would be the effect of any human endeavor to mock the stupendous mechanism of the Creator of the world. His success would terrify the artist; he would rush away from this odious handy-work, horror stricken. (p. xi)

The parable is a familiar one. If life doesn't come from a god or from a "natural" biological system, then it reeks of a demonic power.

The parable goes back further. The reproduction of images, sounds, and life has been, since time immemorial, the work of shamans, artists, and scientists who exerted unique creative forces over life itself. Prometheus, the keeper of the fire, lives in Leonardo, a painter of angels, inventor of aerial perspective, and a designer of the weapons of war. A precursor to Dr. Frankenstein, Leonardo also engaged in the unholy practice of body snatching and dissection for his unique anatomical studies.

With the development of photography and film in the nineteenth century, Renaissance perspective and the camera obscura evolved to become the new, ideologically charged replicating devices. Prior to the invention of the cinema, the reproduced photographic images of the Civil War in the popular press were simultaneously disturbing and wondrous while the sounds coming from Edison's phonograph were probably nothing short of pure magic.[4]

In two separate research studies, Raymond Bellour and Annette Michelson provide historical frames of reference for the merger of biological and mechanistic systems by retelling a fable published over a century ago by Villiers de l'Isle-Adam. It concerns Edison, who by creating an android is compared to a god or even a demon.

"The New Eve, an electro-human machine (almost an animal! . . .), offering a replica of the world's first love, by the astonishing Thomas Alva Edison, the American engineer, Father of the Phonograph" ("Le Traitement du Docteur Tristan," in *Contes cruels*, Villiers de l'Isle-Adam, 1877, cited in Bellour, 1986, p. 111). The story attributes the powers of replication, reproduction, and creation itself to the famous inventor, who was later popularly known as the "Wizard of Menlo Park."

"But," says Edison, "the Android presents nothing like the frightful spectacle of our own vital processes. In her everything is rich, ingenious and somber." "Look!" And he presses his scalpel on the central apparatus riveted to the level of the android's cervical vertebrae. (*L'eve future,* Villiers de l'Isle-Adam, 1889, cited in Michelson, 1984, p. 17)

Bellour (1986) writes in "Ideal Hadaly": "In this story about a sublime robot, Villers offers us an image which both pacified and exhilarated the imagination of his century, a sort of Woman-Computer" (p. 111). With a long history of automata, these examples can lead directly to contemporary thinking machines and artificial intelligence, with the superiority of mind over matter, and the mechanization of nature.

One of the manifestations of the digital age is the categorical simplification of these boundaries, the merging, compression, and reconstruction of industries, disciplines, tools, and concepts. Original and copy, map and territory, have become indistinguishable: not nature and culture, but nature into culture; not art versus science, but art into science. Still, the fundamental questions surrounding the human condition prevail. What is the relationship between the mind and the body, between one civilization and another, between the sexes, and among the races? What does it mean, for example, to be ethnically cleansed?

Ethnic cleansing is an end to the Other. It means the eradication of differences between the body and its culture. As a consequence, it means an end to differences of thinking, an end to the mind.

Unlike Descartes, Vico believed that the human mind had "an indefinite nature." . . . For according to Vico, in becoming more definite more accurate, more scientific, the human mind in time became *less grounded in the body*, more abstract, less able directly to grasp its own essential self, less capable of beginning at the beginning, less capable of defining itself. (Said, 1985, pp. 347-348; italics added)

Is this the beginning of some universal sterilization, some sublime achievement on the road to artificial intelligence, or will the 1990s be like the 1960s?

The 1960s ushered in the postmodern era. Juxtapositions of dominant culture and its alternatives, the Age of Aquarius and the Vietnam War, civil rights, the women's movement, minimalism, and pop art all clashed with the mainstream, eventually commingled, and forced the center to regroup. Low transformed into high. McLuhanism justified medium as message. Society shifted its prejudices, realigned its battlefields, and built new lines of resistance sustained by a conservative worldwide leadership throughout much of the industrialized world during the 1980s.

In the 1990s, information rich and information poor meet at the digital crossroads. Does this digital future harbor bright blue skies ahead, or is there another storm brewing? No matter, life goes on. The new recreational vehicles or virtual realities are on the way. You won't have to leave your home to dial up your own choice brand of prepackaged bliss on the proposed information superhighway.

Where Do We Go From Here?

The lost traveler, after finally asking for directions, hears an all too familiar response: "You can't get there from here." In many cases this means that the limitations of the structure—whether the grid of the city block, roads, rail lines, or even the gaps in electronic information systems—have created a dilemma for reaching an intended destination or any destination at all.

Reaction is not action. To move toward a post-television era, it is important to bring the term *interactivity* into sharper focus. Gregory Bateson's (1979) conceptualization that "information consists of differences that makes a difference" (p. 99) can begin to provide a basis for this pursuit.

One of the "differences" here is that, beyond the immediacy of the senses, a new and remarkable set of circumstances has begun to change the paradigm of human interaction. Within artificially constructed realities, ones that the computer interface are making available for the first time, a cyberspace of globally interconnected networks is beginning to offer myriad possibilities for communication.

How we interact through these systems begins to shape the prevailing values of a post-television culture. Current models predicated on video arcade games featuring the violent shoot-'em-ups staged in theaters of foreign wars or within local arenas of urban decay are merely today's reactionary equivalent to television's vast wasteland. "Dismembering may be a prelude to remembering, which is not merely restoring some past intact but setting it *in living relationship to the present*" (Turner, 1980, pp. 166-167).

New critical theory beckons, yet critique can only follow a radical new arts praxis operating along the boundaries of high-tech and traditional cultures, in the electronic margins of the digital arts and sciences.

As exploratory efforts and pockets of resistance begin to emerge, they may provide an impetus to probe some of the fundamental problems of the human condition. These efforts include the opportunity to build bridges and arrive at solutions to global problems within the context of the socioeconomic, political boundaries being shaped by a post-cold war "new world order." Some of these interactive efforts indeed will affect our survival well into the next millennium.

Notes

1. An oxymoron, the term *virtual reality* presents a contradiction in what is real and what is not. Nevertheless, this new technology is a direct descendant of Renaissance perspective, of the camera obscura, and of the development of photography, film, radio, and television.

2. A recreational vehicle will often be referred to by names specific to a particular market. For example, in certain regions of the world, RVs are known as caravans.

3. HMD was first developed in military-funded labs in the late 1960s.

4. Beyond the mere technics of form and representation, Walter Benjamin's (1955) critical analysis investigated the social, economic, and political implications of "mechanically reproducible works of art."

References

Bateson, G. (1979). *Mind and nature: A necessary unity*. New York: Dutton.

Bellour, R. (1986). Ideal Hadaly. *Camera Obscura, 15*, 111-135.

Benjamin, W. (1955). The work of art in the age of mechanical reproduction. In *Illuminations* (pp. 219-254). New York: Harcourt, Brace and World.

Bolter, J. D. (1984). *Turing's man: Western culture in the computer age*. Chapel Hill: University of North Carolina Press.

Freedman, L., & Karsh, E. (1993). *The Gulf War conflict, 1990-91: Diplomacy and war in the new world order*. Princeton, NJ: Princeton University Press.

Gibson, W. (1984). *Neuromancer*. New York: Ace Book Berkley Publishing Group.

Gibson, W. (1989). *Mona Lisa overdrive*. London: Gratton.

Hall, E. T. (1969). *The hidden dimension*. New York: Doubleday.

Haraway, D. (1985). A manifesto for cyborgs: Science, technology and socialist feminism in the 1980s. *Socialist Review, 80*, 65-107.

Haraway, D. (1991). Cyborgs at large [interview with Donna Haraway]. In C. Penley & A. Ross (Eds.), *Technoculture*. Minneapolis: University of Minnesota Press.

Kosinski, J. (1970). *Being there*. New York: Harcourt Brace Jovanovich.

Kuhn, A. (Ed.). (1990). *Alien zone: Cultural theory and contemporary science fiction cinema*. London: Verso.

Meyrowitz, J. (1985). *No sense of place*. New York: Oxford University Press.

Michelson, A. (1984). On the eve of the future: The reasonable facsimile and the philosophical toy. *October, 29,* 3-22.

RV owner's operation & maintenance manual. (1985). Overland, KS: Intertec.

Said, E. (1985). *Beginnings: Intention and method.* New York: Columbia University Press.

Shattuck, R. (1968). *The banquet years.* New York: Random House.

Shelley, M. (1965). *Frankenstein or, The modern Prometheus.* New York: Signet.

Turner, V. (1980). Social dramas and stories about them. *Critical Inquiry, 7*(1), 141-168.

Bibliography

Aksoy, A., & Robins, K. (1992). Exterminating angels: Morality, violence, and technology in the Gulf War. In H. Mowlana, G. Gerbner, & H. Schiller (Eds.), *Triumph of the image: The media's war in the Persian Gulf—A global perspective* (pp. 322-336). Boulder, CO: Westview.

Armes, R. (1988). *On video.* London: Routledge.

Baggaley, J., & Duck, S. (1976). *Dynamics of television.* London: Gower.

Barnouw, E. (1966). *A tower in Babel: A history of broadcasting in the United States: Vol. 1. — to 1933.* New York: Oxford University Press.

Barnouw, E. (1968). *The golden web: A history of broadcasting in the United States: Vol. 2. 1933 to 1953.* New York: Oxford University Press.

Barnouw, E. (1970). *The image empire: A history of broadcasting in the United States: Vol. 3. — from 1953.* New York: Oxford University Press.

Barnouw, E. (1990). *Tube of plenty.* New York: Oxford University Press.

Barthes, R. (1977). *Image-music-text* (S. Heath, Trans.). New York: Hill and Wang.

Bateson, G. (1972). *Steps to an ecology of mind.* New York: Ballantine.

Bateson, G. (1979). *Mind and nature: A necessary unity.* New York: Dutton.

Battcock, G. (Ed.). (1978). *New artists video.* New York: Dutton.

Baudrillard, J. (1983). *Simulations* (P. Foss, P. Patton, & P. Beitchman, Trans.). New York: Semiotext(e).

Bazin, A. (1967). The myth of total cinema. In *What is cinema?* (H. Gray, Trans.). Berkeley: University of California Press.

Bellour, R. (1986). Ideal Hadaly. *Camera Obscura, 15,* 111-135.

Benedikt, M. (Ed.). (1991). *Cyberspace: First steps.* Cambridge: MIT Press.

Benjamin, W. (1955). The work of art in the age of mechanical reproduction. In *Illuminations.* New York: Harcourt, Brace and World.

Bolter, J. D. (1984). *Turing's man: Western culture in the computer age.* Chapel Hill: University of North Carolina Press.

Boyle, D. (1986). *Video classics: A guide to video art and documentary tapes.* Phoenix, AZ: Oryx.

Brand, S. (1987). *The media lab: Inventing the future at MIT.* New York: Viking Penguin.

Brooks, F. P., Jr. (1988). Grasping reality through illusion: Interactive graphics serving science. In E. Soloway, D. Frye, & S. Sheppard (Eds.), *CHI'88 proceedings* (pp. 1-11). Reading, MA: Addison-Wesley.

Cha, T. H. K. (Ed.). (1980). *Apparatus.* New York: Tanam.

Cirincione, J., & D'Amato, B. (Eds.). (1992). *Through the looking glass: Artists' first encounters with virtual reality.* Jupiter, FL: Softworlds.

Clark, D. (1988, March). Hard lessons for interactive video. *Educational Computing.*

Corea, G. (1986). *The mother machine: Reproductive technologies from artificial insemination to artificial wombs.* New York: Harper & Row.

Cubitt, S. (1991). *Timeshift: On video culture.* London: Routledge.

d'Agostino, P. (Ed.). (1985). *Transmission: Theory and practice for a new television aesthetics.* New York: Tanam Press.

d'Agostino, P. (1991). Interventions of the present: Three interactive videodiscs, 1981-90. In D. Hall & S. J. Fifer (Eds.), *Illuminating video: An essential guide to video art* (pp. 321-327). San Francisco: Aperture/BAVC.

d'Agostino, P. (1980). *TeleGuide—Including proposal for QUBE.* San Francisco: NFS Press.

Davis, D. (1973). *Art and the future.* New York: Praeger.

Deleuze, G., & Guattari, F. (1983). *On the line* (J. Johnston, Trans.). New York: Semiotext(e).

Derrida, J. (1974). *Of grammatology* (G. C. Spivak, Trans.). Baltimore: Johns Hopkins University Press.

Eco, U. (1989). *The open work* (A. Cancogni, Trans.). Cambridge, MA: Harvard University Press.

Eisenstein, S. M. (1949). *Film form* (J. Leyda, Trans.). New York: Harcourt Brace Jovanovich.

Ellis, J. (1982). *Visible fictions: Cinema, television, video.* London: Methuen.

Ellul, J. (1980). *The technological system.* New York: Continuum.

Enloe, C. (1983). *Does khaki become you? The militarization of women's lives.* Boston: Pandora.

Enzensberger, H. M. (1988). *Dreamers of the absolute: Essays on ecology, media and power.* London: Radius.

Faber, M. (Ed.). (1990). *A tool, a weapon, a witness: The new video news crews.* Chicago: Randolph Street Gallery.

Fiske, J. (1988). *Television culture.* London: Methuen.

Fiske, J., & Hartley, J. (1978). *Reading television.* London: Methuen.

Freedman, L., & Karsh, E. (1993). *The Gulf War conflict, 1990-91: Diplomacy and war in the new world order.* Princeton, NJ: Princeton University Press.

Friedrich, O., & the editors of *Time.* (Eds.). (1991). *Desert Storm: The war in the Persian Gulf.* Boston: Little, Brown.

Gardner, H. (1982). *Art, mind, and brain: A cognitive approach to creativity.* New York: Basic Books.

Gayeski, D., & Williams, D. (1985). *Interactive media.* Englewood Cliffs, NJ: Prentice-Hall.

Gibson, W. (1984). *Neuromancer.* New York: Ace Book Berkley Publishing Group.

Gibson, W. (1989). *Mona Lisa overdrive.* London: Gratton.

Gill, K. S. (Ed.). (1986). *Artificial intelligence and society.* London: John Wiley.

Gitlin, T. (1980). *The whole world is watching: Mass media in the making and the unmaking of the new left.* Berkeley: University of California Press.

Gitlin, T. (1983). *Inside prime time.* New York: Pantheon.

Gitlin, T. (Ed.). (1986). *Watching television.* New York: Pantheon.

Gramsci, A. (1971). *Selections from the prison notebooks of Antonio Gramsci* (G. Nowell-Smith & Q. Hoare, Eds. and Trans.). London: Lawrence and Wishart.

Gusterson, H. (1991). Nuclear war, the Gulf War, and the disappearing body. *Journal of Urban and Cultural Studies, 2*(1), 45-56.

Hafer, K., & Markofs, J. (1991). *Cyberpunks: Outlaws and hackers on the computer frontier.* New York: Simon & Schuster.

Hall, D., & Fifer, S. J. (Eds.). (1991). *Illuminating video: An essential guide to video art.* San Francisco: Aperture/BAVC.

Hall, S., Hobson, D., Loew, A., & Willis, P. (Eds.). (1980). *Culture, media, language.* London: University of Birmingham Press.

Hanhardt, J. G. (1986). *Video culture: A critical investigation.* Layton, UT: Peregrine Smith.

Haraway, D. J. (1991). *Simians, cyborgs, and women: The reinvention of nature.* New York: Routledge.

Hartley, J. (1992). *Tele-ology: Studies in television.* London: Routledge.

Hayward, P., & Wollenb, T. (1993). *Future visions: New technologies of the screen.* London: BFI.

Heath, S. (1981). On suture. In *Questions of cinema.* Bloomington: Indiana University Press.

Himmelstein, H. (1981). *On the small screen: New approaches in television and video criticism.* New York: Praeger.

Hofstadter, D. R. (1979). *Gödel, Escher, Bach: An eternal golden braid.* New York: Vintage.

Holloway, R., Fuchs, H., & Robinett, W. (1991, October). *Virtual-worlds research at the University of North Carolina at Chapel Hill.* Unpublished paper.

Horkheimer, M., & Adorno, T. W. (1990). The cultural industry: Enlightenment as mass deception. In *Dialectic of enlightenment* (pp. 120-167). New York: Continuum.

Ihde, D. (1990). *Technology and the lifeworld: From garden to earth.* Bloomington: Indiana University Press.

Innis, H. (1951). *The bias of communication.* Toronto: University of Toronto Press.

Irigaray, L. (1985a). *This sex which is not one* (C. Porter with C. Burke, Trans.). Ithaca, NY: Cornell University Press.

Irigaray, L. (1985b). *Speculum of the other woman* (G. C. Gill, Trans.). Ithaca, NY: Cornell University Press.

Iser, W. (1978). *The act of reading: A theory of aesthetic response.* Baltimore: Johns Hopkins University Press.

Jameson, F. (1991). *Postmodernism, or, The cultural logic of late capitalism.* Durham, NC: Duke University Press.

Jauss, H. R. (1982). *Toward an aesthetic of reception* (T. Bahti, Trans.). Minneapolis: University of Minnesota Press.

Kaku, M. (1994). *Hyperspace: A scientific odyssey through parallel universes, time warps, and the tenth dimension.* New York: Oxford University Press.

Kaplan, E. A. (1987). *Rocking around the clock: Music television, postmodernism and consumer culture.* London: Methuen.

Kaplan, E. A. (Ed.). (1983). *Regarding television* (American Film Institute Monograph 2). Frederick, MD: University Publications of America.

Keller, E. F. (1990). From secrets of life to secrets of death. In M. Jacobus, E. F. Keller, & S. Shuttleworth (Eds.), *Body/politics* (pp. 177-191). New York: Routledge.

Kosinski, J. (1970). *Being there.* New York: Harcourt Brace Jovanovich.

Kuhn, A. (Ed.). (1990). *Alien zone: Cultural theory and contemporary science fiction cinema.* London: Verso.

Lacan, J. (1977). *Écrits: A selection* (A. Sheridan, Trans.). New York: Norton.

Lacan, J. (1987). Television. *October, 40*, 5-50.

Lakoff, G. (1991). Metaphor and war: The metaphor system used to justify war in the Gulf. *Journal of Urban and Cultural Studies, 2*(1).

Landow, G. P. (1992). *Hypertext: The convergence of contemporary critical theory and technology.* Baltimore: Johns Hopkins University Press.

Larsen, E. (1991). Gulf War TV. *Jump Cut, 36*, 3-10.

Leab, D. J. (1983). See it now: A legend reassessed. In J. E. O'Connor (Ed.), *American history/American television: Interpreting the video past* (pp. 1-32). New York: Ungar.

Lyotard, J.-F. (1984). *The post-modern condition: A report on knowledge* (G. Bennington & B. Massumi, Trans.). Minneapolis: University of Minnesota Press.

MacCabe, C. (Ed.). (1986). *High theory/low culture.* Manchester: Manchester University Press.

Marcus, D. (Ed.). (1991). *Roar! The Paper Tiger Television guide to media activism.* New York: Paper Tiger Television Collective.

Marcuse, H. (1955). *Eros and civilization.* Boston: Beacon.

McLuhan, M. (1962). *The Gutenberg galaxy.* Toronto: University of Toronto Press.

Mellencamp, P. (Ed.). (1990). *Logics of television.* Bloomington: University of Indiana Press.

Metz, C. (1977). *Psychoanalysis and cinema: The imaginary signifier.* London: Macmillan.

Meyrowitz, J. (1985). *No sense of place.* New York: Oxford University Press.

Michaels, E. (1986). *Aboriginal invention of television: Central Australia 1982-86* (report). Canberra: Australian Institute of Aboriginal Studies.

Michelson, A. (1984). On the eve of the future: The reasonable facsimile and the philosophical toy. *October, 29*, 3-20.

Mosco, V. (1982). *Pushbutton fantasies.* Norwood, NJ: Ablex.

Newcomb, H. (Ed.). (1976). *Television: The critical view.* New York: Oxford University Press.

Nichols, B. (1988). The work of culture in the age of cybernetic systems. *Screen, 29*(1), 22-47.

Ong, W. J. (1982). *Orality and literacy: The technologizing of the word.* London: Methuen.

O'Regan, T. (Ed.). (1990). Communication & tradition: Essays after Eric Michaels [Special issue]. *Continuum, 3*(2).

Palombo, S. R. (1978). *Dreaming and memory: A new information-processing model.* New York: Basic Books.

Penley, C., & Ross, A. (Eds.). (1991). *Technoculture.* Minneapolis: University of Minnesota Press.

Press, A. L. (1991). *Women watching television: Gender, class, and generation in the American television experience.* Philadelphia: University of Pennsylvania Press.

Rheingold, H. (1991). *Virtual reality.* New York: Simon & Schuster.

Ronell, A. (1989). *The telephone book: Technology, schizophrenia, electric speech.* Lincoln: University of Nebraska Press.

Rosen, R. (1985). Ernie Kovacs: Video artist. In P. d'Agostino (Ed.), *Transmission: Theory and practice for a new television aesthetics.* New York: Tanam Press.

Said, E. (1985). *Beginnings: Intention and method.* New York: Columbia University Press.

Scarry, E. (1985). *The body in pain.* New York: Oxford University Press.

Schechter, D. (1992, January/February). The Gulf War and the death of the TV news. *The Independent,* pp. 28-31.

Schiller, D. (1982). *Telematics and government.* Norwood, NJ: Ablex.

Schiller, H. (1973). *Mind managers.* Boston: Beacon.

Schneider, C., & Wallis, B. (Eds.). (1988). *Global television.* New York: Wedge/Cambridge: MIT Press.

Schneider, I., & Korot, B. (Eds.). (1976). *Video art: An anthology.* New York: Harcourt Brace Jovanovich.

Shamberg, M. (1971). *Guerrilla television.* New York: Holt, Rinehart & Winston.

Shattuck, R. (1968). *The banquet years.* New York: Random House.

Shelley, M. (1965). *Frankenstein or, The modern Prometheus.* New York: Signet.

Skirrow, G. (1986). Hellivision: An analysis of video games. In C. MacCabe (Ed.), *High theory/low culture* (pp. 115-142). Manchester: Manchester University Press.

Stam, R. (1992). Mobilizing fictions: The Gulf War, the media, and the recruitment of the spectator. *Public Culture, 4*(2), 101-126.

Sterling, B. (1988). *Islands in the net.* New York: Arbor House/Morrow.

Tafler, D. (1988). The circular text. *Journal of Film and Video, 40*(3), 27-45.

Tafler, D. (1990a). *The electronic megatext: A theory of telereception and reformation.* Unpublished doctoral dissertation, Columbia University.

Tafler, D. (1990b, Fall). I remember television. . . . In *From receiver to remote control* (catalogue). New York: New Museum.

Tafler, D., & d'Agostino, P. (1993). The techno/cultural interface. *Media Information Australia, 69,* 47-54.

Thede, N., & Ambrosi, A. (Eds.). (1991). *Video the changing world.* Montreal: Black Rose.

Ulmer, G. (1989). *Teletheory: Grammatology in the age of video.* New York: Routledge.

Virilio, P. (1989). *War and cinema* (P. Camiller, Trans.). New York: Verso.

Wark, M. (1991). News bites: War TV in the Gulf. *Meanjin 50*(1), 5-18.

Weiner, N. (1967). *The human use of human beings: Cybernetics and society.* New York: Avon.

Weizenbaum, J. (1984). *Computer power and human reason.* Harmondsworth: Pelican.

Williams, R. (1974). *Television: Technology and cultural form.* London: Fontana.

Worth, S. (1981). *Studying visual communication.* Philadelphia: University of Pennsylvania Press.

Youngblood, G. (1970). *Expanded cinema.* New York: Dutton.

Zerzan, J., & Carnes, A. (Eds.). (1991). *Questioning technology: Tool, toy or tyrant?* Philadelphia: New Society.

Index

About the Authors

Erik Barnouw, Professor Emeritus of Dramatic Arts at Columbia University, organized and chaired the film division of the School of the Arts and started a mass media division of Columbia University Press, the Center for Mass Communication. His books have included *Mass Communication* (1956); *Indian Film* (1980), written under a Fulbright grant with the collaboration of S. Krishnaswamy. Seven other works published by Oxford include a three-volume *History of Broadcasting in the United States* (1966-1970), which won the Bancroft Prize, the Frank Luther Mott Award, and the George Polk Award; *Documentary: A History of the Nonfiction Film* (1974); *Tube of Plenty: The Evolution of American Television* (1975); *The Sponsor: Notes on a Modern Potentate* (1978); and *The Magician and the Cinema* (1981). Since retirement from Columbia University he has been a 1976 Fellow of the Woodrow Wilson International Center for Scholars, Smithsonian Institution; and in 1977 he joined the Library of Congress as a Film and Television Specialist. In 1978 he became chief of the library's newly formed Motion Picture, Broadcasting and Recorded Sound Division, a position he held until a second retirement in 1981. In 1983 he became Editor of the *International Encyclopedia of Communications,* a four-volume reference work published in 1989 by Oxford University Press and the University of Pennsylvania.

Deirdre Boyle is a critic, curator, teacher, and consultant specializing in independent video and film. She is a senior faculty member in the Communications Department at the New School for Social Research in New York. She is the author of over 100 essays and seven books, including *Video Classics: A Guide to Video Art and Documentary Tapes* (1986) and *Video Preservation: Securing the Future of the Past* (1993). She has organized video exhibitions for museums, galleries, universities, and television systems in the United States and abroad. Her clients include Television Española (Madrid), the Finnish Broadcasting Company, Instituto Estudios Norteamericanos (Barcelona), Image Forum

(Tokyo), National Film Board of Canada, Long Beach Museum of Art, American Federation of the Arts, the Learning Channel, and WNET-TV as well as numerous public and private funding agencies. She was awarded a Guggenheim Fellowship in 1983, an ACE award for the best documentary series on cable television in 1988, and a Fulbright Fellowship at Moscow State University in 1992.

John Carey is Director of Greystone Communications, a telecommunication research and planning firm. He is also a consultant to the Freedom Forum Media Studies Center at Columbia University and an Affiliated Research Fellow at the Columbia Institute for Tele-Information.

Sean Cubitt is a Reader in Video and Media Studies at Liverpool John Moores University, England. He is the author of *Timeshift: On Video Culture* and *Videography* and a member of the editorial board of *SCREEN*. He has published widely on art, design, popular music, media, and cultural studies.

Peter d'Agostino is an artist who has been working in video since 1971 and interactive media over the past decade. He is currently Professor of Communications in the Department of Radio-Television-Film and co-director of the HyperMedia Laboratory, Temple University, Philadelphia. He is a Pew Fellow in the Arts, and has been a Japan Foundation fellow, a fellow of the National Endowment for the Arts, a fellow at the Center for Advanced Visual Studies, MIT, an artist-in-residence at the Television Laboratory, WNET, New York, and a visiting artist at the American Academy in Rome. His work has been exhibited internationally and is in the collection of the Museum of Modern Art's Circulating Video Library. His books include *Transmission: Theory and Practice for a New Television Aesthetics* (editor, 1985), *The Un/Necessary Image* (coeditor, 1982), *Comings and Goings* (1982); *Still Photography: The Problematic Model* (coeditor, 1981); and *TeleGuide—including a Proposal for QUBE* (1980).

Todd Gitlin is Professor of Sociology and Director of the Mass Communications Program at the University of California, Berkeley. He has written, among other books, *The Sixties: Years of Hope, Days of Rage* (1987; revised edition forthcoming), *Inside Prime Time* (1983; second edition forthcoming), and *The Whole World Is Watching* (1980), and edited two, including *Watching Television* (1987). His first novel, *The Murder of Albert Einstein,* was published in 1992. He has received grants from the John D. and Catherine T. MacArthur Foundation (for research and writing in international peace and security), the National Endowment for the Humanities, and the Rockefeller Foundation. He is working on a book about multiculturalism and national identity and conducting research on the globalization of media and popular culture.

Fredric R. Jameson is William A. Lane, Jr., Professor of Comparative Literature, Professor of Romance Studies (French), and Chair of the Graduate Program in Literature at Duke University. He received his Ph.D. from Yale in 1959 and taught at Harvard, Yale, and the University of California before coming to Duke in 1985. His most recent books include *Late Marxism* (1990), *Signatures of the Visible* (1990), *Postmodernism, or, The Cultural Logic of Late Capitalism* (1991, which won the MLA Lowell Award), and *The Geopolitical Aesthetic* (1992).

Eric Michaels, an American anthropologist, spent over 5 years in the Northern Territory in Central Australia researching the impact of television and video technology on remote Aboriginal communities. He was Lecturer in Media Studies at Griffith University in Brisbane, Queensland. His major publications include the *The Aboriginal Invention of Television, 1982-1985* (1986), *Kuruwarri: Yuendumu Doors* (with Warlukurlangu Artists, 1987), *For a Cultural Future: Francis Jurpurrurla Makes TV at Yuendumu* (1988), and *Unbecoming: An AIDS Diary* (1987-1988).

Pat O'Hara (formerly Pat Quarles), Ph.D., is Associate Professor in the graduate Interactive Telecommunications Program at the Tisch School of the Arts, New York University. She has been involved in interactive media projects since 1974, working in interactive cable television, videotex, teletext, audio interaction, and interactive multimedia cable projects. She codirects WINDOW, a televirtual cable program exploring the uses of virtual reality as a hypermedia interface for cable television. In addition to teaching, her work includes videography (UJI—*Time Being*) and experimental cable program direction. Her focus is the interaction of computers and video and their relation to empowerment issues of information and telecommunication.

Laurie Ouellette received her M.A. in media studies from the New School for Social Research in New York City. She has long been involved with alternative media, having held positions as librarian of the *Utne Reader* magazine; coeditor of the media criticism newsletter *MediaCulture Review;* researcher and writer for the Institute for Alternative Journalism; and staff writer for the AlterNet, the news service of the alternative press, where she contributed a weekly column of media and cultural criticism that appeared in newsweeklies across the United States.

Andrea L. Press is Assistant Professor of Communication at the University of Michigan at Ann Arbor. She is author of *Women Watching Television: Gender, Class, and Generation in the American Television Experience.*

Avital Ronell is Visiting Scholar at New York University. She is Professor at the University of California, Berkeley. She is the author of a number of books including *Finitude's Score: Essays for the End of the Millennium* (forthcoming); *The Telephone Book: Technology, Schizophrenia, Electric Speech; Crack Wars;* and *Dictations: On Haunted Writing.*

Marita Sturken has written about video and television for over 10 years. She is currently working on a book about the politics of cultural memory in the Vietnam War and the AIDS epidemic, and the role of technologies of memories such as camera images in defining what we remember. She has a Ph.D. from the History of Consciousness program at the University of California, Santa Cruz, and teaches in the Communications Department at the University of California, San Diego.

David Tafler is a member of the Media Studies faculty of Widener University near Philadelphia, Pennsylvania. He received his Ph.D. from Columbia University in 1990. His dissertation, *The Electronic Megatext: A Theory of Tele-Reception and Re-formation,* examines the relations between the viewer-participant and open-ended interactive installations. He has written extensively on interactive media and new technologies. His articles include "I Remember Television . . ." in *From Receiver to Remote Control;* "Der Blick und der Sprung" (The Look and the Leap) in *Kunstforum;* "The Circular Text" in *Journal of Film and Video;* "Autonomy/Community: Marginality and the New Interactive Cinema" in *Cinematograph;* and "Beyond Narrative: Notes Toward a Theory of Interactive Cinema" in *Millennium Film Journal.*